The
Greatest
Hockey Stories
Ever Told

Also from The Lyons Press

The Greatest Adventure Stories Ever Told
The Greatest Baseball Stories Ever Told
The Greatest Boxing Stories Ever Told
The Greatest Cat Stories Ever Told
The Greatest Climbing Stories Ever Told
The Greatest Cowboy Stories Ever Told
The Greatest Disaster Stories Ever Told
The Greatest Dog Stories Ever Told
The Greatest Escape Stories Ever Told
The Greatest Exploration Stories Ever Told
The Greatest Fishing Stories Ever Told
The Greatest Flying Stories Ever Told
The Greatest Football Stories Ever Told
The Greatest Gambling Stories Ever Told
The Greatest Horse Stories Ever Told
The Greatest Hunting Stories Ever Told
The Greatest Golf Stories Ever Told
The Greatest Romance Stories Ever Told
The Greatest Sailing Stories Ever Told
The Greatest Search and Rescue Stories Ever Told
The Greatest Survival Stories Ever Told
The Greatest Treasure-Hunting Stories Ever Told
The Greatest War Stories Ever Told

The Greatest Hockey Stories Ever Told

The Finest Writers on Ice

EDITED BY
BRYANT URSTADT

THE LYONS PRESS
Guilford, Connecticut

An imprint of Globe Pequot Press

The Lyons Press is an imprint of The Globe Pequot Press.

10

Printed in the United States of America

ISBN-13: 978-1-59228-905-9

The Library of Congress has previously cataloged an earlier (hardcover) edition as follows:

The greatest hockey stories ever told : the finest writers on ice / edited by Bryant Urstadt.
   p. cm.
 ISBN 1-59228-530-9 (trade cloth)
 1. Hockey—Anecdotes. I. Urstadt, Bryant.
GV847.G69 2004
796.962—dc22
                                        2004018652

. . . the players mixed like hornets—swift, padded, yellow, black, red, rushing, slashing, whirling over the ice. Above the rink the tobacco smoke lay like a cloud of flash powder, explosive. Over the p.a. system the management begged the spectators not to throw pennies to catch the blades of the skates.

—Saul Bellow, *Herzog*

CONTENTS

Introduction

Hockey, at times, seems like a sport without a literature. There are no well-known poets of hockey, and very few readable novels about the sport. The mysteries of script, in fact, seem largely unknown in the locker room, and after hanging around hockey players for a bit, one begins to suspect that the whole sport is still in the oral, or possibly even pictographic, stage. Is it really so hard to imagine, say, Steve Yzerman there by the fire in the lockers, using the jagged edge of a broken stick to carve into the walls a line drawing of Patrick Roy in his fearsome mask? I don't think so.

Come to think of it, I've only seen two hockey players carrying books. And they were both goalies, which, in a way, disqualifies them from the survey, as goalies are well known to be representative of nothing but their own eccentricity. One of them was a minor minor-leaguer on an overnight bus trip between Corpus Christi, Texas, and Lake Charles, Louisiana. He had sixteen hours to kill, so he was reduced to reading a book about goalies. The other was Mike Richter, the famously intellectual netminder for the New York Rangers, and he was carrying an intimidating brick of a book, probably about logic, or the problems of string theory, so that was a hopeful sighting.

The cynic, or baseball fan, might suggest that all this has something to do with the intelligence of anyone who would join a game that includes real fistfights, getting plastered against inch-thick Plexiglass, swinging sticks, placing one's body in the way of frozen projectiles, and avoiding blades, which are sometimes flying in a chopping motion through the air. The cynic might suggest that there never has been and never will be any great writing about hockey.

But the cynic is wrong. Somehow, intelligent observers have been watching and playing the game, slipping their thoughts quietly onto paper while the mainstream excitedly examines the hollow spaces in Sammy Sosa's bat.

The New Yorker actually runs a good article about hockey once every ten years, and Harper's seems to follow roughly the same schedule. Sports Illustrated commissions a thorough piece about the sport on maybe a biennial basis, and ESPN The Magazine goes deep much more frequently, or at least they did while their sister network was still showing a big chunk of the games. Meanwhile, up in Canada, far out of sight, real books about hockey not only get written and published, but actually appear on the best-seller list.

I've tried to get the best of this underground output in one book. It wasn't terrifically hard to choose the stories. The good ones were just so much better than all the rest. Finding them was the tricky part.

I don't have a favorite, but I find myself rereading Nancy Dowd's screenplay for Slap Shot, Alec Wilkinson's portrait of Richter, and E. M. Swift's phenomenal rendition of the gold-medal-winning 1980 U.S. Olympians. Each of these stories is completely different, and each succeeds as not only a chronicle of hockey, but as pure narrative that even a baseball fan can enjoy.

Peter Gzowski's inspection of the Great One is also up there, and George Plimpton's visit with the 1977 Bruins is the usual Plimpton performance: totally amusing. William Faulkner even weighs in, running hockey through the Faulkner-o-matic language and thought machine, so that it comes out as a metaphor for the American experience.

Of course, there are omissions. Ken Dryden, whose fine book The Game, about his time with the Canadiens, is not excerpted here, on account of it being so well known. (He's a goalie, naturally.) There's nothing about Gordie Howe or Bobby Orr, because I couldn't find anything sharp enough, which is probably more a reflection of my research skills. Roy MacGregor's novel The Last Season isn't here either, but I just didn't feel like including any fiction, unless the author was really making serious fun of hockey, which is why I made an exception for Brian Fawcett's hilarious, and completely made-up, "My Career with the Leafs," which sums up pretty well what would happen if a poet walked on to a hockey team, and all the players turned out to be secret bookworms.

At least, I think it's fiction. As so many of the stories in this book showed me, there's much more to hockey than you can see from the stands.

The
Greatest
Hockey Stories
Ever Told

A Reminder of What We Can Be

BY E. M. SWIFT

Maybe it was just the right writer, in the right rink, at the right moment—that being the peak of the cold war—but E. M. Swift's "A Reminder of What We Can Be," about the U.S. victory over the Russians at the 1980 Olympics in Lake Placid, is simply one of the most moving hockey stories ever written. Swift, a staff writer at *Sports Illustrated,* played hockey at Princeton. A goalie, he finished with a record of 1–22. He would become a better writer. In 2004, Swift, remembering the event, wrote that "A Reminder of What We Can Be" "took on a life of its own. People remembered it. They saved it. In many ways, it overshadowed everything else I would ever write."

The Miracle also overshadowed the players, and Herb Brooks, the coach. The impossibility of their success prevented any of them from ever doing anything nearly like it again. Brooks, who went on to coach four NHL teams without any extravagant successes, died in a car accident in August 2003, at the age of sixty-six in Minnesota, where he was born, where he had coached at the university for eight years, and where he found many of the players that made the miracle happen.

Seven months after the victory, Swift wrote "A Reminder of What We Can Be" for *Sports Illustrated.* The team had been elected "Sportsmen of the Year." The magazine later amended that to "of the century," and that may not be far wrong.

★   ★   ★   ★   ★

The impact was the thing. One morning they were 19 fuzzy-cheeked college kids and a tall guy with a beard, and the next. . . .WE BEAT THE RUSSIANS! In Babbitt, Minnesota, hometown of Forward Buzzie Schneider, guys went into their backyards and began firing shotguns toward the heavens. Kaboom! Kaboom! WE BEAT THE RUSSIANS! In Santa Monica a photographer heard the outcome of the game and went into his local mom-and-pop operation run by an elderly immigrant couple. "Guess what," he said. "Our boys beat the Russians." The old grocer looked at him. "No kidding?" then he started to cry. *"No kidding?"*

In Winthrop, Massachusetts, 70 people gathered outside the home of Mike Eruzione, who had scored the winning goal, and croaked out the national anthem. Not *God Bless America*, which is what the players were singing in Lake Placid. *The Star-Spangled Banner.*

One man was listening to the game in his car, driving through a thunderstorm, with the U.S. clinging to a 4–3 lead. He kept pounding his hands on the steering wheel in excitement. Finally he pulled off the highway and listened as the countdown started . . . 5 . . . 4 . . . 3 . . . 2 . . . 1 . . .WE BEAT THE RUSSIANS! He started to honk his horn. He yelled inside his car. It felt absolutely wonderful. He got out and stared to scream in the rain. There were 10 other cars pulled off to the side of the road, 10 other drivers yelling their fool heads off in the rain. They made a huddle, and then they hollered together—WE BEAT THE RUSSIANS! Perfect strangers dancing beside the highway with 18-wheelers zooming by and spraying them with grime.

We. The U.S. Olympic hockey team wasn't a bunch of weird, freaky commando types. They were our boys. Clean-cut kids from small towns, well-groomed and good-looking, who loved their folks and liked to drink a little beer. Our boys. Young men molded by a coach who wasn't afraid to preach the values of the good old Protestant work ethic, while ever prepared to stuff a hockey stick down an offending opponent's throat. And don't think that didn't matter, given the political climate at the time—the hostages, Afghanistan, the pending Olympic boycott of the Moscow Games.

But there was more to the story then the moment of victory.

The members of the 1980 U.S. Olympic hockey team weren't named Sportsmen of the Year because of the 60 minutes they played one Friday afternoon in February. The game with the Soviet Union meant nothing to the players politically. Even its impact was largely lost on them until much later, confined as they were to the Olympic Village in Lake Placid, listening to one dinky local radio station and reading no newspapers. "If people want to think that performance was for our country, that's fine," says Mark Pavelich, the small, quiet forward who set up Eruzione's winning goal. "But the truth of the matter is, it was just a hockey game. There was enough to worry about without worrying about Afghanistan or winning it for the pride and glory of the United States. We wanted to win it for ourselves."

Not ourselves as in I, me, mine. Ourselves the team. Individually, they were fine, dedicated sportsmen. Some will have excellent pro hockey careers. Others will bust. But collectively, they were a transcendent lot. For seven months they pushed each other on and pulled each other along, from rung to rung, until for two weeks in February they— a bunch of unheralded amateurs—became the best hockey team in the world. The best *team*. The whole was greater than the sum of its parts by a mile. And they were not just a team, they were innovative and exuberant and absolutely unafraid to succeed. They were a perfect reflection of how Americans wanted to perceive themselves. By gum, it's still in us! It was certainly still in *them*.

So for reminding us of some things, and for briefly brightening the days of 220 million people, we doff our caps to them, *in toto*. Sportsmen of the Year.

Leadership, of course, was the key. These guys didn't descend on their skates from a mountaintop preaching teamwork and brotherhood. Are you kidding? They were all-stars, *la crème de la crème*. Many had egos yay big and heads the size of pumpkins. Fifteen of the 20 had been drafted by NHL clubs and considered the Games a stepping-stone to the big time. They could showcase their individual talents, prove they could handle a grueling schedule, and, thank-you-bub, where do I sign? Herb Brooks, the coach, made it the most painful stepping-stone of their lives.

"He treated us all the same," says every last member of the team. "Rotten."

Karl Malden, the actor who plays Brooks in the ABC-TV movie on the team, *Miracle on Ice*, which aired in March 2004, has never met Brooks, but he has studied him on videotape, especially his eyes. "I'd hate to meet him in a dark alley," Malden says. "I think he's a little on the neurotic side. Maybe more than a little. Any moment you think he's going to jump out of his skin."

That's one man's opinion. Malden, that hard-boiled scowler who has no pity in his heart for anyone leaving home without American Express traveler's checks, was brought to tears not once but twice by the sight of Goaltender Jim Craig asking "Where's my father?" after the team had beaten Finland to win the gold medal, first on television, then months later on videotape. Truly, this team plucked many different heartstrings.

Brooks was as sentimental as a stone throughout. After the victory over Finland, he shook hands with two or three people behind the bench, then disappeared into the dressing room. Says Malden, "He could have smiled just once, during the game with Norway, or Romania. But he didn't. Then after working seven months for something, the moment he gets it he walks away from it. You tell me, is that a normal man?"

All right. No. But Malden is wrong about one thing. If you were to meet Brooks in a dark alley, you wouldn't be frightened. He would barely notice you. His mind would be a million miles away. You'd wonder where. He's a driven perfectionist. His wife, Patty, an attractive, bubbly woman, recalls seeing their daughter, Kelly, crawling around and straightening rugs when she was 10 months old. Patty groaned, "Oh, my God, I've got another one!" Brooks is also a brilliant motivator and, like all great coaches, an innovator. He motivates largely through fear. Schneider, who also played under Brooks for three years at the University of Minnesota, says, "He pats you on the back but always lets you know he has the knife in the other hand."

Significantly, the pat is on the back, the knife is front and center. Brooks isn't one to sneak around confrontation. "I gave our guys every opportunity to call me an honest son of a bitch," he says now. "Hockey players are going to call you a son of a bitch at times anyway, in emotion. But they could call me an honest one because everything was up front."

They do, and it requires very little emotion. But most—if not all—of the players realize that if Brooks had been any different, they couldn't possibly have accomplished what they did. "It was a lonely year for me," says Brooks. "Very lonely. But it was by design. I never was close to my university players because they were so young. But this team had everything I wanted to be close to, everything I admired: the talent, the psychological makeup, the personality. But I had to stay away. If I couldn't know all, I didn't want to know one, because there wasn't going to be any favoritism."

Players like Phil Verchota, who played for Brooks for four years at Minnesota then all of last year, have still never heard so much as, "Nice day today, eh, Phil?" out of Brooks. "Say hi, and you'll get hi back," Verchota says. "Not even that sometimes." The man scared the daylights out of them. Gave them the willies. He wasn't human. But he could coach, and they never questioned that for a second.

Which isn't to say they never questioned his methods. (His obsession, of course, was a given.) One of the devices Brooks used to select his final team was a psychological test of more than 300 questions that he had specially prepared. He was looking for a certain type of player, and the test was designed to show how certain people would react under stress. He thought he'd try it. There would be 68 players at the August tryout camp in Colorado Springs, and he had to cut them down to 26 in a matter of days. He would leave no stone unturned.

One player—an eventual Olympic hero—said, "Herb, I'm not taking this. I don't believe in that stuff."

"Why's that?" Brooks asked.

"Oh, it's a lot of bull, psychology."

"Well, wait a minute. Here's what it might show. It's not as important as what goes on out on the ice, but it's something we can use. I don't want to miss anything."

"I don't want to take it," the player said.

Brooks nodded. "O.K. Fine. You just took it. You told me everything I wanted to know." He was steaming.

"How'd I do?"

"You flunked."

The next day the player took the test.

What kind of competitor was Brooks looking for? Big strong kids who could *skate through a wall*? Guys who could *fly*? Who could *pay the price*? Who could make the puck *tap dance*? Good Lord, spare us. Brooks wanted young, educated kids who were willing to break down stereotypes, were willing to throw old wives' tales about conditioning and tactics out the window. He wanted open-minded people who could skate. "The ignorant people, the self-centered people, the people who don't want to expand their thoughts, they're not going to be able to keep that particular moment, that game, that season in the proper perspective. I believe it. Understand this world around you."

When Brooks talks about "ignorant, self-centered people who don't want to expand their thoughts," he's describing 90 percent of the National Hockey League. For better or worse, most of the players trying out for the Olympic team were hoping to jump from there to the pros. So they wanted to show the NHL scouts that they could do it the NHL way—ugh, me fight, me chop, me muck. That doesn't work in international hockey, and Brooks would have none of it. The players had to learn a new style of play in seven months. In simplest terms, they had to learn what any touch-football player knows by the fifth grade—that crisscross patterns and laterals are more effective than the plunge. They had to learn not to retaliate, which is almost un-American.

All that was easy, because weaving, passing, holding onto the puck is simply a more enjoyable way to play the game. Smashing that stereotype was a cinch. But conditioning? There is no mind in the world that is open enough to enjoy the tortures of Herbies.

Herbies are a relatively common form of windsprint that all hockey players do, but only the Olympians call them by that name. End line to blue line and back, to red line and back, to far blue line and back, all the way down and back. Rest. Two or three sets of Herbies at the end of practice is about as much punishment as most coaches are willing to dish out. The day before a game, it's a rare coach indeed who'll submit his players to even one Herbie, and by the time you reach the NHL, your Herbie days are pretty much over. Hey, we're in the bigs now. We play ourselves into shape.

Bull. In the 1979 Challenge Cup the Soviets skated rings around the NHL All-Stars late in the games. The Russians can do Herbies till the cows come home. They skate as hard in the last shift of a game as they do in the first, and it has nothing to do with emotion or adrenaline. They have always been the best-conditioned hockey players in the world.

Peter Stastny, the Czechoslovakian Olympic star who defected last summer to the NHL's Quebec Nordiques, says the one thing that most shocked the international hockey community about the performance of the young Americans (average age: 22) was their conditioning. The Soviets had always been at one level, with everybody else at a level below. Suddenly here are a bunch of *Americans*, for heaven's sake, whom the Russians are huffing and puffing to keep up with in the third period. Who *are* those guys? In the seven games played in the Olympics, the U.S. team was outscored nine goals to six in the first period, but outscored its opponents *16–3* in the third. What got into them? Steroids?

Herbies.

"It's a selling job," says Brooks. "When you want to push people who are living a good life in an affluent society, you have to do a selling job." The sales pitch went like this: Skate or you're off the team. You're gone. No pro contract. No big money. Gone.

In his own words, Brooks was "smart enough to know I was dumb." How do you get a hockey player in shape the way the Russians were in shape? Nobody knew, not in the hockey world. So Brooks went to coaches of track and swimming—areas in which American athletes have been trained to compete successfully on the international level—and found out about anaerobics, flexibility exercises, underloading, overloading, pulse rates, the works. Then he transferred this information to his players, who, because they were educated, because they were open-minded, were willing to listen. Willing to give it a try. Sure, we'll run up and down that hill to the Holiday Inn after practices. Sure, we'll do another Herbie. Twenty-five minutes of sprints today without pucks? Sure, we'll do it. And for six months they hated Brooks's guts.

There was a moment of truth for this team. A moment when they became one. It was back in September of 1979 when they were playing a game in Norway. It ended in a 4–4 tie, and Brooks, to say the least, was dissatisfied. "We're going to skate some time today," he told them afterward. Then he sent them back onto the ice.

Forward Dave Silk recalls it this way: "There were 30 or 40 people still in the stands. First they thought we were putting on a skating exhibition, and they cheered. After a while they realized the coach was mad at us for not playing hard, and they booed. Then they got bored and left. Then the workers got bored, and they turned off the lights."

Doing Herbies in the dark . . . it's terrifying. But they did them. Schneider happened to have been thrown out of the game, and he had already changed into his street clothes. He was watching in horror as his teammates went up and back, up and back. Again and again and again. But instead of feeling reprieved, he felt guilty. "Should I get my skates on, Patty?" he asked Assistant Coach Craig Patrick. "Cool it, Buzz," Patrick replied.

It ended at last, and Brooks had the players coast slowly around the rink so that the lactic acid could work itself out of their muscles. And that was when Forward Mark Johnson broke his stick over the boards. Mark Johnson, who made the team go. Mark Johnson, who was its hardest worker, its smartest player. Mark Johnson, whom Brooks never, *ever* had to yell at. And you know what Brooks said—*screamed*—after skating those kids within an inch of their lives? "If I ever see a kid hit a stick on the boards again, I'll skate you till you *die!*" They believed him. And they *would have died*, just to spite him. Says Silk, "I can remember times when I was so mad at him I tried to skate so hard I'd collapse, so I could say to him, '*See what you did?*' " But they weren't an all-star team anymore. They were together in this, all for one. And Brooks was the enemy. And don't think he didn't know it. It was a lonely year by design, all right.

"He knew exactly where to quit," says John Harrington, a forward whose place on the team was never secure. "He'd push you right to the limit where you were ready to say, 'I've had it, I'm throwing it in'—and then he'd back off."

For Brooks, the trick was knowing where that limit was for every player. They may have been a team, but they were still 20 different personalities. The first time Brooks saw Silk skate at the Colorado Springs training camp, he took him aside and said, "I don't know if you *can't* skate or you *won't* skate, but I intend to find out." Silk had been an All-American at Boston University and had the reputation of playing his best in the biggest games. Brooks wanted him on the Olympic team, but he knew that Silk needed more speed. So he promised to ride him, to embarrass him, to rant and rave at him all season long. And even *then*, Brooks implied, he'd probably be too slow. For three months, Brooks gave Silk not one single word of encouragement. *Silk, you're too damn slow!* Then one day in practice the team was warming up, skating around the rink, when Silk heard, "Keep at it, your skating's getting better." He looked around and saw Brooks. "He never even looked at me," Silk says. "He kind of whispered it on the way by. It made me feel so good I wanted to skate around and holler."

When Brooks was at Minnesota, he had an unofficial rule against facial hair. He would have liked a clean-shaven Olympic team, too. Trouble was, Ken Morrow, the team's steadiest defenseman, a gentle giant who minded his own business, happened to have a beard already. He'd had one in college, and he rather liked it. And the New York Islanders rather liked Morrow. So rather than risk pushing Morrow too far, rather than risk having the little matter of a beard be the straw that sent Morrow to the big money six months ahead of his team-mates, Brooks came up with a rule custom-made to keep Morrow around. Anyone who had had a beard before training camp could keep it. It was new growth that was a no-no.

Brooks treated Johnson differently, too. Johnson is a competitor, one of those rare players who find the puck on their stick all night long. He is absolutely dedicated to hockey, and was dedicated to the team— a leader by example. Yet, until September, Johnson had no idea where he stood. No one did—Brooks had an ax over everyone's head. But Brooks took Johnson aside shortly after the Skate Till You Die episode and told him, "You're the guy who's going to make or break us. When you're really playing, our whole team gets better."

"It was a real shocker," Johnson recalls. "I was just worried about making the club, and he throws a curve like that at you. What can you say? You take a big gulp and swallow it down."

Craig knew he was the man who would be in goal. He had played brilliantly in the 1979 World Cup championship tournament for

Brooks, and by waiting a year to turn professional, he had been all but assured of being the starting goalie for the Olympics. But while the personalities of the rest of the team fit together like a jigsaw puzzle, Craig's cockiness and penchant for yapping kept him apart. He wore on people. For Christmas his teammates gave him a giant jawbreaker, hoping to shut him up. But what the heck, he was the *goalie*, and goalies are kind of ding-y anyway, right? But the psyche of a team is a fragile thing, and when Brooks saw he had a goaltender who wasn't going to fit in, he made sure that he wasn't going to start *messing things up*. So he told Craig to keep his trap shut about whose fault the goals were, shoulder the blame himself, and buy the beer after the game. Don't muddy the waters. It was funny; Craig and Brooks struck up a friendship during the year. They were voluntary outcasts who worked, played, and thought very much as one.

There was a player on the team who had Brooks's ear—the captain, Eruzione. Brooks had wanted him to be captain practically from the start. He was a leader; he was sensitive; he was a catalyst. But the captain had to be elected by the team. So Brooks campaigned. He confided in Eruzione in front of the other players, assigned him responsibilities, showed him respect. He was even prepared to miscount the ballots, but he didn't have to. The players liked Mike, too. But even Eruzione wasn't spared Brooks's menacing knife. With three games remaining in their exhibition schedule and the first Olympic game less than two weeks away. Brooks called Eruzione aside and told him he wasn't playing well. *Uh-huh*. Mike, you're a great captain and a great guy, but you've got to start pulling your oar. *Uh-huh*. Or else I'll have to tell the press you've hurt your back and are coming to Lake Placid as an assistant coach. *SAY WHAT?*

He was going to cut his own captain! After 57 games he was going to say, "Come along and be my assistant—you aren't good enough!" Well, the hell with you. And Eruzione went out and scored five goals in those last three games. Not only that, when word got out that the coach was prepared to cut the *captain*—holy cow, I'd better work my little behind off. And Brooks did the same thing to Craig, telling him it was too bad, but obviously he had worked him too hard, played him in too many games, and now the goalie was fighting the puck and the only thing to do was to get Steve Janaszak, his backup, ready. . . . *SAY WHAT?* You're not giving my job away *now*, not *now*, not after six months of this crud. . . . But you're fighting the puck, Jimmy. . . . I'll fight you, you cur. . . .I'll show you who's ready and who's not.

So they went to Lake Placid united as ever against their coach. *They would show him!* Twenty players, the ones who had survived all the cuts, still hungry to prove themselves. Six who had traveled with the team all year were dropped just before Lake Placid. The last forward to go was a young man named Ralph Cox. Brooks himself had been the last forward cut from the gold-medal-winning 1960 U.S. hockey team, and the one time all year that his callous front came down was when he cut Cox. "He was such a gentleman that I cried on it," says Brooks. "I had a little flashback of myself at the time. And you know what he told me? True story. He said, 'That's all right, coach, I understand. You guys are going to win the gold medal.' *Ralph Cox* said that. And when we won it, that's who I thought of. Ralph Cox."

At the time, though, Brooks was thinking, "What have you been smoking, Coxy?" The U.S. team was seeded No. 7 in the eight-team field and had the toughest draw in the tournament, facing Sweden and Czechoslovakia—the second and third seeds—in the first two games. Further, in the final exhibition game, the Soviets—almost exactly the same team that had whipped the NHL All-Stars a year earlier—had routed the U.S. 10–3. Welcome to the big time, Yanks. The Americans were hoping for a bronze.

They hoped to get two points in those first two games, one win or two ties. If they didn't they could pack it in, because there'd be no chance for a medal. The scouting report on Sweden said that technically the Swedes were as good as any team in the world at skating, passing, and shooting, but in tough games their spirit could be broken. But you couldn't let them get a lead on you. Stay close.

In the first period the young, nervous U.S. team stayed close. The Swedes led 1–0, and they had outshot the Americans 16–7, but Craig had kept the U.S. hopes alive with outstanding work in goal. And the Americans had some chances of their own—both Rob McClanahan and Eric Strobel missed breakaways in the first four minutes. So now it was behind them, those first-period jitters.

But in the dressing room Brooks was furious. *Insane.* McClanahan had suffered a severe charley horse—McClanahan, who played on the first line with Johnson, who was left wing on the power play, who could *fly*—and one of the trainers told him to get his equipment off and put ice on the bruise, that's all for tonight. A *trainer*, for heaven's sake. And McClanahan *did* it. He was sitting in there in his underwear, an ice pack on his thigh, and the door flew open and there came Brooks, and *was he mad!* "You gutless son of a bitch! Nobody's going belly-up now!"

"Instead of coming in and yelling at us as a team, he picked on Robbie," Johnson recalled. "It was the craziest locker room I've ever been in. He's swearing. Everyone else is swearing. Robbie's swearing and crying. Then Robbie follows him out into the hall and is screaming at him, 'I'll show you!' And in a minute here's the door flying open again and Herbie's coming back yelling, 'It's about time you grew up, you baby. . . .'"

At that point Johnson yelled at Eruzione to get Brooks out of there. Can you beat that? *The star player was yelling at the captain to get the coach out of the locker room.* Finally, Jack O'Callahan, a defenseman who wasn't dressed for the game because of an injury, grabbed Brooks from behind; Brooks and McClanahan were jawbone to jawbone and O'Callahan was afraid they'd start swinging. Meanwhile, the rest of the team was sitting there thinking, *"We're one period into the Olympics down one lousy goal, and the coach loses his marbles."*

But had he? McClanahan put his stuff back on, and the U.S. team went onto the ice, outshot the Swedes in the second period and tied the game 1–1. McClanahan couldn't even sit down between shifts; his leg was too sore to bend. He'd stand there at the end of the bench, as far away from Brooks as he could get, then hop out when it came time to play. *I'll show you!* And he finished the tournament with five goals, tying Johnson and Schneider for tops on the team. Sweden scored early in the third period to take a 2–1 lead, but in the final minute the U.S. pulled Craig from the net and Bill Baker boomed home the tying goal off a centering pass from Mark Pavelich with 27 seconds left. The U.S. had pulled out one of the two points it needed and, what's more, everybody got to know each other a little better. "It was mayhem in here," Schneider said afterward. "But that's what's going to win it for us, emotion and talent put together."

Said Brooks, "Maybe I've been a little too nice to some of these guys." Honestly.

The fanfare didn't really start to build until after the U.S. beat Czechoslovakia 7–3 two nights later. That was the game in which, with little time remaining and the game well in hand, Johnson was injured by a dirty check (no pun) and on TV the nation heard the wrath of Herb Brooks firsthand. His proposal to wed a Koho hockey stick with a certain Czechoslovakian gullet provoked 500 irate letters, but it also piqued the curiosity of the non-hockey-minded public. Hey, this guy's *all right!* And those players. They're so *young.* Let's keep an eye on these guys— but what's icing?

Norway . . . Romania . . . West Germany, down they went, each game a struggle in the early going, pulled out in the third period when those nameless kids who looked about 15 simply blew the opposition away. And afterward the players would line up at center ice and smile those great big wonderful smiles, many of which actually displayed teeth, and *salute the fans.* They'd hoist their sticks to the fans on one side of the rink; then they'd turn around and hoist them to the other side. It was a terrific routine.

One of the reasons they still *were* nameless was that Brooks had forbidden them to attend the post-game press conferences, enraging both the U.S. Olympic Committee brass and the players' agents. The players themselves were none too keen on the idea, either, though they understood the reasoning. This team wasn't built around stars, and the press conferences were set up to handle only three players. You couldn't have three players getting all the publicity and not believing they were the stars. So no players attended them. Only Brooks. Then when the press accused Brooks of hogging the limelight, *he* refused to attend any more and sent Craig Patrick in his place. Now everyone was mad at *him.* But without the pressure of the spotlight, the team stayed just as loosey-goosey as a colt on a romp. Hey, this was *fun!* But the Russians were coming.

The day before the U.S.-Soviet game, Brooks held a meeting after practice and told his players that the Russians were ripe; they were lethargic changing lines, their passes had lost their crispness. All season long he had told them that Boris Mikhailov, 13 years the Soviet captain, looked like Stan Laurel. You can't skate against Stan Laurel? The players would roll their eyes: *Here goes Herbie. . . .* But now, 24 hours before the game, they could see it. The Russians were *ripe*. The timing was right. Forget that 10–3 pre-Olympic defeat. That was a lifetime ago. It was, too.

"The Russians were ready to cut their own throats," says Brooks. "But we had to get to the point to be ready to pick up the knife and hand it to them. So the morning of the game I called the team together and told them, 'It's *meant to be*. This is your moment and it's going to happen.' It's kind of corny and I could see them thinking, 'Here goes Herb again. . . .' But I believed it."

The idea was to stay close. "It was in the backs of our minds that we might win," recalls Schneider, "but nobody would say it. They'd think you were off your rocker." Craig made some big saves early, but the Russians scored first. Five minutes later Schneider tied it on a 50-foot shot from the left boards. The Soviets took the lead again, but with one second left in the first period Johnson scored to make it 2–2. That was a big goal. When the Russians came out for the second period, Vladislav Tretiak no longer was in goal; he'd been yanked. Vladimir Myshkin was in the nets, the same Myshkin who had shut out the NHL All-Stars in the 1979 Challenge Cup. The Soviets got the only goal of the second period and outshot the Americans 12–2.

Brooks told his players to divide the third period into four five-minute segments. They didn't have to tie the game in the first segment, or even the second. There was lots of time. Stay with them. Make them skate. The first five minutes of the third period were scoreless. Then at 8:39 Mark Johnson tied the game 3–3 on a power play. Bedlam. Go, clock, go! "I remember thinking we might actually have a chance to tie," says Pavelich. But the U.S. team barely had a chance to think of that improbability when Eruzione scored what Harrington calls "one of the great slop goals of all time." The puck was behind the Soviet net and Harrington and a Soviet defenseman were battling for it. Somehow the puck squirted along the boards to Pavelich, who hammered at it and was promptly smashed face-first into the glass. He never saw the end result. The puck caromed off the boards and slid into the slot, directly to Eruzione, whom Pavelich hadn't seen. Eruzione snapped a wrist shot past Myshkin. There were exactly 10 minutes to go. U.S. 4, U.S.S.R. 3.

That's how it ended. No one remembers much about those final 10 minutes except that they took forever. No one breathed. The shifts were insanely short because, by the players' admission, no one wanted to be on the ice when the Great Red Bear awoke and there was hell to pay. Craig, who had been tying up the puck at every opportunity during the tournament, slowing down the play, now wouldn't touch it. *I don't want it, man, you take it!* He was afraid, and rightly so, that if his teammates lined up for a face-off in their own zone and had time to think about the absurdity of leading the Russians, had time to peer up at the clock and brood about the time remaining, their knees would turn to goo.

But they never panicked. Shoot, this was a ball compared with doing Herbies in the dark. Indeed, if anyone panicked it was the Russians, who started to throw in the puck and chase it—NHL hockey, by gosh—who misfired shots, and who, at the end, never pulled their goalie, never gave it that last desperate try that the U.S. had made work against Sweden.

And then it was over. The horn sounded and there was that unforgettable scene of triumph, the rolling and hugging and flinging of sticks. The flags. My God, what a sight. There was the shaking of hands, the staggered reluctant exit from the ice. But it wasn't until the U.S. players were back in the locker room that the enormity of what they had done hit them. "It was absolutely quiet," recalls Janaszak, "some guys were crying a little. You got the impression that the game wasn't over, because no one is ever up a goal on the Russians when a game is over. No one believed it."

It was then that somebody started a chorus of "God Bless America," 20 sweaty guys in hockey uniforms chanting, ". . . from the mountains, to the valleys, na–na–na–na–na, na–na–na . . . !" Nobody knew the words. And where was Brooks? Holed up in the men's room, afraid to come out and ruin their celebration. "I almost started to cry," he says. "It was probably the most emotional moment I'd ever seen. Finally I snuck out into the hall, and the state troopers were all standing there crying. Now where do you go?"

Of course, the tournament wasn't over yet. If the U.S. had lost to the Finns on Sunday, it would have finished in *fourth place*. No medal. Brooks came into the locker room Saturday, took one look at guys signing sticks and pictures and began throwing things around and telling them, *"You aren't good enough for all this attention! You're too damn young! You don't have the talent!"* So the eyes rolled and the lips buttoned—but they listened, because what he was saying was obvious to all of them by now. They had come too far to blow it. And on Sunday they won the gold medal by beating an excellent Finnish team 4–2, but they needed three goals in the third period to do it. Really, they weren't even worried. They *knew* they would do it, because if you can outscore the Russians in the third period, two goals to none, you can sure as heck outscore the Finns. They believed absolutely in themselves. And Verchota, McClanahan, and Johnson went out and scored—bing, bing, bing.

They counted down the seconds, slapping their sticks on the boards, screaming to each other, to the refs, to the crowd. Again pandemonium, slightly less frenzied than two days before, the handshakes and the gradual retreat from the scene of their triumph. And then a bit of irony. The cameras captured the goalie, Craig, searching the crowd for his father. It brought tears; it made him a hero in the eyes of the country. But, in truth, he was searching for someone to share this moment with. Like Brooks, he was separate, apart from this team. He had no close friendships, and now he needed one.

The final, uplifting moment they gave us was at the gold medal ceremony, when Eruzione called his teammates up on the platform with him. After that they marched around the rink as if they owned the place, singing and carrying on. They were definitely not cooling it; they were happy young men. And they *did* own the place. They owned the whole country for a while. It just made you want to pick up your television set and take it to bed with you. It really made you feel good.

It is over now. Unlike other clubs, Olympic teams self-destruct into 20 different directions and careers afterward—at least in this country. There is never a next year for them. They write their story once. Sportsmen of the Year.

Facing the Shooter

There are few writers as gifted as Alec Wilkinson—not that this is news, for he has been on staff at *The New Yorker* for more than twenty years— and among that small group, he is, sadly, one of the only ones ever to turn his attention to hockey.

Like many of the best hockey writers, Wilkinson played, and still plays. He was captain of his high school team in Connecticut, and he brings to his articles an understanding and sympathy owned only by those who have been at it all their lives.

In 1992, when this profile of Rangers' goalie Mike Richter ran, the Rangers were starting their scramble out of a long stretch of mediocrity, rallying around drafts like Brian Leetch, Alexei Kovalev, and Richter, and acquisitions like Mark Messier. In 1994, they would break their famous drought, with Richter in goal, and win the Stanley Cup.

Wilkinson turned his attention to Richter just as things were getting interesting. It is a long piece, and full of lovely details, like the story of Richter's search for a meal on New Year's Eve in 1989. The final scene, in which Richter describes a goal using fireplace tongs and a wingback chair, may be the most nuanced description of any one-and-a-half seconds in sports. It is a dissection of a breakaway by Rod Brind'Amour, then playing with the Philadelphia Flyers, and Mike Richter's response. For anyone but a hockey fan, it must seem like madness to devote so much to so short a time. For a fan or a player, it is pure pleasure.

★ ★ ★ ★ ★

Mike Richter, the young goaltender for the New York Rangers, has a large, square face, like a detective in a comic strip. The bloodlines in his family run to two types: long-boned and thin, and compact and sturdy. Richter is the latter. He has sloping shoulders and broad hands. He is about five feet ten, and husky. He looks bigger in street clothes than he does in his uniform, because the padding he wears on his chest and shoulders is so bulky that it makes his head look small. When Richter is wearing regular clothes, one notices a wide back, thick legs, and shoulders that seem to descend from his ears. A crescent-shaped scar in the center of his forehead contracts when he lowers his head to think as he usually does before answering a question. The scar is the result of a shot from a teammate which struck his helmet two years ago, during the warmup before a game. Richter's manner is cheerful and generous and cooperative, but guarded. It is not in his character to be introspective. There is a boyishness to his face that suggests he hasn't yet grown into his circumstances—those of a big-time athlete in the world's biggest sports town—and also suggests an openness that is not actually part of his nature.

In June 1985, at the age of eighteen, Richter was selected by the Rangers in the second round of the annual draft of amateur players. He had graduated from high school two weeks earlier and had decided to attend the University of Wisconsin instead of Harvard. Richter is the youngest member of a large family—he has two brothers and four sisters—and his father had been ill, so there was little extra money for tuition. Wisconsin offered a full scholarship, with the expectation that Richter would play for their hockey team. For years, Richter, growing up in Flourtown, Pennsylvania, a suburb of Philadelphia, had privately nurtured the ambition to play in the National Hockey League, and he felt that the program at Wisconsin, which offered more games than Harvard's and a more single-minded atmosphere, would better prepare him to get there. That no one from suburban Philadelphia had ever done so didn't deter him.

It has always been a commonplace in hockey that a singular type of person is drawn to occupying the goal. Goalies have traditionally been thought of as men who nurse grievances, cherish slights, startle easily, brood and suffer nervous complaints. The annals of hockey include at least one goalie who became nauseated and threw up before games. On occasion, he would leave the ice to be sick, then return to the net. Sometimes, asleep on an airplane, he would suddenly kick one foot to the side, as if he were stopping a puck. Ulcers and insomnia have been prominent among goalies. A goalie named Wilf Cude was habitually so tense on days when he was to play that once, at lunch, he threw a steak at his wife, because she asked how a particular goal had got past him. The steak hit the wall behind her, and before it reached the floor he had decided to retire.

Part of the anxiety a goaltender endures is a result of the signal responsibility of his position. A goalie is the only player who plays the entire game, and he is the only player whose lapse of concentration can almost surely guarantee a goal to be scored. He is also the only player who cannot win a game. All he can do is lose one, help preserve a lead, or keep his team in a game that is close. People unfamiliar with the complexities of hockey are more likely to blame a goalie for a goal than any other player, even one whose defensive error may have allowed the person who scored to be unattended. A goaltender once described the pressure all goalies experience by saying, "What other job do you know of where, when you make a mistake, a red light goes on behind you, and fifteen thousand people call you a jerk?"

Richter does not throw steaks. The streak of the exile is strong in him, though. Among his teammates, he is a rarefied species. Young men from Canada still fill the majority of positions on the rosters of National Hockey League teams. While it is no longer exceptional for a professional hockey player to be an American—perhaps one in every five or six is—what nearly all the other Americans have in common is that they grew up in cold climates. Like the Canadians and the Europeans they play alongside, they were raised within the context of a sport that was played widely by children in the towns where they lived. It is not unusual for professional hockey players to have played next to more than one teammate since childhood, and many professionals have played with or against one another, or have heard of one another, or had had friends in common for years before they begin making their living from hockey. In a back room of the house where Richter grew up is a corner with pictures of Richter on teams he belonged to as a child. Each year, several faces are subtracted—boys whose interest was eclipsed, or who no longer played well enough to keep pace with the speed at which Richter was advancing. Richter had the isolated childhood of an athletic prodigy. He played for teams whose members were drawn from ever widening circles of territory. By the time he was sixteen, he was tending goal for a team sponsored by the Tropicana Hotel and Casino in Atlantic City, eighty miles from his parents' house. Playing games on weekends the team traveled as far north as Boston. As the years passed, the pictures on the shelf in the corner of the house featured fewer and fewer boys from Pennsylvania and the states around it, until Richter, at sixteen, was seated among players exclusively from Massachusetts and New Hampshire and Minnesota and Michigan.

Growing up in Philadelphia, Richter developed indefatigable habits of work to overcome his having so little time on the ice compared with boys raised in northern hockey towns. His obsession with hockey caused him to spend long periods of his childhood by himself. Richter's mother says that he was a simple teenager to raise, because she always knew that he would be home Friday night, preparing for Saturday's game. "I was fairly shy," he says. "In some ways, having so much to do was a relief for me. I never went to a prom. I never had an ordinary growing up. I always had a series of tasks in front of me—to do well in this camp, or that tournament. When one has been accomplished, there was always a second on the horizon. One after another, they got me through my childhood."

At summer hockey camps Richter attended as a boy, he met coaches who told him that the best competition was to be found at private schools. In the eighth grade, Richter drew up an estimate of how much money his parents spent on electricity for him to watch television and use lights in the house, and of how many showers he took and what it cost to buy and heat the water and to wash his clothes, and of the expense of the gasoline his family used running him back and forth from practices and games, and of the food that he ate, and tried to convince his parents of how much money could be saved if he were at boarding school with someone else looking after his needs. His parents were unmoved. Eventually, though, they sent him for senior year to Northwood prep, in Lake Placid, a small school known for the quality of its hockey teams.

Richter is accomplished more than gifted. He has extraordinary speed in his feet and his hands, but so do many goalies. More remarkable is his ability to play his position intelligently. As a boy, Richter learned the technical aspects of goaltending, and he devoted himself to perfecting them. He has a tireless desire to better his game. John Davidson, the Rangers' television announcer and a former goalie, says that what distinguishes Richter from the approximately forty-five other goaltenders Davidson observes each season in the National Hockey League is the intensity of his resolve to make himself more proficient. Richter's determination is unusual in someone who has progressed as far as he has. His habits of work are a tenacious response to a permanent feeling of deficiency—of being set back, of having an obstacle to surmount—and the success he has had with them is clear. In his first full season in the league, he was a finalist for the Vezina Trophy, given each year by the league's general managers to the goalie they regard as the best. Even so, there is a solitary and lonesome quality to him, as if he still felt his separation from the kids he grew up with, who were going to movies while Richter did situps and jumping jacks and sat on his bed at night writing entries in the notebooks he kept to record his performances.

Fear preys less on the minds of goaltenders now than it did in the past. The equipment they wear is better designed and more substantial than it used to be; the position is less painful and dangerous. A goalie is the most cumbersomely attired figure in sport. He is also the player in a hockey game least likely to be injured by the puck. The first modern goalie to wear a mask in public was Jacques Plante, of the Montreal Canadiens, who put on a mask on November 1, 1959, at Madison Square Garden. He had been using a mask in practice and in warmups, but his coach would not allow him to wear one in a game. The coach felt sure that the eye slits on the mask were too small to allow Plante to see the puck clearly and, in particular, prevented him from seeing a puck at his feet. Moreover, the coach believed that the mask made Plante less fearful and therefore less alert and less effective. By November 1959, in the course of tending goal, Plante had broken his nose four times and his cheekbones twice, had fractured his skull, and had received more than 150 stitches, without anesthetic, from trainers in locker rooms to close cuts on his face. Eight minutes into the game that night, the Rangers' star right wing, Andy Bathgate, released the puck from his backhand. The puck hit Plante in the face and opened a cut by his nose. Plante fell to the ice and was taken to the dressing room. Hockey teams then employed only one goalie. Each home team kept on hand a man willing to take the ice wearing an injured goalie's equipment. Often the replacement goalies were men with day jobs and a sideline interest in hockey. The Canadiens didn't want to use the replacement, so Plante returned after twenty minutes with seven stitches and wearing the mask. He had refused to go back to the net without it. Before he was hurt, he had made two saves, and then he made twenty-five more. The Canadians won, 3–1. After the game, Plante told reporters, "My head was hurting and I swallowed a lot of blood. I wasn't in any condition to play, but with the mask—well, I felt a littler easier."

When he retired, Plante wrote an instructional book for goaltenders. "People say I was afraid when I started to use the mask in 1959," he wrote, "but I ask them, 'Would you call it brave if you jumped out of a plane and didn't wear a parachute?'"

It wasn't only the lack of a mask that compromised goalies. The padding they wore to protect their chests and arms and shoulders and hands was not thick enough. They frequently lost nails on their hands and feet and had bruises all over their bodies. During the 1960s, players routinely began taking exaggerated swings at the puck in order to send it faster toward the net—a slap shot. A forward would carry the puck into the opponent's end, and if he saw no clear opportunity for a successful shot he might draw his stick back above his shoulder, lean his weight into his swing, and bounce the puck off the goalie's shoulder, or his chest, or his head. The next time the player found himself in a similar position, he might repeat the theatrical arc of his swing. The goalie would flinch, slightly; his shoulder would rise, slightly; the blade of his stick would lift off the ice, slightly. And the player would send the puck underneath it. This kind of manipulation made goaltenders resentful and morose.

Richter says that often, he doesn't see the shape of the puck coming toward him—he sees the streak and knows what direction it's headed in. He says that the puck doesn't hurt when it hits him—that the padding he wears protects him—but I have noticed bruises and welts on his body, and I have one or twice seen him when he takes off his equipment. Occasionally, a bruise will nag him all season, because it keeps being hit by the puck. Jacques Plante writes in his book that if you are the sort of person who worries about being hurt you are not cut out to be a goalie. I have never seen a goaltender, though, who doesn't try to get out of the way of a puck winging toward his head.

Richter says that a goalie is more likely to be hurt in practice than in a game, because there are so many pucks on the ice and not every player checks to be sure he has his goalie's attention before shooting. Also, Richter says, few of his teammates are able to control the elevation or the path of the puck once it leaves their sticks. When they wind up and airmail the puck to him from fifteen or twenty feet away, many of them have no better idea of where it might go than anyone else. More-over, professional hockey includes a motley assortment of personalities, and there is always the teammate who finds headhunting diverting.

A player with a heavy shot can send a puck toward a goalie at a hundred miles an hour. A few players can shoot it even more forcefully. The verb that hockey players use in describing the velocity of a player's shot is "bring." The proper reply to the question "Who shoots the puck hard?" might be, "Well, I guess Al MacInnis can bring it, eh?" Assuming that no opposing players are standing in front of the goalie and inten-tionally blocking his view, or that a puck being brought to him has not struck any of the thicket of sticks that have been thrust in its path, the goalie is expected to stop the puck. A goalie defends a space six feet across and four feet high. In the course of a game, he will usually face be-tween twenty-five and thirty shots. They will come at all speeds and from all directions and in all sorts of sequences and intervals, and mostly with very little warning. The puck will strike all parts of the goalie's body. The shots that miss the net make a sound against the boards or the glass be-hind him like a rifle shot, or a slamming door. The ones that solidly strike the posts of the goal make a sound like someone clanging a wrench against a piece of plumbing pipe. Hockey is a raucous Canadian prairie attraction moved indoors, and it looks chaotic and formless, but it isn't. It's just fast—the fastest team sport in the world. If it were possible to freeze players in the midst of a game and trace their paths, their trails would indicate a plan as plainly as if they were steps on a ballroom dance floor. There are plans of attack and there are plans of defense. A goalie on a team with a feckless defense may face forty shots in an evening, and more is not out of the question. Richter once faced sixty-two, and saved fifty-nine, a Rangers record.

Watching Richter at work—that is, isolating him from the activity of the rest of the game—involves as many moments of boredom as it does to be Richter at work. In any game, he will pass a fair amount of his hour keeping track of the puck at the far end of the rink—"like a fan," he says, except his attention is not diverted by the hot dog vendor, or the drunk with the air horn behind him, or the figures on the out-of-town scoreboard. Richter will actually take part in very little of the game, but the parts he is involved in will be among the most important. As devoted as he is to staying on his feet and facing the puck—what is called "squaring yourself to the shooter"—he will spend a good amount of any game on his back or his stomach or his side, sliding this way and that, lunging toward a player who has carried the puck past his leg, stretching furiously to cover as much of the goal as he can. Because of the nature of the surface he plays on, he can't always be where he would like to be. Once he is down, it isn't easy to get up. He wears thirty-five pounds of equipment. As the game advances, his clothes and the pads he wears on his legs absorb water from the ice and from his body and grow heavier.

Richter is a little bit shorter and far more muscular than goaltenders usually are. With his large thighs and classically molded upper body, his is more like a defenseman. The strength he is able to call on from his legs is at the center of his game: it allows him to move quickly from one side of the net to the other and to drop to his knees and get back up several times in the space of a few seconds. A lot of goals in hockey are scored on a goaltender who has fallen to the ice in making a save and hasn't been able to right himself fast enough to face a second or third attempt. This rarely happens to Richter. Goalies who rely more on their reflexes than on an ability to position themselves strategically move more after the puck has been shot. Richter moves more *before* the puck is shot, and when he is on his game he finds himself always where he wants to be. This forces a shooter to attempt a shot or a pass more complicated than the one he had planned, since the only parts of the net available to him are the corners.

To a shooter, a goalie looks like a piece of geometry. The best shooters see triangles—between the goalie's legs, between the goalie's leg and the side of the net, between the goalie's arm and the side of his body. Shooters will usually send the puck toward the center of an opening. The smaller the opening, the more difficult it is to aim for the center. The kind of battles that take place between a goalie and a shooter are rarely apparent to people in the stands. If a goalie is able by quickness and cunning to restrict a shooter's opportunities so that the shooter sends the puck wide of the net, or buries it in the goalie's pads, or passes instead of shooting, or loses possession of the puck without having taken any shot at all, most people in the stands will believe that the shooter fumbled a chance, not that the goalie gave him nothing to shoot at or forced him to try more than he could manage.

The style of a goalie who is adept at performing the technical movements of his position, who excels at calculating the intricacies of the angles available to a shooter and instantly reducing them to their least promising form, who can move with great speed in any direction, from any posture, and who has learned to let his body rather than his reflexes carry the burden of his work, will appear very unflamboyant. Since he is not likely to be caught out of position, he is not likely to be making the kind of diving, lunging saves that draw a crowd to its feet. It may seem as if the shooters were always sending the puck into his body. On his best nights, he may look as if he were facing an opponent who cannot manage an effective attack. He will demoralize opponents, and depending, of course, on the team in front of him, he will probably win far more often than he loses. A goalie who does this well is likely to be compared to Mike Richter.

For part of November and all of December 1989, Richter lived at Wally's Motor Inn, on the outskirts of Flint, Michigan. The view from his window was of a field with tires in it. Through the walls of his room came sounds representing the full catalog of human nocturnal behavior. Most of his neighbors were solitary men. Fistfights occasionally broke out among them. Wally's premises included a truck stop, and Richter ate most of his meals at the truck stop's restaurant, which was open all night. Often he fell asleep to the sound of diesels idling in the parking lot. Half a mile from Wally's was the rink where Richter practiced and played with his teammates on the Flint Spirits, at that time the minor-league affiliate of the New York Rangers. He was twenty-three. When he wasn't at the rink, he was usually in his room at Wally's reading books on nutrition and fitness and positive thinking.

Richter's father had died in September 1985, a few weeks after Richter had begun his first year at Wisconsin. When his mother called to tell him that his father had passed away, he was so at a loss that he said, "Are you sure?" He went home for the funeral. His father had rarely been sick, and his death cast a pall over the house. After the services, Richter returned to school and the familiar, timeless world of hockey practices and training and traveling and games. Obscurely, he felt that as long as he remained in Wisconsin he could put some distance between himself and what he felt about having lost his father, and to some extent he did. What he really felt about his father's death was waiting for him at the end of the school year, when he returned to Philadelphia and a house that seemed utterly changed without his father's presence. At some point, he found himself saying, "Enough tears, enough sadness—my life has to go on." Richter thinks that his father, a businessman, never thought much of the idea of hockey as a career, and it pains him that his father has not been able to see his successes.

Richter left the University of Wisconsin in 1987, late in his second year, for the team being assembled to represent the United States at the Olympics. At the end of a year and a half of preparation, Richter and his teammates arrived in Calgary, played a week and a half of boisterous, daredevil hockey, and finished seventh in a field of twelve. Richter and his agent felt that it was time that he came to terms with the Rangers. Before the Olympics were over, Richter agreed to a two-way contract—that is, he was to be paid one amount if he played for the Rangers and another if he played for the farm team. The Rangers had two capable goaltenders in Bob Froese and John Vanbiesbrouck, so they assigned Richter to their minor-league franchise, which at the time was in Denver.

"The assistant coach met me at the airport in Kalamazoo, where the team was on a road trip," Richter says. "I practice one day and play the next, and I say, 'OK, I'm in the pros now,' because I'm excited but it turns out I'm in Kalamazoo for a month. There's some reason the team can't play in Denver—arena's booked, I guess. We played five games in eight nights in one stretch, then six in nine in another, but it's OK, I'm in the pros, and I'm playing a lot of hockey. Still, it's different. I had been through college hockey, where you play two games a week and travel by plane and stay in nice hotels, and I had played with the national team, where you travel by air and every time you turn around someone is trying to do something for you or give something to you—'Can I get you something to eat, Mr. Richter? Are you comfortable with that chair?' In addition, everywhere the national team played we were the home team. We went into the spectrum, in Philadelphia, and played the Flyers, and the crowd was cheering for *us*. In the minors, you are just one player among many. You visit Saginaw, Flint, Muskegon, Peoria. The fans were ruthless, because they were mad about the Olympics—no miracle on ice. And even though I'm playing a lot of hockey, and I'm still excited, some part of me can't help noticing that I'm traveling by bus now, and that the players are all different ages, and some have gone as far as they ever will and are thirty years old and holding on to a job that is paying them maybe forty thousand a year—better, still, than anything the world outside has waiting for them—and some are my age but know that the team has no plans for them and that the future is likely to be a version of the present, but again, they at least have a job doing what they love. But even so, regardless of any of that, all of us are putting on wet equipment from the night before which no one has washed.

"As the days go on I begin to see that the team is also made of Western Hockey League players and Quebec League players, and the western Canadians don't particularly care for the Quebec guys, who feel the same way back, but if there's anything they both agree on it's that no one really likes United States college players. The Canadians think the United States players are taking jobs from Canadian kids, and that the Americans don't have the same fire for the game that Canadians do. Also, they think that Americans aren't tough enough. Someone told me soon after I got there not to wear anything like a sweatshirt with a college emblem, because that would be considered inflammatory.

"So it begins to dawn on me that I really do feel a letdown being sent to the minors. That year, 1988, was the last year of the Russian hockey team's true period of greatness, so I had been playing against strong competition, and even if our team hadn't distinguished itself at the Olympics, we had played well. You go to the minors and it's not something you dream of when you're young. Of all the fantasies I entertained about playing professional hockey when I was growing up, I honestly can't recall one that involved taking the ice in an arena that was half empty for a minor-league team where people in the stands shout unspeakable insults, which you hear on the ice. The team pulled itself together, though. We finished in first place in the division on the last day of the season.

"The next fall, Froese and Vanbiesbrouck came into training camp still established as the Rangers' goaltenders, but I played well in the exhibition season, and I was thinking that the Rangers would keep me around, but they didn't, and I was devastated. After I got the news, I went back to the locker room and told a few people, and they were saying, 'Don't go, don't go,' but I didn't see any point in refusing to report.

"I came back to Denver, and this time no one is at the airport to greet me. I'm eating lunches in *Denny's*. All the good players had been traded. I'm in a complete funk. We were going to get creamed—you could see it clear as a road map. We have a lousy team, and I was going to get shelled. We started the year with games where it would be five to nothing at the end of the first period. The year before, the team had been very tough; not only did we win games but we had some punishing physical players. They were all gone, though, and the guys on the other teams would remember how they'd been pummeled the year before, and they'd take it out on this team and just beat us up. We had a road trip that lasted a month, because the rodeo came to town. I looked at the schedule, and there were seventeen games away. We made the playoffs but we didn't win a game. I was called up then to the Rangers for the playoffs. The team was down three games to none to the Pittsburgh Penguins in the first round, and Phil Esposito, the general manager, who had fired the coach with two games to go in the regular season and had taken over as coach, put me in goal to start the fourth game. It was a desperate tactic—the team was demoralized and things were more or less hopeless—but I looked at it as an opportunity to steal the game. Which I didn't. Pittsburgh scored three goals in almost no time, and although I settled down after that, we still lost the game and went home for the season. David McNab, the Ranger scout who had first spoken to me, when I was a teenager, and who was partly responsible for my being drafted, called me and said, 'Congratulations, you're the only goalie in history to lose the playoffs for two Ranger teams.'

"The next fall in training camp I worked as hard as I could. Vanbiesbrouck and Froese were still ahead of me, but I began the year in New York. The Rangers had a new coach, Roger Neilson. By November, though, he had grown tired of trying to play three goalies. Also, it was hard for me to get time in the net in practice. It wasn't my place to ask Froese or Vanbiesbrouck to step aside, and I had to find time where I could, piecemeal. Mainly I was just sitting and not practicing, so they decided to send me down once again—this time to Flint, where the team had moved. Roger took me aside and said, 'It's tough; you're a good young goalie, but you're not getting the chances here.' Then he said, 'The bad news is you'll take a pay cut to play in the minors'—and I'm thinking, *A pay cut, I'm going from a hundred and twenty thousand to twenty-five thousand*—'but', he says, 'the good new is that Flint's not really a bad place, and you'll have a chance to play, and maybe some other team will pick you up.' I just felt my chest constrict, because I had been drafted by the Rangers and really wanted to play for them and I hadn't even really had the chance, and here we were talking about leaving.

"So now I'm living at Wally's. I didn't want to move into a house or an apartment, because that was a step toward a permanent stay, and I waned to be ready to be out of there, should the phone ring. The Rangers were playing an exhibition game against a traveling Soviet team on New Year's Day of 1990, and I had been told that I would be called up for the game. I began to get some sense from my coach, though, that maybe the Rangers had changed their minds and didn't really want me to come, and I felt like I was being manipulated, and didn't like it and got angry and said I was going. My girlfriend had come to Flint for New Year's, and I knew I was going to miss the team party, but I also knew I could go to New York, play the game against the Soviets, and be back in Flint in time to play the game on the schedule for the day after New Year's.

"I get to La Guardia. It's New Year's Eve. There's no one at the airport to meet me. It's Sunday night, dark, a pouring-down rain. No cabs, because they're all in the city taking people to parties. I finally get one of those vans that take you to the city and stop every ten minutes along the way. I had just enough cash to pay the fare. I hadn't brought any money, because I'd expected someone to be at the airport to meet me. The Rangers had reserved a room for me at a hotel by Madison Square Garden. I'm carrying my goalie equipment into the lobby, and the bellhop asks if he can help me, but I don't have any money to tip him, so even though I'm practically falling down and had barely made it through the revolving door, I say, 'Oh no, that's fine, I can get it.' All I had was a credit card and my bank card from Flint. I couldn't see, I'm so hungry. The hotel's room service was closed for the night. It's New Year's, and probably everyone else in the city knows you want to be on the twentieth floor or above to get away from the noise, but I'm from Flint and they give me a room on the fourth floor. I go out on the street and start walking around, looking for someplace I can eat with my credit card, but everything's closed, and the places I find open don't take credit cards. I'm standing in the coffee shops looking at the desserts in those turning display racks and those cabinets with the mirrors behind them. I come back to my hotel room. I had half a granola bar in my suitcase, and I eat that. Everyone in the world is drunk and is outside my window shouting and tooting those little tin horns. I had a glass of water and went to bed.

"The next morning, I walk over to the Garden, but it's locked. I go to a diner, where there's this old Greek man behind the counter, and I say, 'Hi, my name's Mike Richter, I'm a goalie in the Rangers' organization.' I tell him he can take my credit card, my bank card, my license—whatever he wants—but can I order some food and promise I'll pay him back? He said, 'Order what you want, we'll deliver it to your room, and you better pay me back.' So I had some ham and eggs and some toast and I felt better, and I go over to the Garden, and we lose, three to one, but I play OK. After the game, I take my shower and pack up my stuff and find the team guy who's supposed to get my ticket back to Flint, and tell him I'm in a hurry because there's a game back there and I want to be home in time to play. I figure the Rangers don't really want me around anyway, so I don't want to be there. Besides, my girl-friend is back in my room at Wally's. The guy goes to talk to Roger, the coach, and he says, 'Better have him hold off.' So I call my girlfriend at Wally's and give her the news, and get a ride to the Ramada Inn up in Westchester, where the Rangers have a room for me. Then I went with the team on a road trip in January and when I get back they put me in a hotel in Armonk, and after a few weeks the real-estate agent who rents most of the players their places says to Roger, 'What about Richter? Don't you think you should get him a house? He's at the hotel,' and Roger says, 'Jeez, is he still there?'

"So I get a house, and I'm playing at Madison Square Garden. I lose my first game, then I play seven in a row without losing and get named the league Rookie of the Month, and I'm really excited, and I never see Wally's again."

One day I showed Richter an arresting picture of himself from the *New York Daily News*. The photograph appears on the back page of the paper—that is, on the front page of the sports section. It took up most of the page—it was the biggest picture of Richter I have ever seen— and it showed him making a bell-ringing save on the shifty Philadelphia player Rod Brind'Amour, who had skated in alone on a breakaway. Richter looked like one of those soldier dolls whose legs and arms have been twisted into unnatural positions His legs were split and his arms were flung to the sides like wings. His left arm was behind him, and his right arm held his stick so that the blade defended the triangular space between his legs.

Richter was living by himself at the time, in a house with five bed-rooms and maids' quarters, in a neighborhood of big houses by the golf course of the Westchester Country Club, in Rye. He had rented the house in the fall with two other players, and both had been sent to the minors early in the season. The house was cold and enormous and drafty and dark. The only evidence in it of Richter was some cereal boxes in a row on the counter in the kitchen, a few books and pictures in the room where he slept, and a closet with his clothes. The house was on the market. People would arrive with real-estate agents and walk through it without Richter's knowing they were coming, or would be there while he was away and leave lights on in parts of the house he didn't often visit, and he would find them several days later.

Richter likes to use props when he talks. In a restaurant, he will collect anything at hand to depict a hockey player. "Say you're a forward," he will begin and start shifting the salt and pepper shakers and the sugar packets around as if they were cards in the hands of a monte dealer. At home, he liked to answer questions about goaltending by standing in front of the fireplace.

"That save was right near the beginning of the game," he said. "We were on a power play. Brian Leetch had carried the puck into the Philadelphia end and lost it. A Philadelphia player knocked it back up against the boards, a pool shot, and it came to center ice, where the only player was Brind'Amour. Everyone on our team was in the Philadelphia end—they'd been trapped by that quick clear—and they hadn't even started back by the time Brind'Amour got the puck. I skated about ten feet forward so that I could reduce the angle he had on the net, but I couldn't get out as far as I wanted, because he was traveling full speed, and I had to stop and begin traveling full speed in reverse to stay with him. I want always to be a barrier in front of him, with no holes, if I can help it, so that he has no way to shoot through me. The most difficult place to protect is the space between your legs. When you're in position, your knees are bent and your feet are apart, so there's a gap between your shins, called the five hole—the corners of the net are one, two, three, and four. For all the other saves, you make your body explode to reach the puck, but with the five hole everything is moving in. You have to, I don't know—I guess, implode, and that's very difficult. Anyway, my eyes are watching the puck on his stick. If I'd had more time, I might have tried to see where he was looking, but a player like Brind'Amour is tricky enough that he'll skate with his head down and only look quickly, or barely raise his eyes."

I called Brind'Amour, and he said, "Once I had the puck on my stick, I took a quick look but mostly I kept my head down. I can see what I'm looking for—how far out of the net he is, whether he's leaning one way or the other, or maybe leaving more space to one side, if he's got his arms close to his body, or if there's any room between his legs—but I don't want *him* to know that. All I could tell as I got closer was that no one else was with me, and that there wasn't much available. Richter was where he wanted to be, and he wasn't giving much away."

Richter: "Brind'Amour has a clear lead on everyone else, no one is going to catch him, and he must have realized that, because about twenty-five feet from me he changes from having his arms extended and the puck out in front of him to carrying the puck on his forehand, close to his body with his arms relaxed, which means that he can either shoot now or throw a fake. As long as his arms are extended and he's skating hard, he can't shoot—he has no force available to propel the puck."

Brind'Amour: "I'm going forward, trying to find the first hole I can, but I don't see one. I know he doesn't very often make a first move, and he's quick to recover, so I thought I'd probably only get one chance."

Richter: "What he wants is for me to move first. If I lean one way or the other, or move my feet, or respond to any gesture of his head or his hands or his shoulders or his stick, then I've committed my body, and he will have a fraction of a second to act before I can move in another direction."

Brind'Amour: "Sometimes you don't even think about what you're going to do—you just trust your body to come up with something—and sometimes you plan. It depends on how you feel, and it depends on the goalie. If you know he has a weakness, you might try and take advantage of it, but I didn't know of any weakness with Richter. I made up my mind to walk in and cut wide to the forehand once I got close to him, which would make him open his legs to stay with me, and then try to slide the puck between them."

Richter: "Brind'Amour's feet are planted and set apart, and he's gliding, but he hasn't yet dipped his shoulder or turned his blade to fake a shot, or moved the puck to either side to try and draw me with it. I'm lined up with the puck in front of him, and it looks to me like he is going to his left, because he's traveling in that direction and, as fast as he's moving, I don't think there is room anymore between him and me for him to reverse himself. I have to honor every one of his possibilities, though, because he's flying—if I go down too soon, he'll just chip the puck over me—and how I'm doing it is by taking little tiny steps, so that I'm not thrown off balance or caught leaning to one side of the other, which opens up holes. Also, you take small steps because it's very difficult to move a leg you have put your weight on. By cutting wide,

Brind'Amour's trying to make me open my legs, but I'm making sure my stick is in place to protect the space between them."

Richter turned around and picked up the fireplace tongs to use as a goal stick. Then he moved a wingback chair to a position a few feet in front of him and a little to his right, to represent Brind'Amour. "Brind'Amour got to the net," he said, facing the chair, "and I remember it seemed like he almost came to a stop and faded to the left, because he ran out of room, which is ideal; it means that I gave him nothing to exploit, that he used up his chances, and the advantage suddenly began to shift toward me. When he cut wide to the forehand, I had to explode my right leg out in case he was going to shoot, and that was how I ended up in a split. The momentum threw my left arm behind me. And then I fell over backwards. Before I did, he shot the puck toward the space between my legs, but I had my stick blade in front of me so that he had only a couple of inches between the top of the blade and my body, and if he's good enough to fit the puck through that slot he gets the goal."

Brind'Amour: "I didn't have anything, so I tried to make something."

Richter: "Instead he hit me with the puck."

Brind'Amour: "If you're going to write that he stoned me, you better put in that I got two goals on him later in the game."

Richter doesn't return phone calls. It is something he says he is working on. His tolerance for talking on the phone is limited anyway. A phone call to him usually ends by his abruptly invoking some variation on the theme of urgency. "OK, buddy, I'm running a little late. I was supposed to be at the gym/meet a guy/be at the airport an hour ago." Richter lives modestly, especially compared with his teammates. He is the only Ranger who does not have a fancy car; he drives a Honda several years old. Usually, the first purchase a hockey player makes is the best showcase car he can afford. Richter is frugal. He puts his money in the bank. There is a joke among his teammates that if you want to find Richter you announce that you are buying lunch. He was paid approximately seven hundred thousand dollars to play hockey last season, and he managed to save most of what didn't go to taxes and rent. He bought his mother a trip to Ireland, where her family is from, and over the summer he took a trip to France. One of his sisters works for a man who has a chateau in the country south of Paris, and he offered Richter the use of it. It took him a while to make up his mind to go. Visiting France meant giving up summer school—he has been attending Cornell during the summers—and resigning himself to making it up later; it will take ten years of summer classes to complete the year and a half he has left. His father conveyed to him the feeling that a person is hopeless without a college degree.

There are stories of Rangers wearing lampshades, and stepping from limousines in funny costumes after the team's Halloween party, and livening up the atmosphere of this or that club, but except for a little sing-along two years ago in an obscure Irish bar on the Upper East Side, I don't know of any such episodes that involve Richter. After games, his teammates head for bars where models gather. Richter, though, is often on his way home early, in order to have sufficient rest for practice the next day and the game on the day after that. Richter's adherence to sensible policies of diet and rest give him the air of an ascetic, or a priest. Without any difficulty, I can imagine Father Richter superintending a parish among the leafy precincts of suburban Philadelphia—not dynamic, perhaps, but admired for his deliberateness and reserve—which his parishioners read as wisdom—and beloved for his tenacity and humor. I see him as never insisting to his flock on the need for moral behavior but striving by example to convey its advantages. I do not see him as entirely comfortable with sympathy calls—shyness would restrict his natural feelings. I see him living in a small parish house, his light on late into the night, writing sermons on the subject of what might be said to be the goaltender's creed: Only the most rigorous vigilance can see a person safely through this life.

Open Net

BY GEORGE PLIMPTON

George Plimpton was the first, and, for fifty years, the only, editor of *The Paris Review,* which he joined in 1953, when it was just a year old. He is more widely known, perhaps, as writer of a series of books in which he tried his hand at a variety of sports, starting with *Out of My League* (1961), in which he attempted to pitch to a roster of major leaguers. It was a huge success, and produced a string of follow-ups. Among other things, he boxed with Archie Moore, played tennis with Pancho Gonzalez, and lost badly in a round of golf with Arnold Palmer and Jack Nicklaus. In the best-selling *Paper Lion* (1963), he tried playing quarterback for the Detroit Lions.

For *Open Net,* Plimpton, sticking to his m.o., spent several weeks with the Bruins in 1977, and, in this excerpt, suits up as a goalie for an exhibition game against the Philadelphia Flyers. *Open Net* is still one of the only, if not the only, truly funny books about hockey. It's too bad Plimpton didn't have time to write one more. He died in 2003.

★   ★   ★   ★   ★

My game jersey was handed to me. It had a big pair of zeroes on it like the spectacles on the back of a cobra's head. Two zeroes. With the Detroit Lions I had worn a single zero, which they joked was an indication of my talent. Presumably, the Bruins had the same sort of thing in mind, compounding it with an extra zero. When I skinned it on, I was fully dressed, goalie's pads strapped on and all. It was almost an hour before we were due on the ice. It seemed as good a way to pass the time as any. The rest of the Bruins sat around in the Spectrum's visitors' locker room in the first layer of their hockey apparel—the long white union suits—and played cards, or chatted easily . . . distanced increasingly from me now by their nonchalant calm. From time to time a player took a skate into an adjoining room to have its edges sharpened. A slight hum rose. Each hockey team carries its own skate-sharpening machine with it—a small electric lathe with a steel attachment for holding the skate in place. The equipment manager is responsible for the device and he strains his way through the airline terminals hauling the big tin-surfaced suitcases with the assembly within—the overall weight well over eighty pounds. Years ago the home team provided skate-sharpening facilities for the visitors, but it was feared that home-team chauvinism would ultimately prevail and that the machine would be tampered with—the edges of the skates dulled rather than sharpened, so that a player would rush onto the ice at a crucial moment to discover he was skating on what felt like a pair of spoons. A few years ago the Pittsburgh Penguins had their skate-sharpening suitcase stolen—presumably by a thief first threatened by the weight of his booty as he tried to scamper away with it, and then excited by the prospect of its contents—"What could be in this thing . . . so damn heavy . . . full of watches perhaps"—and then his ultimate bewilderment at wedging open the tin lid to discover what must surely be one of the more specialized machines around—a skate sharpener.

Don Cherry sat down next to me. He saw me fully dressed and said, "Well, at least I've got one man ready to send out."

I smiled at him weakly. He went on to say how amazing it was that nothing was consistent about how professionals prepared for a game. "Bobby Orr was the earliest I ever saw in the locker room," he said. "If it was an eight o'clock game, he'd get there at three in the afternoon. He'd pace around with a big weighted stick like he had nothing in his hands. He'd get half-dressed. He'd tape and retape his sticks until game time. Then you have the guys who come in late. Wayne Cashman comes in late. Brad Park comes in ten minutes before the team's due on the ice for the warm-ups. It doesn't seem to make any difference." Cherry paused and tapped my goalie's pads. "But I don't know any players who get completely dressed so early before a game. When are you going to put on your face mask?"

"Very soon," I said.

He began telling me about some of the pregame rituals. Phil Esposito laid out his sticks in a certain way, and his gloves too, and if anyone rearranged them, or stepped on a stick, there was always a big commotion. Just before going out on the ice Bobby Orr always went around the locker room and touched everyone with his stick and Terry O'Reilly carried on the ritual with the current team.

"Do you have any rituals?" Cherry asked.

"A lot of sweating," I said.

"I can see."

A few nights before, during one of our lengthy talk sessions, Seaweed had described a curious pregame ritual—the behavior of a fellow goaltender named David Reese with whom he played on the Bruins' farm club at Rochester. "Dave and I were sitting on our stools talking before a game," Seaweed had told me, "discussing the players on the other team . . . just a normal sort of conversation except that I noticed Reese kept looking up at the clock on the locker room wall like he had an appointment. Suddenly he quit talking in the middle of a sentence. He had just said, 'Now you've got to watch this guy because he comes down the ice and cuts . . .' and that was the end of it, like he'd been gagged. And from that time on he never spoke a word. That was his ritual—that exactly an hour before play he'd quit talking."

"That's the damnedest thing."

"That's why he kept peeking a look at the clock," Seaweed said. "So's to know when to clam up. He made it hard on himself, because if he wanted something real bad, or had something real important on his mind to say, he wouldn't allow himself to break that ritual. If he wanted something to drink he'd point down his throat with his fingers, or if it was something else, he'd wave his hand around and look at you with this pleading look, hoping you'd understand what he wanted. But he never said anything, ever. In fact, he never said a word until after a game was over . . . just a lot of nodding and finger waving."

I told Don Cherry about Reese and he nodded and said it didn't surprise him a bit. Tension could make hockey players do amazing things. He told me about the 1975 play-offs, when the New York Islanders carried around a fifty-pound sack of elephant dung to bring them luck. It had mysteriously arrived special delivery when the club was three games down to the Pittsburgh Penguins. It came with no return address in a big potato sack. Nobody knew who had sent it, or the significance of it being sent. Obviously, it could have been an indication of someone's extreme displeasure. On the other hand, the Islanders had been successful in Madison Square Garden in the first play-off series against the Rangers. The Ringling Brothers Circus was in town; a strong circus smell was in the locker room; somebody may have made the connection. So they took the sack to Pittsburgh and it worked. By then a talisman of high value, it disappeared just before their final play-off game with the Philadelphia Flyers. As Cherry told this, I could not help imagining the same thief who had snitched the skate-sharpening suitcase from the Penguins also snatching up the elephant dung from the Islanders' locker room ("Boy! A double heist") and his reaction after opening first one, then the other, in a back alley somewhere.

Sitting in the Spectrum locker room, it was oddly intimidating, a foreign place—stools, the wire mesh of the lockers, the colors . . . all were jarring. The players said you could always tell by looking at a visiting locker room whether the team occupying it was winning or losing. The losing clubs tended to creep into a locker room and leave it in the same condition they found it, almost as if they didn't wish to leave the slightest evidence of their presence. A locker room attendant in Madison Square Garden described to me a Washington goaltender in the early, dismaying days of that franchise carefully arranging a towel at his feet in the locker room before hawking and spitting into it. The Capital players sucked oranges and lobbed the rinds toward a big plastic barrel in the middle of the room with dead-center accuracy—the oranges arcing and dropping in like perfectly executed foul shots in basketball . . . almost as if to prove that this was one physical act they could pull off without humiliation.

That was not the way, apparently, with the great dynastic powers—the Montreal Canadiens, the Bruins, the Islanders, the Oilers, and so forth. As soon as they walked in, the place began to go to pieces. Their people sucked the oranges dry and simply dropped them on the floor. Then they stood up and stomped over them with their skates and ground the rinds into the carpet; the towels were strewn everywhere. They did not set a towel down like the Capital goalie. They went ahead and spit.

The attendant who told me this said he had always looked forward to the Capitals coming to town. "It's a pleasure working for these guys," he said. "But I wouldn't want to bet on them."

We went out on the ice for the warm-ups—fifteen minutes. The Flyers populated a half of the ice. It was true what Seaweed had observed—that the sight of them in the white and orange of their jerseys was an intrusion—like the strangeness of the Spectrum locker room—on one's sense of well-being . . . as if a gang of complete strangers had suddenly materialized in one's house. My tendency was to sneak awed looks at them. Which one was Dornhoefer? There was not much time to speculate because the pregame drills were hectic—a lot of activity all very carefully programmed to the minute. Skating drills to get the muscles loose. Shooting drills. The goalies took their turns. The arena was filling—a low hum starting to rise as the moments passed. A buzzer went off. Our time was done.

"How was the warm-up?" Cheevers asked in the locker room.

I replied. "Tense, I felt tense, and afterwards there were enough pucks in the back of the net to remove with a shovel."

"Don't worry about it," he said. "I'm always terrible in the warm-ups. In fact, the Bruins worry if I stop too many in the warm-ups. The thing about the warm-up is to get loose, get a little sweaty and feel the puck a little bit."

"I understand," I said.

"Remember, stand up. Going down is a reaction. You're less mobile. You've got to do your best to get up as soon as possible."

I gave a small groan . . . thinking of the laborious effort involved in hoisting myself up, rather—a friend of mine reported who had seen me at it—like a movie monster trying to pull himself out of a bog. . . .

Some of the players came by to pass the time—some to offer encouragement, others to pass on a quip: "Cherry has a surprise for you. A big one. You're staying in for the whole game."

No one else seemed at all perturbed. "That shouldn't surprise you," one of the Bruins said to me. "There's nothing you can do except carry on. I mean they all knew what Rocky Marciano was going to do to them."

"Well, thanks a lot."

Finally the tension in the Bruins' locker room began to settle in. The sticks lay in front of each player, fanning out into the room. The constant sound was the rip of tape; the players applied the strips of it to their skate boot tops; they worked strips onto their sticks. Through the locker room door we could hear the organ playing out in the arena, and the distant and increasing murmur of the crowd. From time to time a thin, squeaky voice emerged from a squawk box on the wall: "ten minutes"—intruding periodically to count down the time the team was due back on the ice . . . such a sudden, foreign presence in the locker room that it broke the quiet concentration and ignited a number of exhortations from the more voluble of the Bruins. "Keep loose and tramp 'em!" someone called out. "Stick it to them." "Everybody works out there!" Bobby Schmautz made a series of loud racing car "vroom! vroom! vroom!" sounds, and from back in the toilet stalls one of the players produced a perfect imitation of a hen laying an egg. I sat glumly looking out into the room. The goalies flanked me on their stools. Cheevers leaned across and had some more last minute suggestions to make.

"The Flyers have two incredible cannons at the point—Bladon and Daily," he told me. "Look out for them. When MacLeish gets the puck, as he comes across the middle he cuts loose, usually high, a shot he can do in full stride. MacLeish and Leach will always shoot if they have half a chance, and remember they don't have to get set to shoot."

"Right."

"Bobby Clarke is so good at the face-off in your zone that you'll have to rearrange your stance in the nets." He stood up to show me how. "As for Dornhoefer, he'll jam you in the crease," he went on. "He's not supposed to touch you, but you'll think he's part of your uniform. Get rid of him. Crack him with your stick!"

"Crack him with my stick?"

"That's right. Chop him."

"Chop him. You expect me to chop Dornhoefer."

"Why not?"

"I can hardly lift my stick up. Much less chop anyone with it."

"Use both hands," Cheevers said. "The main thing is just to keep telling yourself what to do."

I could not resist asking Cheevers if *he* ever talked to himself out there on the ice.

"No." He laughed and said, "I'd be afraid I might answer! Hey," he said. "One more thing. If you catch the puck, try to drop it out of your glove so your defensemen can move it up the ice and kill the clock. Your sentence will be up sooner."

The others along the bench were grinning. Schmautz fell to his knees and offered a mournful prayer on my behalf—pleading that I had sinned, but not so deeply as to be worthy of punishment by a Flyer slap shot. "Spare him that!" he cried, rolling his eyes at the ceiling.

Gilles Gilbert, who was assigned to play in the goal that night, pretended to drop a skate on his bare foot—incapacitating himself. "I can't go on," he called out. "Send in the new guy."

Cheevers said: "You've got to hope Kate Smith's not out there to sing the National Anthem." He was referring to the hefty singer from Philadelphia whose singing of "God Bless America" had been such an emotional catalyst during the championship years of 1974 and 1975. "If she is," Cheever was saying, "you're in for a serious five minutes."

Someone called out, "Hey, Georgie, give them the Northland sandwich!"

"What's the Northland sandwich?"

"That's the brand name on your stick, for Chrissake . . . stick it in their teeth is what I'm saying!"

"Oh."

I clumped over and sat down next to Terry O'Reilly to get away from the taunting. He seemed a lot more concerned than the others—grief-stricken and tormented. "I hate these people," he murmured to me. "They took the Stanley Cup away from us."

"Bastards," I said. I tried to work up some hatred, but the thought of the Flyers in the locker room just a few doors down the corridor, doubtless doing just what we were doing—staring at the floor between the fans of their hockey sticks, and working up *their* hatred for the Bruins—meant so little to me; I knew nothing of them. I had not seen them beat up on my friends; they had not scored a goal on me, or embarrassed me . . . at least not yet. Perhaps by the end of the evening I would work up some venom, but at the moment they were simply a vague foreign presence, like two dozen Finns. On the other hand, O'Reilly knew them as people who had contributed to the little stitch marks on his face and the deprivation of honors, money, winter after winter of this—indignities suffered so that animosity slowly built like adding charcoal to a fire until a torrent of heat was the result. One wondered how these people ever calmed down.

I went back to my seat next to Cheevers just as Don Cherry called for our attention and began his pregame talk.

He lashed at us; his voice rose. "There's a full house out there. Every jack one of them remembers the play-offs last year when you beat them and they'll really be standing up to you." His vocabulary was formidably peppered with cusswords, which was odd since in ordinary conversation with him there was little of this. It was as if the official language of the peroration required this sort of embellishment. He glared at us. "Take it to them! If they ever have one of our guys down, I don't care about the third-man rule; the rest of you be there to help him."

It crossed my mind that Cherry was pumping the team up too much . . . at least for my own good . . . that the Bruins would go out and "muck it up in the corners" so heartily that the Flyers would begin to bristle and retaliate, perhaps by shutting high and ringing a few zingers off the goaltender's melon.

Cherry kept railing at us. He said he didn't care if the Bruins were getting beaten 15–0 in the first five minutes (he looked grimly over at me as he said this) but he'd remember every time a check was made along the boards. That was the sort of pressure he wanted.

How many times had the Bruins heard these same words?—subjected before every game to this appeal to be physical, to go out and "muck it up in the corners." It was the Bruins' trademark. It was essential to their success. It was a simple principle: tough players got more room on the ice, owned it, like lepers being avoided—and that was worth any amount of finesse. Physical pressure was what made one team dominate another. Peter McNab said that it was possible to sense when the other team sagged under pressure—the analogy he used was that of a wounded animal on the veldt weakening, and the predators knowing it, and closing in—and the great pros especially could feel when it was happening to the other team and then they would increase the pressure. You never could be reminded enough.

And that, too, was why Cherry kept emphasizing the team to-getherness, even urging the players to break the third-man rule, which was that players could not break into a fight between two opponents without incurring heavy fines and penalties. The official wording for this is "entering an altercation." The French-Canadians refer to a bench clearing as a *bagarre générale*. The rules are very rough on the *bagarre générale*. In theory, two linesmen can handle a fight between two hockey players, but when seventeen men from each team get on the ice with their gloves off, things tend to get really out of hand. It was rare, even with the Bruins, that this rule was broken, because the fines came out of one's own pocketbook . . . but to hear it so obviously flaunted in a locker room tirade made a player feel sacrosanct: he was being told he was one who was above the rules.

When Cherry was done, we had just a few minutes left. Bridge-work was removed: when the teeth came out, the face took on a slightly different aspect, collapsing slightly, like the first twinge of an umbrella being closed. Cheevers leaned across from his stool. He looked very serious. He had one last thing he wanted me to remember. "Stand up! Stand up!" he said, meaning, of course, to remind me to keep myself aloft on the ice, that I was useless if I fell down. Under the stress of the moment I misunderstood him. I thought he was telling me, for some odd reason, to stand up there in the locker room. I shot up from my bench abruptly, towering over him on my skates, and looked down at him questioningly.

"Not in here, for God's sake," Cheevers said. "Out on the ice." He shook his head. "A basket case."

Cherry read out the lines: Mike Forbes and Al Sims at defense, and the McNab line, with Dave Forbes and Terry O'Reilly at the wings, would start. He read out my name as the goaltender somewhat per-functorily, I thought, making nothing of it in any jocular way, as if it were a perfectly natural choice to make, and then he looked over at me and said: "It's time. Lead them out."

I put on my mask and clumped to the locker room door. I had forgotten my stick. Someone handed it to me. I was the first Bruin in the tunnel. I could hear the Bruins beginning to yell behind me as we started out.

The tunnel to the rink is dark, with the ice right there at its lip, so that one flies out of it, like a bat emerging from a cast-iron pipe, into the brightest sort of light—the ice a giant opaque glass. The great banks of spectators rose up from it in a bordering mass out of which cascaded a thunderous assault of boos and catcalls. Cherry was right. The Bruins were not at all popular in Philadelphia.

We wheeled around in our half of the ice . . . the Flyers in theirs. There was no communication between the two teams; indeed the players seemed to put their heads down as they approached the center line, sailing by within feet of each other without so much as a glance. Seaweed had told me: "In hockey you don't talk to the guys from the other team at all, ever. You don't pick him up when he falls down, like in football." He told me about a pregame warm-up in the Soviet-Canada series in which Wayne Cashman had spotted a Russian player coming across the center line to chase down a puck that had escaped their zone; Cashman had skated over to intercept him and checked him violently into the boards. "Well, the guy was in the wrong place," Seaweed said when I expressed my astonishment. "He should have known better."

I skated over to the boards, working at the clasp at my chin to adjust my mask. The fans leaned forward and peered in at me through the bars of the mask—as if looking into a menagerie cage at some strange inmate within. "Hey, lemme see." A face came into view, just inches away, the mouth ajar, and then it withdrew to be replaced by another, craning to see. I could hear the voice on the public address system announcing me as the goaltender for a special five-minute game. The Bruins were motioning me to get in the goal. We were a minute or so away. I pushed off the boards and reached the goal in a slow glide, stopping, and turning myself around slowly and carefully.

The three officials came out onto the ice. The organist was playing a bouncy waltzlike tune that one's feet tapped to almost automati-

cally, but I noticed the officials pointedly tried not to skate to its rhythm
as they whirled around the rink to warm up, perhaps because they would
seem to demean their standings as keepers of order and decorum if they
got into the swing of the music. They too came up and inspected me
briefly, glancing through the bars of my mask without a word and with
the same look of vague wonder that I had noticed from the fans.

The Bruins began skating by, cuffing at my pads with their sticks
as they passed. Tapping the goaltender's pads is perhaps the most universal procedure just before the game—in most cases, of course, a simple
gesture of encouragement, like a pat on the back, but in other instances
a most distinctive act of superstition. The Buffalo Sabres had a player, Ric
Seiling, their rightwing, who had it fixed in his head that things would
go badly if he were not the last of the starters on the ice to top the goaltender's pads. The trouble was that the Sabres had another player, a big
defenseman, Jerry Korab, of exactly the same inclination. On one odd
occasion Bill Inglis, the Sabres' coach, put both men on the ice to start
the game; the two of them, as the other players got set, began wheeling
around the net, tapping the goaltender's pads, one after the other, to be
sure to be the last before the puck was dropped—a sight so worrisome
that Inglis made a quick substitution and got one of them out of there.

For me, even as I wobbled slightly in the crease from the impact of some of the stronger blows from my Bruin teammates as they
skated by, I felt a surge of appreciation and warmth towards them for
doing it. Two of the Bruins stopped and helped me rough up the ice in
front of the cage—this is a procedure so the goalie gets a decent purchase with his skate blades. Invariably, it is done by the goalie himself—
long, scraping side thrusts with skates to remove the sheen from the new
ice. It occurred to me later that to be helped with this ritual was com-
parable to a pair of baseball players coming out to help a teammate get
set in the batter's box, kneeling down and scuffing toe-holds for him,
smoothing out the dirt, dusting his bat handle, and generally preparing
things for him, as if the batter were as unable to shift for himself as a
store-front mannequin. However odd this may have appeared from the
stands—the three of us toiling away in front of the net—it added to my
sense of common endeavor. "Thank you, thank you," I murmured.

Other Bruins stopped by while this was going on, and peering into my mask they offered last-minute advice. "Chop 'em down! Chop 'em down!" I looked out at Bobby Schmautz and nodded. His jaw was moving furiously on some substance. "Chop 'em down!" he repeated as he skated off. Slowly the other Bruins withdrew, skating up the ice toward the bench or their positions to stand for the National Anthem.

I spent the anthem (which was a Kate Smith recording rather than the real article) wondering vaguely whether my face mask constituted a hat, and if I should remove it. My worry was that if I tampered with any of the equipment I might not have it in proper working order at the opening face-off. The puck would be dropped . . . and the Flyers would sail down the ice toward a goaltender who would be standing bare-headed, face down, fiddling with the chin strap of his mask, his big mitt tucked under his arm to free his fingers for picking at the clasp, his stick lying across the top of the net . . . no, it was not worth contemplating. I sang loudly inside my mask to compensate for any irreverence.

A roar went up at the anthem's conclusion—something grim and anticipatory about that welter of sound, as if, Oh my! we're really gong to see something good now, and I saw the players at the center of the rink slide their skates apart, legs spread and stiff, their sticks down, the upper parts of their bodies now horizontal to the ice—a frieze of tension—and I knew the referee in his striped shirt, himself poised at the circle and ready for flight once he had dropped the puck, was about to trigger things off. I remember thinking, "Please. Lord, don't let them score more than five"—feeling that a goal a minute was a dismaying enough fate to plead against to a Higher Authority—and then I heard the sharp cracking of sticks against the puck.

For the first two minutes the Bruins kept the play in the Flyer end. Perhaps they realized that a torrid offense was the only hope of staving off an awkward-sounding score. They played as if the net behind them were empty . . . as if their goalie had been pulled in the last minute of a game they had hoped to tie with the use of an extra forward. I saw the leg-pad of the Flyers goaltender fly up to deflect a shot.

Well, this isn't bad at all, I thought.

There can be nothing easier in sport than being a hockey goalie when the puck is at the opposite end. Nonchalance is the proper attitude. One can do a little housekeeping, sliding the ice shavings off to one side with the big stick. Humming a short tune is possible. Tretiak, the Russian goaltender, had a number of relaxing exercises he would put himself through when the puck was at the opposite end of the rink. He would hunch his shoulder muscles, relaxing them, and he would make a conscious effort to get the wrinkles out of his brow. "To relax, pay attention to your face. Make it smooth," he would add, the sort of advice a fashion model might tend to.

It is a time for reflection and observation. During a static spell, Ken Dryden from the Montreal goal noticed that the great game clock that hung above the Boston Garden was slightly askew.

With the puck at the other end, it was not unlike (it occurred to me) standing at the edge of a mill pond, looking out across a quiet expanse at some vague activity at the opposite end almost too far to be discernible—could they be bass fishing out there?—but then suddenly the distant, aimless, waterbug scurrying becomes an oncoming surge of movement as everything—players, sticks, the puck—starts coming on a direct line, almost as if a *tsunami*, that awesome tidal wave of the south Pacific had suddenly materialized at the far end of the mill pond and was beginning to sweep down toward one.

"A tsunami?" a friend of mine had asked.

"Well, it *is* like that," I said. "A great encroaching wave full of things being borne along toward you full tilt—hockey sticks, helmets, faces with no teeth in them, those black, barrel-like hockey pants, the skates, and somewhere in there that awful puck. And then, of course, the noise."

"The noise?"

"Well, the crowd roars as the wings come down the ice, and so the noise seems as if it were being generated by the wave itself. And then there's the racket of the skates against the ice, and the thump of bodies against the boards, and the crack of the puck against the sticks. And then you're inclined to do a little yelling yourself inside your face mask—the kind of sounds cartoon characters make when they're agonized."

"Arrrgh?"

"Exactly. The fact is it's very noisy all of a sudden, and not only that, but it's very crowded. You're joined by an awful lot of people," I said, "and very quickly. There's so much movement and scuffling at the top of the crease that you feel almost smothered."

What one was trained to do in this situation (I told my friend) was to keep one's eye on the puck at all costs. I only had fleeting glimpses of it—it sailed elusively between the skates and sticks as shifty as a rat in a hedgerow: it seemed impossible to forecast its whereabouts . . . my body jumped and swayed in a series of false starts. Cheevers had explained to me that at such moments he instinctively understood what was going on, acutely aware of the patterns developing, to whose stick the puck had gone, and what the player was likely to do with it. The motion of the puck was as significant to him as the movement of a knight on a chess board. His mind busied itself with possibilities and solutions. For me, it was enough to remember the simplest of Cheever's instructions: "Stand up! Keep your stick on the ice!"

The first shot the Flyers took went in. I had only the briefest peek at the puck . . . speeding in from the point off to my right, a zinger, and catching the net at the far post, tipped in on the fly, as it turned out, by a Philadelphia player named Kindrachuk, who was standing just off the crease. The assists were credited to Rick Lapointe and Barry Dean. I heard this melancholy news over the public address system, just barely distinguishing the names over the uproar of a Philadelphia crowd pleased as punch that a Bruins team had been scored on, however circumspect and porous their goaltender.

Seaweed had given me some additional last minute tips at training camp on what to do if scored upon. His theory was that the goaltender should never suggest by his actions on the ice that he was in any way responsible for what had happened. The goalie should continue staring out at the rink in a poised crouch (even if he was aware that the puck had smacked into the nets behind) as if he had been thoroughly screened and did not know the shot had been taken. In cases where being screened from the shot was obviously not a contributing cause of the score, Seaweed suggested making a violent, abusive gesture at a defenseman, as if that unfortunate had made the responsible error.

When the Flyer goal was scored, I had not the presence or the inclination to do any of the things Seaweed had recommended. I yelled loudly in dismay and beat the side of my face mask with my catching glove. I must have seemed a portrait of guilt and ineptitude. "I didn't see the damn thing!" I called out. As I reached back to remove the puck, the thought pressed in on my mind that the Flyers had scored on their very first attempt—their shooting average was perfect.

What small sense of confidence I might have had was further eroded when soon after the face-off following the Philadelphia goal, one of the Bruins went to the penalty box for tripping; the Flyers were able to employ their power play, and for the remainder of the action, the puck stayed in the Bruins zone.

I have seen a film taken of those minutes—in slow motion so that my delayed reactions to the puck's whereabouts are emphasized. The big catching mitt rises and flaps slowly long after the puck has passed. There seems to be a near-studied attempt to keep my back to the puck. The puck hits my pads and turns me around, so that then my posture is as if I wished to see if anything interesting happened to be going on in the nets behind me. While the players struggle over the puck, enticingly in front of the crease, the camera catches me staring into the depths of the goal, apparently oblivious of the melee immediately behind me.

The film also shows that I spent a great deal of the time flat on the ice, alas, just where Cheevers and Seaweed had warned me not to be. Not much had to happen to put me there—a nudge, the blow of the puck. Once, a hard shot missed the far post, and in reaching for it, down I went, as if blown over by the passage of the puck going by. The film shows me for an instant grasping one of my defensemen's legs, his stick and skates locked in my grasp, as I try to haul myself back upright, using him like a drunk enveloping a lamppost.

Actually, my most spectacular save was made when I was prostrate on the ice . . . the puck appearing under my nose, quite inexplicably, and I was able to clap my glove over it. I could hear the Bruins breathing and chortling as they clustered over me to protect the puck from being probed out by a Flyer stick.

What was astonishing about those hectic moments was that the Flyers did not score. Five of their shots were actually on goal . . . but by chance my body, in its whirlygig fashion, completely independent of what was going on, happened to be in the right place when the puck appeared.

A friend, who was observing from the seats, said the highest moment of comic relief during all this was when one of the Flyers' shots came in over my shoulder and hit the top bar of the cage and ricocheted away.

"What was funny," my friend said, "was that at first there was absolutely no reaction from you at all—there you were in the prescribed position slightly crouched, facing out towards the action, stick properly down on the ice and all, and then the puck went by you, head-high, and went off that cross-bar like a golf ball cracking off a branch; it wasn't until four or five seconds, it seemed, before your head slowly turned and sneaked a look at where the puck had . . . well . . . *clanged*. It was the ultimate in the slow double-take."

"I don't remember," I said. "I don't recall any clanging."

"Hilarious," my friend said. "Our whole section was in stitches."

Then, just a few seconds before my five-minute stint was up, Mike Milbury, one of the Bruins defensemen out in front of me, threw his stick across the path of a Flyers wing coming down the ice with the puck. I never asked him why. Perhaps I had fallen down and slid off somewhere, leaving the mouth of the net ajar, and he felt some sort of desperate measure was called for. More likely, he had been put up to it by his teammates and Don Cherry. Actually, I was told a *number* of sticks had been thrown. The Bruins wanted to be sure that my experience would include the most nightmarish challenge a goaltender can suffer . . . alone on the ice and defending against a shooter coming down on him one-on-one. The penalty shot!

At first, I did not know what was happening. I heard the whistles going. I got back to the nets. I assumed a face-off was going to be called. But the Bruins started coming by the goal mouth, tapping me on the pads with their hockey sticks as they had at the start of things, faint smiles, and then they headed for the bench, leaving the rink enormous and stretching out bare from where I stood. I noticed a huddle of players over by the Philadelphia bench.

Up in Fitchburg I had been coached on what the goaltender is supposed to do against the penalty shot . . . which is, in fact, how he maneuvers against the breakaway: as the shooter comes across the blue line with the puck, the goaltender must emerge from the goal mouth and skate out toward him—this in order to cut down the angle on the goal behind him. The shooter at this point has two choices: he can shoot, if he thinks he can whip the puck past the oncoming, hustling bulk of the goaltender, slapping it by on either side, or he can keep the puck on his stick and try to come around the goalie; in this case, of course, the goalie must brake sharply, and then scuttle backwards swiftly, always maneuvering to keep himself between the shooter and the goal mouth. I would always tell Seaweed or Cheevers, whomever I was chatting with about the penalty shot, that I had to hope the shooter, if this situation ever came up, did not know that I was not able to stop. All the shooter had to do was come to a stop himself, stand aside, and I would go sailing by him, headed for the boards at the opposite end of the rink.

Penalty shots do not come up that often. Gump Worsley in his twenty-one-year career had only faced two, both of which he was unsuccessful against—not surprising perhaps because the goals came off the sticks of Gordie Howe and Boom-Boom Geoffrion. But Seaweed had told me—despite the Gump Worsley statistics—that he thought the chances favored the goaltender . . . that by skating out and controlling the angle the goalie could force the shooter to commit himself. Also, he pointed out that since the shooter was the only other player on the ice, the goaltender always had a bead on the puck, whereas in the flurry of a game he had often lost sight of it in a melee, or had it tipped in by another player, or passed across the ice to a position requiring a quick shift in the goal. Others agreed with him. Emile Francis believed that the goaltender should come up with a save three times out of five. He pointed out that while the goaltender is under considerable pressure, so is the other fellow—the humiliation of missing increased because the shooter *seems* to have the advantage . . . the predator, swift and rapacious, swooping in on a comparatively immobile defender. The compiled statistics seem to bear him out. Up until the time I joined the Bruins, only one penalty shot out of the ten taken in Stanley Cup play has resulted in a score—Wayne Connelly's of the Minnesota North Stars in 1968 off Terry Sawchuck.

The confidence that might have been instilled by knowing such statistics was by no means evident in my own case. I stood in the cage, staring out at the empty rink, feeling lonely and put upon, the vast focus of the crowd narrowing on me as it was announced over the public address system that Reggie Leach would take the penalty shot. Leach? Leach? The name meant little to me. I had heard only one thing that I could remember about him from my résumé of Flyers players, which was that he had scored five goals in a play-off game. A record. I dimly recalled that he was an Indian by birth. Also a slap shot specialist . . . just enough information to make me prickle with sweat under my mask.

I gave one final instruction to myself—murmuring audibly inside the cage of my face mask that I was not to remain rooted helplessly in the goal mouth, mesmerized, but to launch myself out toward Leach . . . and just then I spotted him, moving out from the boards, just beyond the blue line, picking up speed, and I saw the puck cradled in the curve of his stick blade.

As he came over the blue line, I pushed off and skated briskly out to meet him windmilling my arms in my haste, and as we converged I committed myself utterly to the hope that he would shoot rather than try to come around me. I flung my self sideways to the ice (someone said later that it looked like the collapse of an ancient sofa), and sure enough he *did* shoot. Somewhat perfunctorily, he lifted the puck and it hit the edge of one of my skates and skidded away, wide of the goal behind me.

A very decent roar of surprise and pleasure exploded from the stands. By this time, I think, the Philadelphia fans thought of me less as a despised Bruin than a surrogate member of their own kind. The team identification was unimportant, for an instant. I represented a manifestation of their own curiosity if they happened to find themselves down there on the ice. As for the Bruins, they came quickly off the bench, scrambling over the boards to skate out in a wave of black and gold. It occurred to me that they were coming out simply to get me back up on my skates—after all, I was flat out on the ice—but they wore big grins: they pulled me up and began cuffing me around in delight, the big gloves smothering my mask so I could barely see as in a thick joyous clump we moved slowly to the bench. Halfway there, my skates went out from under me—tripped up perhaps or knocked askew by the congratulatory pummels—and once again I found myself down at ice level; they hauled me up like a sack of potatoes and got me to the

bench. I sat down. It was a very heady time. I beamed at them. Someone stuck the tube of a plastic bottle in my mouth. The water squirted
in and I choked briefly. A towel was spread around my shoulders.

"How many saves?"

"Oh, twenty or thirty. At least."

"What about that penalty shot?"

"Leach is finished. He may not play again. To miss a penalty shot
against you? The Flyers may not recover."

I luxuriated in what they were saying.

"Is that right?"

But their attention began to shift back to the ice. The game was
starting up again. The sound of the crowd was different: full and violent.
I looked up and down the bench for more recognition. I wanted to hear
more. I wanted to tell them what it had been like. Their faces were
turned away now.

The Game of Our Lives

BY PETER GZOWSKI

Peter Gzowski is unknown in the United States, but he was a legendary radio broadcaster in Canada, so much so that he was often referred to as "Mr. Canada," or "Mr. Broadcasting." As a morning host on the CBC, he conducted more than twenty-seven thousand interviews, reaching about one million people a day. He started as a journalist, however, and wrote eleven books. He died in 2002.

Peter Gzowski followed Wayne Gretzky and the Edmonton Oilers almost daily during the 1980–81 season, traveling with the team, and interviewing all of the players extensively. The result, a book about that year called *The Game of Our Lives,* was an immediate success in Canada, and stuck on the best-seller lists there for twenty-one weeks.

In this excerpt, Gzowski catches the greatest player of all time on one of his finest nights, and tries to find out what makes the Great One tick.

★   ★   ★   ★   ★

On the evening of February 18, Gretzky put on one of the most remarkable demonstrations anyone in the NHL had ever seen. Watching it was what it must have been like to see Nijinsky dance in his prime, or hear Caruso sing. Throughout the season, Billy Harris had been saying that one night, when all Gretzky's perfect passes were received perfectly by his teammates, and all his perfect shots went in, he would score fifteen points. In his February display, he didn't quite do that. Some of his passes were missed (he made some bad ones, too), and some of his shots were blocked. But he accumulated as many points in one game as all but five players in league history, scored as many *goals* in one game as all but an historic few, and in one period, scored as many goals as anyone, ever.

At lunch the day before, he had looked tired. After practice, we had ridden in his four-wheel-drive Jeep downtown to Walden's, one of Edmonton's smarter restaurants, which has more ferns than Guatemala, but was one of the few places where he felt we might not be bothered by his fans. He was enjoying the adulation that had now become part of his life. When it became too much for him, he would remind himself of his own boyhood worship of hockey stars—Gordie Howe in particular—and the grace with which they had treated him (or, in some cases, the lack of grace) and he would be patient and outgoing. For all the shyness he still retained from his boyhood, he did not like to be alone, as indeed he almost never had been. He was raised in a large family, and all the homes he lived in during his hockey travels had had other children present. Rooming with Kevin Lowe was good for him, since Kevin was as good at cooking as Wayne was bored by it—although never with eating—and as neat as Wayne was inclined to be sloppy. By the middle of his second season, however, there were places in Edmonton where he could not go. On the way to lunch, he told a charming story about this part of his life, which was also a measure of Vickie Moss, the young woman who had become his steady companion.

"Vickie sometimes forgets," he said. "Last night we went to dinner at the Edmonton Plaza"—he had been there to receive one of the endless array of plaques and trophies he was collecting, this one as Edmonton's athlete of the year—"and we could hear music coming from the convention room next door. It was that Edmonton group, you know, the Emeralds, that Vickie had sung with last year. When she heard them she wanted to go and say hello, and maybe sing with them for part of a set. 'Let's go,' she said, and grabbed me by the arm. Well, outside the door I saw a sign saying it was some kind of business gathering, Imperial Oil, I think. 'I can't go in there,' I said, but she just grabbed me and dragged me, and when I looked up there were about a thousand pencils coming at me. Sometimes on Saturday afternoons she'll say, 'Let's go to McDonald's and have a hamburger.' Well, I can't go to McDonald's on a Saturday afternoon. I couldn't get near the counter. She just seems to forget."

"Stick with her," I said.

"I'm going to," he said. "She's one of thirteen children and when I go over there it's just like I'm one of the family."

"One of her brothers is retarded, isn't he?"

"Yes. Joey. He's terrific. When I go to visit he puts on an Oiler sweater and he grins at me and says my name. Last week there was a Leaf game on TV, and he spelled Toronto. I got a real kick out of that."

"I wonder if people know why you put so much effort into your work for the retarded."

"My dad's sister, you mean?"

"Yes."

"Well, I was very fond of her. I was really close to my grand-parents, you know. I used to go down there and visit every weekend. They had a great place on the Nith River, not far from Brantford, trees and all that. I'd like to have a place like that someday. My aunt used to go there, and yes, I guess that's why I do the work I do."

"Some people think you're getting overexposed."

"Oh. Who?" He looked up to challenge me.

"I don't know. Just some people. Do you ever worry about that?"

"I guess I'd worry if they stopped asking for me. Gus is pretty good about handling requests."

"You're having a good time, aren't you?"

"Jeez." He laughed. "I must be about the luckiest guy in the world. Can you imagine getting paid as much as I do for playing hockey? I've only had one real job in my life, you know. One summer I had to haul myself out of bed at six-thirty and go shovel gravel off a truck for the highway department. I hated it. Later on, when I didn't want to practice hockey very hard, my dad would say, 'Do you want to get up every morning at six-thirty?' and I'd sure go and practice. You hear guys complain about the schedule and that. But for me this is just the perfect life. I'm having, well, you know, I just can't think of anything better than this."

"Are you ever embarrassed by the amount of money you're making?"

"No. Why should I be? There are guys making a lot more, and I'm supposed to be the biggest draw in hockey. It must be worth it for somebody."

"Pocklington says he wants to make you rich."

Wayne laughed. "Yeah. I don't know what that would be like. Right now, we're just trying to make sure the family will be okay." Most of the money he was earning was going into annuities for his siblings. It was something that Walter Gretzky had wanted from the beginning— although he had asked nothing for himself.

I told him I thought he looked tired.

"Do I?" He said. "I can't be too worn out. I'm gaining weight. I started the season at 166 and I'm 172 now. I've been gaining five pounds a year. Anyway, after lunch I'll go get some sleep." Making a confident U-turn, he pulled the Jeep into a parking spot near Walden's.

Wayne Gretzky is as unaffected by his fame as it is possible to be. He has kept in touch with boyhood friends, and still regularly calls the various families with whom he boarded on his way to maturity. He is diffident and polite with his elders and considerate of the children who crowd around him as if Edmonton were Hamelin and he the Pied Piper. Through the season I tailed around after him, he would amaze me off the ice nearly as often as he would on it. He has a capacity for making people feel welcome around him, of sharing even the pleasure of his accomplishments. When friends would ask me what he was like, for in the season of 1980–81 he became as celebrated as any Canadian alive, I would tell them, and they would be skeptical of my enthusiasm.

At Walden's he ordered a quiche and a wine cooler with 7-Up (one of his sponsors) instead of ginger ale. The waitress brought a mix called Bubble-Up. "You're getting closer," he said, laughing. I told him I wanted to ask a favor of him. I said that to help with some work I had been doing about how he thought when he was on the ice, I would like him to make a tape for me. We would select, together, one of his goals on videotape, and he would look at it several times, dictating notes about what had been going through his mind as he made his moves. He responded with enthusiasm.

"When can you do it?" I said.

"Well, I'm going home right after lunch," he said. "And tomorrow after practice I've got some interviews I have to do. But I'll do it before the game. I'll get there early."

"Gretz," I protested, "there are a million things you do well. But one of them is not getting to places on time, never mind early. You've never been early for anything in your life."

"I'll do it," he said. "We'll choose the goal tomorrow morning and I'll do your tape before the game."

NORTHLANDS: The display begins early. The Oilers are playing St. Louis, who are still in first place, and have lost only three of their last twenty-seven games. Tonight could be another showdown between Liut and the Kid. In the first period, Gretzky is concentrating on setting other people up. At 2:25, he takes a pass from Paul Coffey in the middle of the St. Louis zone, fakes a shot and sends a backhand pass to Callighen, who makes a smart move to score. At 12:30, on a power play, he is an intermediary again, this time between Siltanen and Kurri, who pops his twenty-first of the year. With Pat Price off for his usual first-period penalty, Bernie Federko scores for St. Louis; a minute later, Wayne Babych adds another, and the period ends 2–2.

I have my tape. Wayne did not arrive early at the rink, but when he did, he went right to the video machine, my tape recorder in hand, and sat down to work. This morning we chose one of the goals he had scored in the 9–1 romp over Montreal. This afternoon he played it through once at regular speed and once at slow motion, recording his comments. When Sather arrived in the coaches' room, where the video machine sits, he found Wayne still in street clothes. "We have a hockey game tonight," he said.

At 4:44 of the second period, he sets up Brackenbury, who is out to create some action. Brackenbury shoots, Liut saves, and Wayne pokes in the rebound. 3–2. At 7:03, Mark Messier, who is playing with the abandon we have expected from him all along, combines with Glenn Anderson to make it 4–2.

Stan Weir wins the opening face-off of the third period, and passes to B.J. MacDonald. B.J. drops it back for Paul Coffey. Coffey carries it to the blue line, feints twice, appears indecisive, and then swerves to his backhand to beat Liut again. 5–2.

And then the deluge starts. At 5:49, with Pat Price and Perry Turnbull off for roughing, Gretzky picks up a loose puck, cuts to his left and drifts a shot along the ice back across in front of Liut and into the furthermost corner of the net.

Bill Tuele, the Oilers' publicity man, begins an announcement in the press box that this is Gretzky's thirteenth goal and thirty-eighth scoring point in the last sixteen games, when . . .

He does it again. Nine seconds after the unassisted goal, he takes a pass from Coffey and moves in alone toward the goal. Liut comes out. Gretzky moves to his left again and shoots with the same motion as for his last goal, but this time aims it instead for the closest corner, and Liut misses.

The crowd, without Krazy George, gives Gretzky a standing ovation.

With the hat trick, Liut publicly acknowledges his loss of tonight's showdown, and takes himself out of the game. In his place comes Ed Staniowski, who has been doing yeoman service all year as his more celebrated colleague's back-up.

At 8:17, with the Oilers shorthanded, Gretzky scores again. Stealing the puck, he cuts yet again to his left, and this time, as Staniowski tries to outguess him, he repeats the low, short, cross-corner shot that first beat Liut. There is no power to these shots that are going in, but they are as accurate as a surgeon's needle, and there is something about their timing that is keeping the goalies off-balance.

The pressbox is buzzing. The three consecutive goals are among the fastest ever scored by one player, although Jean Beliveau once got three in 44 seconds. The crowd stands again, this time mixing their applause with merriment. The Oilers are whipping the first-place Blues 8–2. Tuele is chattering statistics into the press box PA.

And then Gretzky does it again. He is standing in the attacking zone when Doug Hicks, taking a pass at the blue line from Siltanen, rips an apparently harmless snapshot in the vague direction of the goal. As the puck is about to whistle by Gretzky, he flicks his stick in the air and directs it into an open corner of the goal.

Are these the fastest *four* goals ever scored? No one in the press-box knows. But the record he has tied—four in one period—goes back to 1934, when Busher Jackson did it for Toronto against a team called the St. Louis Eagles. And what about Gretzky's five goals in one game? In all the NHL's history, only seventeen men have scored five goals in one game; one was Maurice Richard, one was Howie Morenz, and five of them were Joe Malone.

There is an unhurried grace to everything Gretzky does on the ice. Winding up for a slapshot, he will stop for an almost imperceptible moment at the top of his arc, like a golfer with a rhythmic swing. Often the difference between what Wayne does with the puck and what a less accomplished player would have done with it is simply a *pause*, as if, as time freezes, he is enjoying an extra handful of milliseconds. Time seems to slow down for him, and indeed, it may actually do so. Dr. Adrian R. M. Upton, the head neurologist at McMaster University in Hamilton, Ontario, has done some fascinating experiments with elite sprinters that suggest (the reservations about the work are that it is very hard to get a sufficiently large sample to test) that their motor neurons fire faster than those of mere mortals; the quicker their reaction times were to even simple tap tests, the faster they were liable to run. If this is true, it may account for much of what we see among the champions of a lot of sports. When Bjorn Borg, playing tennis as fast as any human can play it, appears to have the same control the rest of us would have in a casual Sunday morning knock-up, it may well be that for him the pace *is* slower; his neurological motor is running with such efficiency that his response to his opponent's actions is as deliberate as ours would be at a more turgid pace. Dr. Upton, who has published several technical papers about his work with athletes, compares the difference between the neurological systems of the superstars and those of the rest of us to the difference between a highly tuned sports car and the family sedan. The sports car is simply capable of firing faster. When George Brett claims that he can see the stitches on a baseball spinning toward his hitting zone, he may be telling us something about his motoneurological capacity. Wayne, too, if

Dr. Upton's suppositions are correct (and from neurological evidence alone he was able to predict the 1976 Olympic sprint victory of Hasely Crawford of Trinidad), is reacting to the situation of the games he plays as if it were being played for him in slow-motion film.

In the fall of 1980, John Jerome, a former editor of *Skiing* magazine, brought out a book called *The Sweet Spot in Time*, in which he examined much of the most recent exploration of athletic anatomy. His title was an echo of one of his central observations, that just as there is a physical "sweet spot" on a tennis racquet or a baseball bat, so is there, for the exceptional athlete, an almost immeasurably brief moment in time that is precisely right for performing his action. In explaining this thesis, Jerome cited a musical analogy. He wrote:

> I happened to hear violinist Isaac Stern discuss his art one night, and a jazz musician [whose name escapes me] the next. Both of these immensely talented individuals would sing wordless snatches—"dum dum ti dum," and so on—to illustrate points about their very different forms of music. I am not a musician, and could barely catch the significant differences they were demonstrating so effortlessly. I could discern, but I'm sure I did not fully comprehend, these differences—in emphasis and tone, but mostly just in timing. Each man would illustrate one way to play a phrase, then an alternate, varying the timing of the notes subtly without violating the form, changing in major ways the emotional content of the music without changing a note. I suddenly realized that for musicians—and for athletes—there must be a great deal more *room*, in effect, in the flow of time than there is for the rest of us.

Gretzky uses this room to insert an extra beat into his actions. In front of the net, eyeball to eyeball with the goaltender, he will . . . hold the puck one . . . extra instant, upsetting the anticipated rhythm of the game, extending his moment, as he did against Liut and Staniowski, the way a ballet dancer extends the time of his leap. He distorts time, and not always by slowing it down. Sometimes he will release the puck before he appears to be ready, threading a pass through a maze of players precisely to the blade of a teammate's stick, or finding a chink in a goaltender's armor and slipping the puck into it before the goaltender is ready to react. Because of hockey's speed, the differences between his actions and those of anyone else are invisible from the stands (as they often are, for that matter, from a position next to him on the ice). If he did not repeat their results so many times it would be possible to dismiss many of them as luck. If there is such a thing as sleight of body, he performs it.

On top of his neurological advantages, Gretzky seems to bring certain special qualities of metabolism to the game. With Gordie Howe, he shares an exceptional capacity to renew his energy resources quickly. Even when Howe had been out on the ice longer than any of his team-mates he would be the first man on the bench to lift his head. Similarly with Gretzky, who often, as against St. Louis, or in the turnaround of the game in Toronto in November, has his best moments in the third period. When Dave Smith, a University of Alberta exercise physiologist who tested all the Oilers in the spring of 1980, first saw the results of Gret-zky's test of recuperative abilities, he thought the machine had broken.

In the simplest terms, Gretzky is an exceptional pure athlete. Bearing out Dr. Upton's suppositions, he is a runner fast enough to compete at respectable levels. (His sister, Kim, was a provincial cham-pion.) In baseball, he batted .492 for the Brantford CKCP Braves in the summer of 1980, and he was offered—seriously—a contract by the Toronto Blue Jays. But he is hardly a superman. Smith's tests showed him to be the weakest of the Oilers. ("Am I stronger than my Mom?" he asked when he saw the results.)

His physical gifts, in any case, are not enough to account for Gretzky's supremacy. Each year in Canada alone, some hundred thou-sand boys totter out on the ice for their first game of organized hockey. By the time they reach puberty, about half of them will have dropped out. Some of those who leave will have done so for reasons that have little to do with ability: girls, school, their parents' unwillingness to con-tinue the Saturday dawn drive to the rink, or simply because they don't like playing hockey. At about the age of twelve, however, those who are playing at the most competitive levels will include a high percentage of gifted and ambitious athletes. As with my own contemporaries from Galt, all that will keep most of them from professional hockey is that somehow they are not good enough. I asked various sports physiologists how many of, say, a hundred elite Canadian peewees they could eliminate from potential stardom in the NHL through physical measurements alone. The highest guess was twenty, which came at the University of Alberta; the lowest was none, which came at Waterloo, in Ontario. Given a certain minimum standard of size-for-age, in other words, and a general aptitude for sports, there is almost nothing in the human body—unless Dr. Upton's sophisticated tests are someday made universal—that can separate the potential million-dollar hockey player from the potential weekend racquetballer.

Much of the most interesting work in sports physiology has been done with muscle fibers. Researchers have taken painful biopsies of athletes to see what they could learn. While much of this work has been of value in understanding how muscles work—what fast-twitch fibers (the dark meat) do, as opposed to slow-twitch fibers—it has not been of much predictive use. "Little, if any, of the information has been of any value to the athletes studied," wrote the authors of an overview of their work in *The Physician and Sportsmedicine* in January 1980. For an even more exhaustive view of "Physiological and anthropometric characteristics of elite Canadian ice hockey players" published in *The Journal of Sports Medicine and Physical Fitness*, Drs. William Houston and Howard Green of the Waterloo department of kinesiology studied various characteristics of two teams of different levels. They concluded: "The absence of significant physiological differences emphasizes the fact that physiological criteria were not differentiating factors."

And yet by the time the hundred thousand boys who started hockey reach an eligible age, perhaps fifty of them—in a very good year—will win places in the NHL, making the odds against a young hockey player reaching the pinnacle of that profession higher than they are against a random student in grade one becoming a university teacher. What has winnowed them out, finally, is not their ability but the way they are able to apply it, to put together the various small components of hockey that are so painstakingly measured on the Oilers' scouting chart. As Drs. Houston and Green concluded: "In the absence of a fundamental understanding of the physiological systems involved, coaches tend to differentiate between hockey players on that aspect with which they are most familiar, skill."

Even skill, however, is not a sufficient standard by which to measure Gretzky's mastery. At many of the skating techniques the Oilers' scouts would rate, he would be, perhaps, seven out of nine; at shooting less. And yet scrawled across his reports are only the words "can't miss." What separates him from his peers in the end, the quality that has led him to the very point of the pyramid, may well have nothing to do with physical characteristics at all, but instead be a matter of perception, not so much of what he sees—he does not have exceptional vision—but of *how* he sees it and how he absorbs it. Here, some work in fields that at first glance seem a long way from hockey yield some enlightening clues.

Much of this work is recent, but it is an extension of experiments carried out in the late 1930s by the Dutch psychologist Adrian de Groot. De Groot worked with chess players, whom he divided into groups according to their level of play: grand master, experts, and club players. In one experiment he had each player look for a limited time at a number of chess pieces arranged on a board in a fairly complex middle-game position. Then he asked his subjects to reconstruct that position. Perhaps not surprisingly, the grand masters did much better than the experts, and the experts much better than the club players. Then, however, de Groot exposed all three groups to yet another set of positions, only this time the pieces were arranged not in game situations but at random. This time, there was no measurable difference in the participants' ability to recall the arrangement. What the better players had remembered, in other words, was not so much the positions of the chess pieces but the overall situations. Later experiments confirmed these findings; the more highly gifted the chess player was, the more likely he was to see on a board not individual pieces, but the combinations they formed, the forces in play. In the 1970s, Neil Charness a professor of psychology at the University of Waterloo, himself a chess player who had carried on work in the de Groot tradition, extended these explorations to the field of bridge. Charness found—to oversimplify—that expert bridge players could remember bridge hands much better than beginners, but at remembering combinations of cards that had no relationship to bridge they were no better at all. And in a recent PhD thesis, an Ontario psychologist named Lynne Beal showed that the same principle held for music: accomplished musicians could recall and repeat sets of chords better than nonaccomplished musicians could, but when notes were assembled in random clusters, the experts fared no better than their less well-trained partners in the experiment.

The more we are trained in a given field, then, the more we tend to understand that field in combinations of familiar information, or what the psychologists call "chunks." A chunk, to use one of Neil Charness's examples, might be a telephone number. If you are familiar with a telephone number—your own—you can summon it up at will. If you're learning a new one, you will stumble over it as you begin to dial. Given two new numbers at once, you will almost certainly get them confused. This is the difference between short-term memory and long-term memory. Short term is what you pick up and use instantly. Long term is what has become part of your bank account of information. When a *chunk* of information becomes part of your long-term memory, it can be summoned up as a single piece. The chess player can react to a combination he has seen before, and expert chess players carry around as many as 50,000 combinations in their memory bank. A concert pianist tends to practice longer phrases from his musical repertoire, and recall them as longer phrases, than a Sunday thumper.

In the 1970s a sociologist named David Sudnow set out to teach himself to play jazz piano like a professional. When he had progressed to the state he was happy with, he wrote a book called *Ways of the Hand*. At the beginning of his experiments, Sudnow wrote: "I wrote down the names of the notes under each finger, then went home and duplicated the songs. I gained a little repertoire of tunes this way, but I didn't know what I was doing." At the end, he concluded, he had absorbed a new language. "I learned this language through five years of overhearing it spoken. I had come to learn it in a terrain . . . of hands and keyboard whose respective surfaces had become known as the respective surfaces of my tongue and teeth and palate are known to each other."

In 1965, the American journalist John McPhee set out to discover some of the secrets that at the time appeared to set the basketball player Bill Bradley (now a U.S. senator) as far apart from his peers as Gretzky now appears from his. McPhee found that Bradley, who, like Wayne, had an impressive ability to articulate his own performance, had an almost mystical sense of the shape and situation of the basketball court. McPhee wrote:

All shots in basketball are supposed to have names—the set, the hook, the lay-up, the jump shot, and so on—and one weekend last July, while Bradley was in Princeton working on his senior thesis and putting in some time in the Princeton gymnasium to keep himself in form for the Olympics, I asked him what he called his over-the-shoulder shot. He said he had never heard a name for it, but that he had seen Oscar Robertson, of the Cincinnati Royals, and Jerry West, of the Los Angeles Lakers, do it, and had worked it out for himself. He went on to say that it is a much simpler shot than it appears to be and, to illustrate, he tossed the ball over his shoulder and into the basket while he was talking and looking me in the eye. I retrieved the ball and handed it back to him. "When you have played basketball for a while, you don't need to look at the basket for a while when you are in close like this," he said, throwing it over his shoulder again and right through the hoop. "You develop a sense of where you are."

In 1980, Fran Allard, a colleague of Neil Charness's at Waterloo, did some tests whose results seem to bring together both the conclusions of the work done on chess, bridge, and music, and the "court sense"— a phrase Allard used in the publication of her work—that Bill Bradley had exhibited for McPhee. First, Allard exposed basketball players of various levels of accomplishment to photographs of basketball situations that were both structured and unstructured—real game positions or arbitrary ones. As with the more exotic disciplines, she found the better the basketball player the more likely he was to be able to recall a real situation; with the unstructured positions there was no difference. Elite basketball players, Allard and her fellows wrote in *The Journal of Sports Psychology*, "as do chess and bridge players, encode structured information more deeply."

With volleyball players, however, Allard at first seemed to have found an exception. Exposed for a short time to slides of players on a volleyball court, expert players seemed no better able than nonplayers to answer questions about whether or not there was a ball in the picture. Puzzled, Allard and her partner, Janet Starkes of McMaster, began running the same test with a timer. Now, there was a difference. The good players were able to figure out the situation more *quickly* than the rest of their group. The principle had held.

Elite athletes, then, like chess masters or artists of the jazz piano, may not so much think differently as perceive differently. Moreover, because they can quickly recall chunks of information from their long-term memories, they can react to those perceptions more efficiently. What Gretzky perceives on a hockey rink is, in a curious way, more simple than what a less accomplished player perceives. He sees not so much a set of moving players as a number of situations—chunks. Moving in on the Montreal blueline, as he was able to recall while he watched a videotape of himself, he was aware of the position of all the other players on the ice. The pattern they formed was, to him, one fact, and he reacted to that fact. When he sends a pass to what the rest of us appears an empty space on the ice, and when a teammate magically appears in that space to collect the puck, he has in reality simply summoned up from his bank account of knowledge the fact that in a particular situation, someone is likely to be in a particular spot, and if he is not there now he will be there presently.

The corollary, of course, is that Gretzky has seen all these situations before, and that what we take to be creative genius is in fact a reaction to a situation that he has stored in his brain as deeply and firmly as his own telephone number. When I put this possibility to him, he agreed.

"Absolutely," he said. "That's a hundred percent right. It's all practice. I got it from my dad. Nine out of ten people think it's instinct, and it isn't. Nobody would ever say a doctor had learned his profession by instinct; yet in my own way I've put in almost as much time studying hockey as a medical student puts in studying medicine."

Even before he got on skates, Wayne seemed to have an almost spiritual attraction to hockey. Once, when Walter and Phyllis were both working, Wayne, not yet two, was staying with his grandparents at their home on the Nith River. His grandmother had a Saturday afternoon hockey game on television. Wayne imitated the players, sliding back and forth on the linoleum. When the game was over, he cried, thinking his grandmother had turned it off to punish him.

He started skating before he was three years old; there are films of him on the ice, taken by his father, when he was two and a half. Walter built a rink in the backyard. He couldn't flood it with a hose; a hose might have made it too lumpy. He got out his lawn sprinkler, and laid on coat after coat. Every night, when he got home from his job as a technician with the telephone company, he would turn on the sprinkler and lay down another smooth coat. One year, the sprinkler broke, and Walter asked Phyllis to get him another one. When she got home from the store, she told him that was the last time for that. The clerks had thought she was crazy, buying a lawn sprinkler in February.

Walter had played Junior B himself, but he had been too small, they said, to make it to the pros. He was determined to give his children every chance. Wayne's first skates were single bladed, not the bob-skates so many kids wasted time on. When Walter couldn't find a hockey stick small enough for Wayne, he bought the lightest he could find, then shaved it down with a plane. Even today, the Titan stick Wayne uses is shaved thin.

Walter had a lot of ideas. He got some tin cans, and Wayne would skate patterns through them. He'd set sticks down on the ice and Wayne would hop over them while Walter sent him passes. There were balance drills and target shooting. Walter would put targets up on the net he had bought for the backyard rink, and Wayne would fire at them for hours, going in for supper and coming back out again under the lights Walter strung, and practicing again until bedtime. Walter put a picnic table on edge so that it blocked all but the outer edges of the net. Wayne would shoot for the corners.

"When the Russians came over here in 1972 and '73," Wayne once said, "people said, 'Wow, this is something incredible.' Not to me it wasn't. I'd been doing those drills since I was three years old. My dad was very smart."

When Wayne was five, Walter drove him all around the Brantford area, looking for an organized team that would take him. No one would let him play until he was six. Walter coached him anyway, and when was finally old enough, Walter took over his team.

"People say you can't teach anticipation," Walter says now. "I'm not so sure. I used to get them out on the ice and I'd shoot the puck down the boards toward a corner and I'd say, 'Chase that.' Well, they'd all go right into the end after it. Then I'd say, 'Wait, watch me.' I'd shoot it in again, and let it roll around the net. Instead of following it around the boards, I'd cut across to where it was rolling. 'There,' I'd say. 'You've got to know where it's *going* to go.'"

The concentration, the dedication, has never relaxed. From training camp on, none of the Oilers, not even the laboring Brackenbury, practiced skills with more single-mindedness than Gretzky. At training camp, long after everyone else had headed for the showers, he would still be out on the ice. Sometimes, he would lay a stick down beside the net and take a bucket of pucks behind it, and practice flipping them just high enough to clear the stick and lie in the goal-crease. Often Glenn Anderson would work on this drill with him. But sometimes Wayne would just stand alone and shoot at a crossbar or a goalpost. The trick he does in the 7-Up commercial—the one that he pretends to let his little brother Keith, teach him—is one he does at practice all the time, hoisting a puck in the air with the blade of his stick and then bouncing it as long as he can. In the summers, when he cannot skate, he still works for hours in his driveway, honing his stick-handling skills or trying to figure out, as he did in the summer of 1980, what he was doing wrong on breakaways.

The practice alone, of course, had not made him what he is, nor even the early beginnings. Although all the superstars whose boyhood stories we know, from Morenz to Orr, started skating at amazingly early ages, so did millions of other boys who never made it past peewee. It is a combination of things, the neurology, the metabolism, the father, the coaches, the Kid's own determination to succeed, and the gift of mind he has. In various permutations, these elements have combined in modern hockey's brief history to give us all our superstars, and if Gretzky is unique in the pantheon it is in his knack of articulating his skills. Today, the ability he showed as a young teenager to re-create game situations has become uncanny. There is scarcely a goal he has scored, or a chance he has missed, which, if asked, he cannot re-create in detail, setting each teammate and opponent into place with the precision of a chess master replaying a game. The joy of it all is that we have found him, that the game is so much a part of our lives that when a Wayne Gretzky is born we will find him. The sorrow is that there may also be Wayne Gretzkys of the piano or the paint brush, who, because we expose our young to hockey so much more than to the arts, we will never know about.

In the dressing room after the St. Louis game, the Oilers crowded around a television set. The Kid had gone down to the ITV studio under the stands, to accept his praises as the game's star, and to look at replays of his goals. The other players were shaking their heads in wonder. "Jeez," they were saying. "Look at *that*. How did he ever put it *there*?"

I remembered I was supposed to appear on the post-game show myself. I left the dressing room and headed for the studio. Along the barriers that separate the paying customers from the participants and the press, fans were lined up four and five deep waiting to catch a glimpse of Gretzky as he went back to shower. As I approached the studio, he emerged, still in skates and uniform. He was keeping his head down, trying to avoid the eye contact with his fans that would have kept him there, acknowledging their applause. As we passed, I reached out to touch his arm—a gesture of congratulation.

"Was the tape I made okay?" he asked.

Steaua Wears a Black Hat

BY DAVE BIDINI

In 1998 and 1999, author Dave Bidini undertook a hockey odyssey, searching out the game around the world, visiting spots as disparate and unlikely as northern China, Dubai, and the Transylvanian Alps. He watched local contests, and often joined them, traveling with a full complement of gear. The result was *Tropic of Hockey*, a wonderful tribute to the game, and a best seller in Canada.

This excerpt describes hockey in Romania, specifically the bloody team rivalry between Ciuc, a city in the province of Szekely, and Bucharest, the capital. Ciuc is ethnically a largely Hungarian city, and so it is always under the thumb of Bucharest's Romanian population, who have dominated politics in the country for nearly a century, with particular brutality during the reign of the communist dictator Ceauşescu. The Bucharest team, Steaua, not only draws the lion's share of state funding, but has first dibs on all of the country's best players. That Ciuc's Sport Klub is constantly bested by Steaua only seems to fire the passion of the Ciuc fans, and the rivalry has become a battle not just between two nearby cities, but between the weak and the strong, repression and freedom, the passionate amateur and the professional ringer.

★　★　★　★　★

"Do you like Boston?" asked Karolina, standing in the lobby.
"I used to."
"I think they are very good."
"You mean Boston, the group, right?"

"Yes. The music. Later, we will take a drive in the boss's car and I will play for you my tape of Boston."

Karolina walked us to the rink through a park. She wore a smart grey coat and had long, black hair pinned high on her head. Karolina was elegant and young and among the brightest of the post-revolution youth. She'd attended seminars in Bucharest, where the most promising of the next generation of Romanians, selected by their schools, assembled to discuss politics and culture. She was Ferenc's assistant and our guide and translator.

It was midmorning in Ciuc, and the scene was still, the chatter of our voices filling the park. At the top of the grounds was a cenotaph. The sky was cold and grey and I had to pull my hood over my head to stay warm in the frigid wind that swept down the Ciuc Depression.

The arena lay at the bottom of the park; a grey building that looked like a giant concrete accordion, PATINOARUL VAKAR LAJOS JEGPALYA painted in blue on a wooden marquee over the entrance. As we approached it, we passed two sets of statues, both of hockey players. Once was a wire-work sculpture of a player positioning himself for a face-off. It was set flat against a large silver disc rooted in a bed of black-eyed susans. To its right was a much bigger, more impressive rendering: two ten-foot-tall, constructivist metal figures in full stride, their sticks stretched out in pursuit of the puck, eyes peeled, skates kicking out behind them, silver blades knifing the air. They made me think of fearsome Tin Men, their welds like veins through which molten steel was coursing. Their names were engraved on the shafts of their sticks—Czka Istun and Vakar Lajos—and sometimes, when the sun found them, light shot from their elbows, boots, and sticks, bringing the park to life.

Erected in 1975, these were the first statues of hockey players in Europe, predating those in Russia, Sweden, and the Czech Republic. Transylvania, it seemed, had a jump on the rest of the hockey world and, as I passed into the lobby of the Vakar Lajos rink, this became obvious. On one wall of the foyer hung a set of black-and-white photos. It was, more or less, the Vakar Lajos Hall of Fame. Ferenc joined us as we studied the photos, and, with Karolina's help, he guided us through Lajos's life, a legacy that includes being quite possibly the first ever European hockey player.

Vakar's stick hung diagonally against the wall. It looked like an old ruler, thin and straight-bladed, with his name penciled along the shaft. It was this stick, said Ferenc, that changed the face of hockey in Europe.

"This is the one he made for himself, after he saw the Canadians playing hockey. He made it from a tree, so excited to have discovered the game."

"Where did he see the Canadians?" I asked.

"In a film."

"What film?"

"I don't know; no one knows. It was a film before another film."

"Another film?"

"You mean like a newsreel?" asked Janet.

Ferenc and Karolina conferred.

"Yes! There was a ten-second film of Canadians on the ice, playing hockey."

"When was this?"

"Nineteen twenty-three."

In 1923, Frank Calder was the president of the four-team NHL. Babe Dye of the Toronto St. Pats won the scoring title and Lester Patrick announced his retirement. In a game between the Montreal Canadiens and the Hamilton Tigers, Bert Corbeau attacked Habs goalie (and ex-teammate) Georges Vézina and broke his nose with a punch. The next time the two teams played—for which Vézina dressed despite his broken nose—the Montreal crowd became unruly and littered the ice with lemons, hitting referee Lou Marsh in the face; Marsh attacked his assailant and landed a few blows. In the Stanley Cup final that year, King Clancy of the Senators played every position, including goal, which he was forced to occupy after netminder Clint Benedict received a penalty. In those days, goalies had to serve the full two minutes in the box, so Clancy bravely stepped in and didn't allow a goal.

Teams iced seven men in 1923 and, in March of that year, Foster Hewitt of the *Toronto Star*'s new radio station, CFCA, was assigned to broadcast a game between Kitchener and Parkdale at Mutual Street Arena, his first game behind the microphone. At the beginning of the season, Newsy Lalonde was traded to the Saskatoon team of the Western Hockey League for Aurel Joliat, who would go on to play with

Howie Morenz and Black Cat Gagnon for the Montreal Canadiens. The NHL champions in 1923 were the Ottawa Senators, who defeated the Edmonton Eskimos, led by Bullet Joe Simpson, in two games. Frank Nighbor was one of the Senators' stars. Early in the season, he played in six consecutive games without relief, not once coming off the ice. He was supposed to be chased out of Edmonton by rival Duke Keats, but it never happened. Nighbor and the boys took the train back east, bringing with them the Stanley Cup, parading their silverware on the platform of each stop en route. And, in Romania, Vakar Lajos watched them on the flickering screen, thinking to himself, *We can do that*.

It was a staggeringly early beginning for hockey in Europe, and it proved why there was such a deep love and closeness for the game in Ciuc. I studied the photos and was particularly drawn to one of Lajos's team showing some of the players in berets and short pants with knee socks, and others in wool cardigans with striped ties and upturned collars. Lajos himself was a handsome man, with a narrow chin supporting an enormous forehead and crest of wavy hair. But the two goalies who were kneeling at the front of the picture fascinated me the most. One of them wore a flat white cap and a sweater borrowed from the Michelin Man. It was bulky around the middle and ribbed along the arms and shoulders, giving the illusion of a muscular upper body. It looked as if whalebone padding had been sewn into the sweater itself, which is what Cyclone Taylor's mother did back at the turn of the century. She removed the ribbing from her old corsets and sewed it straight into Cy's hockey jersey, revolutionizing the skater's ensemble.

But the team's other goaltender was even more compelling. She was Vakar's wife, Elizabeth. She was the only player smiling in the photo—a beautiful dark smile, at that—and she wore a black toque and over her ribbed sweater was the team's jersey—a black jersey with a white stripe and the team's Transylvania logo across the middle. But the most astonishing thing about her equipment was her noncatching glove, which had a flat, rectangular panel above her hand: a blocker. Many hockey historians credit Frank "Mr. Zero" Brimsek with inventing the blocker—he was the first to insert bamboo piping into his glove to stop shots with the back of his hand—but he played in the late 1930s. This photo was from the late 1920s. Mrs. Lajos's blocker predates the NHL's by ten years.

Elizabeth Lajos was very important to Sport Klub. Denes told me that, in her retirement, she was "part of the equipment" and occupied a special chair just to the left of the goalie, from where she watched the games. She became something of a good luck charm for the team, and if ever she was late for a game, the Sport Klub would delay the start. Elizabeth and Vakar first met during a pickup game. I imagine him coming in on a breakaway, looking up for an instant and being captivated by her beauty, the puck rolling off his stick. Co-ed hockey games were popular among the Ciuc youth in the 1920s and 1930s and, like teen dances in North America, they were the center of their social lives.

I moved over to the next wall. There was another set of photos, these more modern and in color. They were of a junior tournament staged here in 1987. The teams entered were Yugoslavia, Bulgaria, the Czech Republic, Russian, Romania, and North Korea. For years, Romania had been linked, as had China, to the great Soviet hockey program, and there'd been an unofficial arrangement between Communist Bloc nations for their national teams to play each other a certain number of times per year. It's one of the reasons Jin Guang visited here in the 1970s with the Chinese Nats, and had played against the Romanians and others in unofficial tournaments set up to further each other's domestic programs.

Ferenc didn't know too much about the tournament, only that North Korea had finished without a win, and that the Romanians had played an inspired game against the Soviets, but lost. I was about to be led away by Karolina into the rink itself, but something caught my eye. I looked closer, and there he was, a teenager, smaller than the rest, looking in:

Jagr.

There was no Navratilovian mullet to give him away, no earring. But there were his trademark flushed cheeks, his wonky eye, his bubble helmet. Jagr. I recognized a few others, too, but couldn't place their names (Jiri Slegr and Jaroslav Modry were on the team, as well). It was 1987, before the fall of Communism, and Jagr was all of fifteen. He was not yet a glimmer in a scout's eye, three years away from being drafted fifth overall by the Penguins of Pittsburgh, where he would ask for, and be given, the number 68, to remember the year that Soviet tanks crossed the Czech border and seized power. He had not yet grown to tower above the rest of the players, nor were his shoulders as big as they would be when he ascended to the pros. In 1987, his life was spent in tournaments like these, games in small, hockey-crazed towns across Eastern Europe, twenty-four hours from Prague by train. He had rolled through the forest, eating salted meat and bread, withdrawn from the rest of the world, yet looking out, as I had, at the endless trees and dark woods and mountains, wondering what kind of hockey lay ahead, and against whom he'd be playing. At fifteen, he was within reach of the skills that would make him one of the most elegant scorers of his time, eleven years removed from waving his Olympic gold medal from the stage in Prague's Old Town Square. When Jagr took to the ice at Vakar Lajos rink in 1987, could he have imagined that his life would work out the way it did? Or did he just play?

Jagr. A swooping bird.

I moved over to the photo of the Soviet team, and spotted Pavel Bure. Small features and tiny arms, peeking out from behind a defense-man's elbow. A mite, a scamp. Taught the game in Moscow by his fa-ther—whom neither he, nor his brother, Valeri, speak to anymore—a disciplinarian. Pavel. Scampering across the pond, his speed coming not from his hips or thighs, but his feet, a zealous windup toy, a skittler, wav-ing his hockey stick in front of him. In the 1996 Olympics, he scored five goals against the Finns in the semi-final, then moved on to play Jagr in the gold-medal game, both players the focus of systems designed to make the ice theirs. Bure, Moscow. Saucy, elite; a player whose speed and deft hands were obvious from the beginning. The bus rides were an af-front to him. He bit his lip and ploughed through, stopping in places like Ciuc, only to play against North Koreans whose equipment was the worst he'd seen. But also . . . Jagr. They met. The two great stars of the beginning of the twenty-first century skated head-to-head for the first time. It was here, in Vakar Lajos arena, where the future of the game took shape, where the styles of these two players mixed in a form that later gave the game identity and shape after Lemieux and Gretzky passed into history. A game being born. In the final game of the tournament, Bure met Jagr. "It was extraordinary game," one Transylvanian hockey fan told me later. "So fast. So exciting. Tied four to four."

I left the photographs and walked into the rink. Progrym Gheorgeni were playing Ciuc Sport Klub. Karolina led us up to the VIP section ten rows above the ice, where long, purple, upholstered benches fronted by a dark rosewood railing stretched out below the press gallery. It was a little wine-colored salon in the middle of the rink, which had maybe 2,000 seats, all but a hundred of them empty. There was an old, 1960s-style score-clock at one end, where seconds elapsed in illuminated pixels around the circumference of a circle. Both ends of the rink were protected with floor-to-ceiling webbing that trapped flown pucks. Below them, goal judges sat in steel cages operating a series of lights: green (the play is on), red (a goal is scored), and white (a whistle, or stoppage in play). The rink was evidently well used: the plastic seats were scuffed and the walkways spread with years of grime. A banner for Ciuc Beer hung around the boards, and Karolina told me that Miercurea Ciuc was known throughout Eastern Europe for two exports, hockey and beer. That, I told her, was familiar to Canadians. Under another banner I spotted six soldiers in grey riot helmets and blue-and-white camouflage uniforms, their backs to the game, smoking cigarettes.

Ciuc dominated play for most of the game. Gheorgheni was a town about fifty kilometers from Ciuc, where the players trained and played outdoors, on artificial ice in a closed valley between two mountains (Vakar Lajos and the state rink in Bucharest were the only two indoor rinks in Romania). Though Gheorgheni was one of the few teams in Romania to have city council pay their full wages—it was a staggering notion considering how desperate the local economics were—they didn't have the skill or team play of Sport Klub. The Ciuc attack was driven by two defensemen—number 6, Attila Nagy, and number 5, Jozsef Andordjan. Neither wore a face guard, and both played in the style of a young Randy Carlyle: fast and thick-bodied, rushing whenever they got the puck. I was also drawn to a forward, Istvan Gereb, a sad-faced forty-year-old Ciuc veteran who skated stiffly and with his head down, but possessed just enough Mike Waltonian savvy to stand out from his teammates, most of whom were a lot younger. Among this youthful group was the tiniest of forwards, a little buzz saw of a player who filled the ice with puck-carrying razzmatazz. His slipperiness allowed him to avoid being hit (even though it wasn't a physical game) and when I asked Ferenc who he was, he pointed to the ice and said "Vakar Lajos!" then moved his hand halfway up his chest.

"Laszlo Kovacs," said Karolina, smiling.

"Who?"

"Vakar Lajos's grandson."

Ciuc won the game easily. The crowd was quiet during most of the play, but stirred as a group of players in athletic sweats walked into the rink and stood together between the two benches. Fans on one side of the arena signaled across to the other, who stood up and started shouting and whistling at the players. An old man shook his fist and bellowed "*Kazuku!*" which meant Gypsy, a racist taunt common throughout Romania. The skaters on the ice noticed this and looked around, slowing the action. The unwelcome newcomers moved closer together and formed a cordon. Ferenc shook his head and scoffed while Karolina looked at the floor.

Steaua.

Most of our time in Ciuc was spent either at the rink or the hotel. We'd rise early in the day, eat breakfast, then head out with Karolina.

At the rink, Karolina introduced us to a passel of Romanian hockey dignitaries—ex-players, coaches, and broadcasters—who gave us insight into the history and development of the local game. There was only one figure from Romanian hockey I didn't meet, although I spent much of the trip waiting for him to appear. His nickname was Whiskey. The dashing Robin Hood of Romanian hockey, Whiskey was a former player from Hungary turned bank robber. I anticipated a covert meeting with him—maybe in the park after sundown, in a cold flat on the fringe of town, under the rafters during a game—but he never appeared. He was considered public enemy number one by the Hungarian authorities, even though, as Karolina and others liked to point out, "He only steals from banks, never the people. He is also very polite and very gentle. All the people from Ciuc are behind him, especially the fans because he was a player, too. He is very clever, and his actions hurt no one." Whiskey was linked to twenty-seven robberies, in which, along with Orbin Gbor, a fellow Hungarian player, he'd stolen 140 million Hungarian forints. He was the most wanted man in Hungary, a reputa-

tion that no doubt increased his popularity among the hockey fans of
Szekely land, and a Barilkoesque legend had developed around it.

There was a rumor that Whiskey would attend the final Ciuc
game against Steaua, which organizers had moved up to Saturday afternoon so that it could be broadcast nationally. This was done because the
previous year's game had been the second-highest rated sporting event of
the year after Romania's first ever soccer victory over Hungary. The pitch
of the tournament seemed geared toward the clash between these two
teams, and you could feel the tension tighten as the tourney progressed.
Both Sport Klub and Steaua disposed of teams from Gheorgheni and
Galati, the latter team having ignominiously traded their starting goaltender to Steaua for a bag of secondhand equipment, which they needed
to keep their program alive. One of the first people to tell us about the
Steaua-Ciuc rivalry was a fellow named Zoltan Becze, a small, garrulous
man who pointed his finger at me when he spoke; that is, when he was-
n't grabbing my jacket and pulling my face to his. A writer for the local
Hungarian-language newspaper, he was proud to call himself a member
of the international sports press. Zoltan was Romania's Foster Hewitt. He
was both the play-by-play and color commentator whenever games were
televised nationally (usually one or two matches a year). On my last day
in Ciuc, he took me to the local television studio and showed me footage
of the finals of the Romanian championships from the 1980s, which
were played outdoors in Gheorgheni, snow falling as the players scrab-
bled after the puck, the beautiful Transylvanian Alps rising above the end
boards. Zoltan's play-by-play technique was to describe the action in a
reserved, bordering on moribund, tone, then screech breathlessly into the
microphone whenever a goal was scored. When I told him that Foster
Hewitt's gondola in Maple Leaf Gardens used to be considered the
Noah's Ark of Canadian radio, he exclaimed, "I too have an ark. From
where I sit and tell people the truth!"

Zoltan was a wealth of information. Upon first being introduced to me at the arena, he took me to the Sport Klub's director's
lounge, which, besides being the only heated room in Ciuc, was decorated like a '60s party pad. "This is a place for chiefs!" exclaimed Zoltan,
calling out the door, at which point the secretary of the Ciuc sports federation came in with a tray of beer and an urn of coffee. As I turned on

my tape recorder Zoltan squeezed my shoulder, and said, "We must start with Steaua."

"What's the history between the two teams?" I asked.

"Well, in hockey, you see, we in Ciuc have demonstrated to Romania that we are the best. We have shown the world that, even though we are a minority, hockey is ours, it is our voice. In seventy years, we have not had one Romanian play for us, only Hungarians. Out of this has evolved a great love for the team, and in 1989 Miercurea Ciuc became the first place in Romania where five thousand men were heard singing in public a song in the Hungarian language! It was our team's hymn— what you'd hear in a church—that had been composed by a very talented local composer and whose text had been written by my father, Anton Becze. You will hear them sing this song tomorrow when we play against Steaua, and millions of people will watch on TV and hear this Hungarian song! They will hear our voices right across the country!

"We sang this song even though we knew that the rest of Romania did not want to hear it. We sang it in victory and in defeat. Our voices came out, out, out!" he said, putting his hand to his mouth as if pulling out string. "We did this even though we knew that Sport Klub would be prevented from winning by the Communists. It goes back to Ceaușescu, I believe. Ceaușescu liked to think he was a sportsman, so he gave a lot of money for sports, but it was more out of propaganda, like the Third Reich. Steaua got most of the money and became the military's team, Ceaușescu's team, the Communist's team. They were the team from the city, Bucharest. Because we came from a small town and were a Hungarian team, we got very little of this money, still do. They would only support us if we would give away our best players to Steaua. Of course, we would not let them do this, so we suffered, and during Ceaușescu's reign, they did every thing they could to stop us from winning. The Steaua team traveled with soldiers and the Securitate. One time, in 1985, they took away our best player and had him committed to the madhouse. They put him away for three days so he could not play. Then they told the rest of the Ciuc team, 'If you do not lose this game, the rest of you will go to the hospital, too!'

"Ceaușescu was afraid, of course. He was worried that if he sent a team with Hungarian names to the European championships, the leaders of other countries would get the wrong idea. He would be embarrassed. So he ordered that the winning team must be Steaua and that the players with Hungarian names would have to change them if they wanted to advance. Could you imagine that? To play for your country, to have to change your name? They threatened and intimidated the referees, and after a while, they didn't even have to do that. The referees knew that if they called a game against Steaua, they would be paid a visit by the Securitate. Perhaps it is hard for you to understand, but it was a matter of life or death."

The Securitate were Ceauşescu's security police, and were all-encompassing in their powers. They were a vast network of informers recruited from the ordinary population, common spies. Citizens were played against each other, and the most loyal were trained to be part of Romania's secret police. They tapped phone lines, intercepted mail, and reported conversations overheard in public places, resulting in, as Denes had told me, a fear of gathering, even in small groups. There were more than a million informers in the Securitate, each of them backed up by a militia responsible for keeping track of those citizens considered unreliable—kids who sang in coffee bars, writers, painters, former activists. Under Ceauşescu's regime, no person was allowed to change dwellings without permission from the militia, and anyone who made a visit of more then twenty-four hours to a town they did not live in had to report to the authorities.

In this political climate, hockey provided one of the few forums for self-expression, a place where citizens could be together in great numbers and form a unified voice. At the rink fans were able to scream and yell and taunt Steaua. Even though some fans were jailed before games—one of them, an old man who'd played in the Lajos era, had been prohibited from going within one hundred feet of the rink—the Ciuc crowd were brave and resilient, and for many years, those who sang their Hungarian freedom hymn from the stands were the most defiant voices heard in all of Romania.

"The government has always resented the Sport Klub fans," said Zoltan, sipping coffee from a small porcelain cup. "This was the case even after Ceauşescu. During one game a few years ago between Steaua and Ciuc, the Steaua team invited their soccer fans to come to a game simply to outnumber the Ciuc fans. These were people who had never seen a hockey game in their lives: hooligans, thugs. They taunted the Ciuc fans, chanting: '*Criminals!*' and '*Out with Hungarians from Romania!*' Since there were no police at the game, fans fought. Knives were drawn. There was no Plexiglas on the boards, so the hooligans hopped onto the ice and attacked the players from Sport Klub. In the Romanian papers the next day, they talked about how the Ciuc fans were not to be trusted, how they incited violence and were a bad influence and should not be allowed to participate. The papers used this as a tool, or a tactic, to influence opinion; they still do. They told people that it was not safe for Romanians to come here to visit. They tried to get us banned from all games away from Ciuc, going so far as to suggest that no championship be played at Vakar Lajos for fear of the safety of the people. These writers have never been to Ciuc, and still like to think that we live in a Communist country."

We finished our coffee, and the secretary came in and took away our cups. I told Zoltan that his insight was valuable, and his final words were "Be careful of yourself and your wife at the game. You sit in the VIPs, you'll be okay, but beware of the crowd. You just sit, listen, and learn, yes?" With this, he swept me out of the room. I walked down a hallway tacked with finger paintings of Sport Klub players by children from a nearby school.

To celebrate game day, Karolina, Ferenc, Janet, and I made a pilgrimage. It seemed like the right thing to do on the afternoon of Ciuc's most important game of the year, so we hopped in Ferenc's car and drove to the top of a hill outside of town, part of the same range I'd admired from the city.

Karolina played her Boston tape. It sounded great, but I don't think it was Boston. I didn't have the heart to tell Karolina.

"Do you like this tape of Boston?" she asked.

"Love it!"

From the top of the hill, I was able to look down at Vakar Lajos arena and think, "There's where the shit's gonna happen." I did this while sitting on a large stone pulpit surrounded by old-growth forest and crosses erected by small villages around the region. It was the ancestral center of the Szekelys, the site where they gathered by the thousands each year to drink, fight, party, and pray. The pulpit gave way to a steep slope that had been shaved up the middle, a ski run used by Sport Klub members to train.

At the bottom of the hill was a well with water gushing from two spouts. A pair of soot-faced young men drew the water into dirty wine bottles. The water was an offering to those who'd made the pilgrimage to the top of the hill, so Karolina asked us if we'd like to have a drink.

"Try. Try. Is good," said Ferenc.

"Is it safe?" asked Janet.

"Yes. Yes. Very," said Karolina.

We took deep gulps, regretfully. The water was cool and fresh-tasting, but dense with mineral deposits. It was like drinking sand at the bottom of a beach bucket.

Before the revolution, there had been a forty-team national league in Romania, but now there were only six teams. After 1989, many Romanian and Hungarian players left the country to play elsewhere, some of them going to Hungary, others to Austria, others to colleges in the United States. Ciuc lost more than fifty men to foreign clubs, depleting Sport Klub as a national power. With the demise of Ceauşescu's national sport program, the Steaua team grew even stronger relative to teams in Ciuc, Galati, and Gheorgheni. The benefit of playing for a big-city team that was closely linked to the sports federation meant a job at a sub-officer's salary, as well as guaranteed sponsorship. By contrast, only ten percent of the government's hockey budget went to Ciuc, the result of Romania's long-standing denial of Hungarian culture, as well as the theory that putting the lion's share of money toward maintaining one high-level team was more effective than supporting several middling ones. Besides, there was only one Hungarian in the Romanian Sports Federation to fight for Ciuc, and it was only the previous year that the town had elected their first representative to sit in the Romanian house of parliament.

It was hard for Sport Klub to keep pace with the Army team. While Ciuc had been the first champions of Romania in 1949 and had won six titles altogether (the last coming in 1997), Steaua were the dominant force, winning a total of twenty-eight championships from 1963 to 1999. In its own way Ciuc suffered the small-market blues, only this was not the result of some greedy owner's power game or a player flexing his dollar signs, but rather years of political and cultural hardship. That the fans in Ciuc continued to hold out hope that they would one day rise to their rightful place as kings of Romanian hockey exposed the North American pro sports scene for the obnoxious entity that it has become. In Ciuc, fans showed their devotion to the game by turning out in great numbers for big games, even though they lived in a country where it was considered a good year if inflation rose by only fifty percent, as it had the previous year. For local fans to spend a handful of lei on a game they couldn't afford to go to was a show of faith that, with the exception of a few cities and towns, was rare in North America. Paying for a ticket in Ciuc was like dropping pennies in hockey's collection plate.

The last time Steaua and Sport Klub clashed, in Bucharest, Steaua won 5–3, capturing the Romanian championship. But this was a new season (the Romanian Cup was played at the beginning of the schedule, the Romanian Championships at the end) and the local fans were optimistic.

That afternoon, we made our way to the rink. We fell in step with a stream of people and walked through the park, which was filled with families picnicking before the start of the game. The scene around Vakar Lajos arena was no different than that outside old Maple Leaf Gardens. There was a scrum of a few hundred people outside the rink, their voices high with chatter: men with their hands plugged inside their jackets; boys in blue-face; young girls waving flags and pennants; old men sipping coffee; women smoking and talking about the game. A kid with an old-fashioned air horn stood in front of the rink going *whaoooonk!* and shouting in Hungarian with his friends, who had blue and white S's and C's drawn on their cheeks. We met Denes under the marquee and I asked him what they were saying.

"Go back to Romania," he said, rubbing his hands.

"For Steaua or their fans?"

"Steaua have no fans!" he said, laughing.

"What do you mean?"

"If they had fans, they would travel here. They would come and watch the games like the supporters of Ciuc. But they don't. They are afraid," he said.

I showed my pass to a rumple-faced man with a bushy mustache, handing him my accreditation—a white greeting card that had been stamped and signed by the organizer of the local sports federation—and he held it in front of him, eyeing me suspiciously as if I were a local nogoodnik trying to bust my way into the rink.

I complimented him on the hat he was wearing.

He grunted and handed my papers back.

In the lobby, Sandor Gal, a former player whom I'd met briefly, called Karolina over and asked her to clarify a point he'd made to me in an interview I'd done the day before. Sandor was the assistant trainer of Ciuc and had played for Romania in the world championships in Vienna, Austria, in 1978.

He waved his hands when he spoke, breathlessly rattling off the details of a trip to Vienna in 1977, when Romania had defeated the USA 4–3. "The trainer remembers," said Karolina, looking at Sandor, "that in 1977, the teams were the Soviet Union, Czechoslovakia, Canada, Sweden, the USA, Finland, and Germany." With each country, Sandor nodded and said: "Ya. Ya."

"He remembers playing with Espo . . . Espo . . . Espo . . ."

"Espo-sito!" said Sandor.

"Yes, Esposito," repeated Karolina. "Phil Esposito?"

"Ya. Ya."

"Phil Esposito."

"I know him," I said.

"Oh! You know this Esposito?" asked Karolina.

"No. Not know. I mean, I've heard of him."

"Well, the trainer says that he remembers Esposito because he was the biggest player. He had the biggest head of hair, too. There was another one, Tony, his brother. The Romanian team was very excited, nervous, to be playing his team, but Esposito was relaxed. He met Esposito and he has a photo."

"A photo?"

"Yes. A picture. Trainer says he will bring it."

"Thank you, thank you," I told him, shaking his hand.

"Ya!" he said, turning away into the rink.

The arena was stuffed with fans. And riot police, hundreds of them. They'd fastened heavy Plexiglas visors to their helmets and were carrying billy clubs. The crowd was already singing the Hungarian freedom song for which Zoltan's father had written the words. It was a great, throaty anthem. Fans locked arms and swayed when they sang, calling out for one side of the stands to join the other. Janet and I settled in a section above the purple benches, which were occupied by invited guests: a Hungarian MP, sports writers from Bucharest, the head of the Romanian sports federation, and local hockey cognoscenti. Around us, fans cracked the sunflower seeds sold in paper cones, nervously snapping and chewing as the rosters were announced over a scratchy public-address system. Denes gave me a sheet of paper with a hand-written starting lineup, which he'd got from one of the local writers. He circled the names of the players from Steaua who were born or bred around Ciuc. They were Andreas Kodstandi and Laszlo Bazilidesz—both members of the top line—as well as Ioan Timaru, raised just thirty kilometers outside of Ciuc, who would prove to be Steaua's most effective, and nastiest, forward, a Kenny "the Rat" Linseman of Eastern Europe.

Once the Ciuc lineup was announced, Denes realized that Sport Klub was missing some of its better players. One of them, Kolozsi Lorant, was in jail for having beaten up someone outside a nightclub. Three or four others had decided to skate for the Gheorgheni team, while a couple of Ciuc-born forwards were away playing in the Hungarian league. It was a depleted squad but, Denes said, "Not bad. We'll only see what this will mean to Sport Klub once the game begins. At this point, it is hard to tell. Before the game, anything is possible." The referees skated out to the ice, and the crowd readied itself for the appearance of Steaua.

Steaua wore national team jerseys: ROMANIA written in red across royal blue. This was an immediate affront to the crowd. It would be like the Toronto Maple Leafs playing against Montreal in the seventh game of the Stanley Cup finals in Team Canada jerseys. The Steaua sweaters said to the crowd, "We don't even acknowledge you; you don't exist." It would be revealed a few days later that the Romanian Sports

Minister had given Steaua the sweaters to help boost their confidence and defeat Ciuc.

The crowd wailed, louder still. Clusters of fans shook their fists and sang the freedom song. There was a veil of smoke hanging over the rink. Toothless old men wearing fedoras and smoking cigarettes cried "*Hungaria!*" and "*Freedom!*" If I hadn't known better I would have sworn I was at the Felt Forum, circa 1942. Although the section in which we were sitting was mostly occupied by middle-aged men, the crowd was all ages. In the stands nearest to the home side, young men waved blue and white Sport Klub flags. Janet went to photograph them, and when she returned, she reported seeing a tiny girl wearing little pink gloves who thrust her middle finger furiously at Steaua when they hit the ice.

While Steaua warmed up their goalie—he was tiny and quick, like Arturs Irbe—Sport Klub skated out to great applause and, of course, more singing. I'd never heard such singing from a crowd. I couldn't tell where one anthem started and where the other ended. There were fans in each section who stood in the front row and directed the tune in whatever direction they saw fit. They were like conductors in sweats, calling up tunes among the supporters. This resulted in a great, booming wall of sound, a mad sports opera that, once it kicked into high gear with the face-off, shook me to the bone.

Sport Klub's jerseys were a crazy billboard of logos. Compared to Steaua's—which were new and perfect and had only one name, Gillette, stitched below the crest—Sport Klub's looked like Bobby Unser's bumper. The faces of the players were different, too. Steaua had quite a few clean-shaven, square-shouldered forwards whose physiques showed their training regimen, while the Ciuc players were more individual, scruff-faced, and lumpen. Sport Klub was young and old, big and small, and instead of looking like they'd been equipped by the same outfitter, some of them—like Istvan Gereb, the forty-six-year-old veteran—wore gloves that they might have had since childhood, while Laszlo Kovacs, Vakar's grandson, had modern equipment untouched by time.

I looked across at the Steaua bench and saw that the fellow with the air horn had taken a seat just above the players. He hung the horn over the railing until it was a few feet above the coach's ear, then began pumping it. *Whaoooonk! Whaoooonk!* The coach, a grim-looking man, waved his hand above his head like a man swatting bees. *Whaoooonk! Whaoooonk!* The referees called the players to center ice, where a Finlandia vodka logo bled across the middle of the rink. Ciuc iced a starting five that included Attila Nagy, the visorless defensemen and Ciuc captain. Nagy skated back to his goalie, put his hand on the back of his head and whispered something to him. The goalie nodded and Nagy drifted, stick across his knees to the blue line. As he did this, the antagonist from Steaua, Timaru, stood in the face-off circle with his hand on his hip. Nagy gestured to the ref and the game began.

The game started slick and exciting and, with the crowd charged the way it was, it had all the drama of a Stanley Cup final. Gereb had Ciuc's best chance early, but he was called for an offside. As the whistle sounded, he floated over the blue line and fired a shot that zoomed just past the head of the Steaua goalie, Viorel Radu. It looked like Gereb couldn't stop his shot in time but, considering the history of these two teams, one couldn't know for sure. As Gereb circled behind the net, Radu shot his stick out, catching the Ciuc veteran just under the shoulder. Gereb spun around and skated backwards outside the zone, glaring at the little Army goalie.

There was more hitting in this game than I'd seen the previous afternoon, but it wasn't the kind of open-ice stuff you'd find at home (or used to find). Instead, collisions happened along the boards and in the corners. Neither team played a physical game, but whenever they had a chance to get a stick or a leg on an opponent, they did. Steaua had two rangy defensemen who did this well. Their first goal came when one of them stole the puck from a Ciuc forward trying to avoid a check. The defenseman stepped over the line like Larry Robinson or Rob Blake and beat the Ciuc goalie, Ladai, with a slapshot low along the ice. If you'd asked him, Ladai probaby would have told you that it was the kind of shot that he usually stops in practice. But, like the rest of us, his nerves were crawling along a knife's edge. The crowd let out a groan, but soon resumed its chanting. I looked over at Denes, who was shaking his head and smiling.

"What're they saying?" I asked.

"Steaua player's mother is a pig gypsy scoundrel!"

"What about that guy?" I asked, pointing to an enormous, bearded fellow dressed like a woodsman who was clapping his hands above his head and shouting in a deep, growling baritone.

"He is talking about possible urination on the head of the player from Steaua!"

"And him?" I asked, gesturing to another fan.

"Gypsy pig traitor!"

There was one Ciuc supporter, as imposing as Sasquatch, who spent the period leaning into our section and giving the sports federation rep from Bucharest the what-for. To his credit, the rep stared straight ahead despite the visceral verbal assault. I was reminded of the night of the Richard riots, when Clarence Campbell was approached by a fan with a program asking for an autograph. Campbell responded implacably, writing his name. The fellow looked at the signature, then raised the magazine and brought it down over the president's head. After that: smoke bombs and busted windows. Campbell's assailant was a little wraith of a man, but the Ciuc fan who was giving the federation rep an earful looked big enough to pick him up and hurl him over the stands to the ice. And we were only ten minutes into the game.

About five minutes after their first goal, Steaua scored again. This time, when the players arrived at their bench, they taunted the fans with their sticks poking them into the air. They waved their hands and made gestures of strength like posing bodybuilders.

"The idiots from Steaua!"

"*Traitor!*"

"*Hungareeeeaaaaa!*"

The guy with the air horn went mental, sounding it for the whole of the next shift, which resulted in a goal by Ciuc. While this narrowed the score to 2–1, provoking more singing and cheers from the crowd, it also meant that Mr. Air Horn was convinced that his instrument had been the cause of the goal, meaning that the rest of the game featured the kind of air horn solo usually reserved for sax players falling through the circles of hell. The crowd pickup up a new chant, so I poked Denes and asked him.

"*The idiots from Steaua!*" he screamed, his voice barely heard over the din.

The period ended 2–1, and so did the noise. The crowd caught its breath. We made our way out to the concourse, where people were milling around, some wandering into the sunshine, others cruising the concession stands, which were two long tables manned by a team of young women. Denes, Ferenc, and I talked about the game and the consensus was that, while Ciuc were still in the game, they had to play better to match Steaua's skill. But in sudden-death games, anything was possible. Besides, if anybody could run Steaua out of the rink, Mr. Air Horn had as good a chance as anyone.

Ciuc perked up in the second period. Kovac, their heir to the Lajos legacy, buzzed around the Steaua zone, wreaking havoc in the goal crease. He skated like Cliff Ronning, snowing the goalie, poking after loose pucks, and burrowing like a beetle under Radu's skin. Radu was petulant, and Ciuc played this to their advantage. They followed Kovac's lead and pressed on his doorstep until the little goalie took to flailing his stick like an egg beater whenever anyone came close, often putting himself out of position. Still, no matter how hard Sport Klub ran him, he was able to command the game in his end. My sense was that if Ciuc had any real chance of getting back into the game, the second period was the only time. Many of the Steaua players were preoccupied with jibing the crowd, leaving room for Nagy to rush the puck, which he did often and effectively.

Over the course of the period, Radu's behavior worsened and the tension between the two teams mounted. Tiramu, the little devil, had a chance in close, but he was stopped by the Ciuc goalie, Ladai, whom he promptly punched in the neck. There was a frenetic scrum around the goal with players hanging on to each other, but the referees skated in and broke it up. No penalty was called on Tiramu—"*Gypsy! Traitor!*"—which the gritty Army forward took as a moral victory. This appeared to energize his team and, on the following shift, Steaua scored their third goal, which they celebrated at great length, hugging and jumping and skating as a group back to the bench. It was an obnoxious display of mock joy. As well as sounding his contraption, Mr. Air Horn leaned over the railing and screamed insults at the players. There was shuffling throughout the crowd and I noticed the first sign of activity among the riot police, who shuttled from one side of the rink to the other, thickening on the top level above the taunting fans.

The crowd chanted, "*It's now or never!*"

Whaoooonk!

The mantle of smoke on the ceiling was beginning to spread out into the crowd, and the game took on an ethereal quality, as if I were watching it through the foggy rear window of a car. Tiramu skated to the face-off circle and waved his hand at the crowd, prodding them like a relentless insult comic. But the veterans Gereb and Nagy, realizing the threat, led their team up-ice. They pinned Steaua in their zone until they scored, making it 3–2. It was enthralling hockey. During Ciuc's play, the Hungarian fans threw their shoulders against each other, arms flailing, necks pulled back, hands gripping their faces. They'd willed Sport Klub to find the net, the puck popping in from a seemingly impossible angle. After the goal, Radu lay prone in his crease like a snow angel. The kids directly above him leaned over the railing and yowled. Tiramu stood next to him, tapping his pads and looking worriedly up into the stands.

After the second period, the score 3–2 for Steaua, Karolina asked if I wanted to interview a former Romanian national team member in the Sport Klub's lounge. I said that I did, and so we descended into the bowels of the rink. We were taken to the president's quarters, a small drawing room with pennants of obscure international teams pinned to the wall: Nederlander Ijshockey Bond, Ice Hockey Federation of Slovenia, CSSLH, Sg Dynamo, Trebic, and others. There was also a glass cabinet filled with the vases, cups, trophies, plates, goblets, urns, and chalices won by Ciuc over the years.

I took a chair across from Istvan Takacs. He was a gentle, frosty-haired fellow who had played for the Romanian Nats in the 1959 World Championships in Geneva, and then in 1963 in Stockholm. He answered my questions slowly, but in Hungarian, as if speaking deliberately would help me understand him better. Karolina translated. I asked him why he started playing.

"It was in 1946," he said. "I started because, really, it is what all of us did, and still do. It is our way of life, the way it is for you in Canada. My philosophy is: hockey is life. What you learn on the ice, you take to your home, your office. Nothing that you accomplish on the ice is unnecessary."

"What are some of the things hockey has taught you?"

"So much about life, about other people, and getting along with them," he said. "Through hockey, you learn to respect life and to value people. You learn to listen to your coach, and to your heart. You learn how to let your mind speak with your body, because the two become close after playing all these years," he sighed, building a house with his fingers.

"Did you ever play under circumstances like today's game?" I asked.

"It wasn't quite the same for me. My greatest games were international, when I competed around the world. The Olympic ideal was enforced, to play only for the game and my country, never for money."

"Did you ever play against Canada?"

"Yes, many times."

"Can you remember one particular player?"

The old-timer paused. He looked over my shoulder and narrowed his eyes. They became misty as he stared off into the distance, pausing a long time.

"Yes, I remember one."

"Who?" I asked.

"Jules Berry," he said.

The old-timer's eyes grew wet.

"Jules Berry," he repeated, shaking his head.

The room was quiet. I could hear the sounds of fans outside, smoking and drinking and arguing about hockey. The old-timer repeated the name: "Jules Berry."

I have no idea who Jules Berry is. When I returned to Canada, I dug through the pro, minor pro and national team records, but Berry's name did not appear anywhere. No one in Canadian hockey had heard of him. To Ivan Takacs, however, the memory of Jules Berry was clear as a bell. His name had sent him into a sweet, sad trance. This phantom Canadian Nat represented a time in Takacs' life when he'd crossed the European continent by train and visited two of Europe's great cities, playing outdoors with his countrymen on torchlit rinks in front of hearty crowds of men in scarves and fur hats, children packed in wool, and girls with alabaster skin and golden hair, their voices soft as snowflakes. Discotheques, cobblestones, cafés, raisin buns, reporters with great whooshing cameras, automobiles snorting black smoke, mountain slopes and ski runs, salted fish, sweet beer.

In the world of international hockey, players steal memories from each other. They mark each other's lives without ever being aware of it. International hockey shrinks the world so that two people who come from places on opposite sides of the earth are allowed to skate their names on the insides of each other's hearts. Their lives are tilted simply by playing together, by crossing paths in a game. During the 1987 Canada Cup in Hamilton, Wayne Gretzky invited members of the Soviet Union National team to his parents' home in Brantford for a barbecue. They talked hockey and ate burgers and two days later played one of the most beautiful exhibitions of hockey ever—passing their lives back and forth just as Jules Berry and Ivan Takacs, Sandor Gal and Espo once had.

"I will try to find Jules Berry," I told the old man.

"Thank you," he said, unfolding his hands.

"Death to the fucking federation!"

The third period started with more smoke and more police. The Sasquatch was now standing a few feet from the Romanian hockey rep, pointing at him. Steaua were the first to score, making it 4–2 with about fifteen minutes left to play. What happened next came in such a flurry that it's difficult to remember the sequence of events. I only know that it came in a flash and set wildfire to what, until then, had been an intense, well-played game.

Timaru was at the center of what eventually set Ciuc's blood to boil. This was a shame because, as easy as it was to despise his behavior, he was clearly the best skater on the ice. But I suppose it was his arrogance that had led him in the first place to play for the Army team instead of his home club in Gheorgheni. Timaru's best hockey came in the third period. He was so involved with the play that the Ciuc players did everything they could to try and take the puck off him, resulting in more incidental contact than we'd seen up until that point. Finally, Nagy hit Timaru with his hip and he went down in the corner. The referee hurried in with one hand raised above his head as Nagy stood over the fallen Timaru, poking his foot with his stick, trying to get him to rise.

The ref grabbed Nagy around the waist and pushed him away. The Steaua team skated over to Nagy, insulting him:

"*Pig!*"

"*Outsider!*"

"*Go back to Hungary, pig!*"

Nagy, to his credit, said nothing. He allowed himself to be led to the penalty box. Timaru lay still until the Ciuc captain was removed, then he rose to his feet, shaking his head as if emerging from a nightmare. The first thing he did was try to spear the Sport Klub player closest to him. The crowd hollered at Timaru, calling for his blood as he prowled the ice before lining up for the face-off. He skated around the ice trying to run at the entire team, but he was on the bench when Steaua scored on the power play, making it 5–2. Captain Nagy came out of the box, and you could see him talking to the players on the bench, telling them, "This game isn't over! Don't let them goad you!"

After their three-goal lead, Steaua tried to slow the action. They fell on the puck whenever they could and lagged it through the neutral zone, spinning back in their own end to kill the clock and diving to the ice whenever a Ciuc player skated near. This did not discourage the home team, however, because they came back with pressure, peppering Radu with shots from every spot on the ice, each volley a gesture of defiance. But the little goalie turned them away easily and kept a lid on his temper until, with about three minutes left to go, all hell broke loose at Vakar Lajos.

There was a goalmouth scramble in front of Radu followed by a whistle and some slashing between players. One of the Army players took exception and cross-checked the veteran Gereb. The veteran stood his ground and hacked him across the arm, crumpling the player to the ice. The Steaua team exploded off the bench. Radu, wielding his blocker, punched the Ciuc player nearest to him. Jozsef Andorjan. Jozsef grabbed the back of the goalie's helmet and tried to pull it off his head. Radu windmilled his arms and caught three different players—including one of his own—with clobbering shots. With this, Ladai sprinted from the other end of the ice and was met at the blue line by Tiramu, who pulled him to the ice, obliging the Ciuc coach to release his players, who jumped from the boards and headed straight for the Steaua Rat.

One of the Army players headed to the bench and started swinging his stick at the crowd. Fans were leaning over the railing, their arms and legs draped over the sides, faces wide with panic. The player thrashed up at Mr. Air Horn, whacking the sides of the contraption while the fan pumped frantically *Whaoooonk!* I could hear the rumbling of boots and, before I knew it, the cops had reached the bottom of the stands to, as it turned out, protect Mr. Air Horn from the player. Kids with blue faces stood up and pelted the visiting team with cups. One of the Steaua players turned around on the ice and landed a haymaker on the Ciuc trainer, sending him sprawling to the ice. Bottles exploded like firecrackers as the crowd sang:

"*Hungareeaaaa!*"

The police gathered near where we were sitting. They stationed themselves in front of the VIPs, and I looked down at the Romanian sports rep and the Hungarian MP. Their faces were frozen. Sasquatch was screaming from behind the cops, snaking his arms over their shoulders to get at the Romanian hockey emissary. On the ice, a Steaua player, Robert Mihai, skated over to where we were sitting. He looked up into the stands and pointed at the Hungarian MP. The player held out his finger until the crowd knew exactly at whom he was pointing. Then brought his stick over his shoulder and steadied it there as if aiming a rifle. He leaned his head against the wood, and paused. Then fired a blast that rocked him back on his skates.

Hockey Fan-Antics, or . . . Why the Rangers Will Never Finish on Top or Win the Cup!

BY JEFF GREENFIELD

Jeff Greenfield, the author of the following, remains something of a mystery to this editor, but his tribute to the fans of the New York Rangers is still fresh twenty-five years later. The Rangers have always been a frustrating team to watch, and were true to form when Greenfield followed them in the early seventies. It is a perfect portrait of the angry oddballs who show up night after night to watch an expensive team lose.

The Rangers did break the curse, of course, in 1994, when they won the Cup. But the decade afterward has returned fans of the team to the dark swamp of frustration, which Greenfield's piece describes so well, and the story could have been written yesterday.

★   ★   ★   ★   ★

G*ave proof, through the night, that our flag was still there. . . .*
A stirring.
. . . Oh, say does th-at star-spangled ba-a-nne-er ye-et wa-ave . . .
The clapping and whistling start, faintly, somewhere in the far reaches of the balcony.
. . . O'er the la-and of the free . . .
It is spreading—cheers, claps, whistles, shrieks from Air Blast horns and plastic trumpets, from every part of the arena.

...And the home ...

Forget it. When the New York Rangers are at Madison Square Garden, you never hear the last words of the National Anthem. A continuous roar explodes through the Garden; the skaters, lined up at attention along the blue lines, break from their stances, wheel, and skate by their nets, tapping the leg pads of the goalies for luck. The referee hovers over the circle at center ice, ready to drop the frozen rubber puck between the sticks of the players and begin the game.

From her permanent seat in the first row on the balcony—it's called the "mezzanine," for the same reason that the smallest tubes of toothpaste you can buy are called "large"—Wanda performs her face-off ritual. As the last strains of the National Anthem are swallowed by the crowd, she shuts her eyes, makes the sign of the cross, and clasps her hands to the sky in prayer. This affirmation of faith complete, Wanda leans over the railing, cups her hands to her mouth, and screams with unbelievable power, "Come on, you sons of bitches—*kill 'em!*"

Wanda and the 17,000 others who filled Madison Square Garden for every Ranger home game are not "enthusiasts" or "fans." Communicants, perhaps. More accurately, they are witnesses—witnesses to a tragedy.

As everyone remembers, Aristotle taught that tragedy is a catharsis of emotion through pity and terror; an exercise in which we learn something of life by watching heroic mortals struggle in a web spun by Higher Forces. We do not watch *Oedipus Rex* or *Hamlet* to find out whether Rex will reign happily ever after, or because we hope Hamlet and Ophelia will settle down at Elsinore. We go to be moved by the spectacle of man challenging his inexorable fate. For the followers of the New York Rangers, this winter marks the resumption of one of the longest-running tragedies in history.

The New York Rangers never win: such is the Eternal Verity that decrees their fate and imprisons their fans. Yes, they win games. Yes, they field respectable, even enviable teams. But when the final test comes, the Rangers never win. They have not won the Stanley Cup, symbol of major-league-hockey supremacy, for thirty-four years; of the five other veteran clubs, only Detroit has gone as long as sixteen years without tasting ultimate victory. The Rangers until 1972 had not even been in the final round of Cup play for more than twenty years; another record of futility unmatched by the established clubs. Even in the regular season standings, a matter only of pride, the Rangers have not finished first in thirty-two years.

Losing is nothing new to the sports fans of New York City; indeed, they treat failure with the kind of wry affection offered by an eminently rich, respectable family to a black-sheep uncle whose catastrophes are international, explosive, and slightly risqué. New York is the Big Apple: failure is dealt with summarily and ruthlessly in the world of commerce, industry, finance, politics, and the arts. In forgiving the failure of our teams, we New Yorkers can offer the kind of compassion we are ourselves unlikely to receive.

What is different about Ranger fans, however, is that they are the only group of New York sports fans *never* to have tasted the big victory in more than thirty years. The Dodgers *did* win a World Series finally (beating the unbeatable Yankees in seven games in 1955). The Mets went from a nine-place finish in 1968 to a 1969 World Series; so explosive was the celebration that bus drivers let passengers on for free, and Mayor Lindsay's reelection was demonstrably assisted by the goodwill that spread over the city. And the fans of every other New York team have the remembered taste of victory. Yankee rooters live with the memory of dynasty; the Jets have Joe Namath and a Super Bowl trophy; Giant football fans, reading their road maps to Hackensack, remember the Eastern Division championships of the late fifties and early sixties and a once-impregnable defense; the Knicks have a 1973 basketball championship and a still-powerful team.

But to be a Ranger fan is to hold to the term's original meaning: fanatic. Moreover, rooting for the Rangers has afflicted all of us—for I am one of them—with a nearly incurable schizophrenic rage that removes Ranger hockey from the realm of Sport. Ranger fans, for example, do not stand by their heroes; they are the ultimate summer soldiers of winter sports. A single missed check or bad pass can instantly erase a night or a week or a season of spectacular play. Indeed, there are those who make insult their chief obsession.

Take Wanda (I have changed her name for fear of physical reprisal), the girl who sends up a prayer at the start of each game. Wanda has the most recognizable, piercing voice in the Garden. She also seems to have learned her vocabulary by speed-reading men's-room walls: the breadth and imagery of her obscenities are breathtaking. Often, Wanda arrives forty-five minutes before game time, when the teams are practicing and the arena is empty and quiet. If Wanda is in good form, endearments like these greet the Rangers:

"Rod Seiling, you stink. You're smelling up the ice, Seiling. Get cancer."

"Gilbert, you fairy! Drop dead! You're no superstar, Gilbert, you're a superfart!"

"You bum, Neilson, why don't you get hit by a truck, you c——r!"

Throughout the game, Wanda questions—graphically—the manhood, ancestry, sanitary habits, patriotism, and sobriety of every Ranger player. But it is *her team*—she wants them to win. When a Ranger scores, it is Wanda who leaps to her feet, embracing whoever is next to her, suffused with ecstasy. When the Rangers win a game, it is Wanda who is chief celebrant. Her joy at their triumphs and her anger at their failures are constantly at war with each other, and the sounds of combat fill the Garden every Wednesday and Sunday night.

Or consider Red: one of the authentic communicants. Red and his colleagues know everything about the Rangers. They know where the players live. They show up at practice sessions to roar encouragement and abuse. They study the yearbooks and the charts. They can remember—and will tell you, with very little urging—every mistake every player made in every game over the last four seasons.

Hard-core fans like Red hold a place of honor at the Garden; through him, the ordinary fan can test his judgment. There are two fifteen-minute rest periods in a hockey game, natural occasions for Instant Analysis and Querulous Commentary. At any given moment, clusters of communicants and acolytes are grouped around refreshment stands or in the aisles, reviewing the shortcomings of the Rangers.

Here, Red is in his element. Somewhere in his early twenties, Red has all the makings of a loser. He is very overweight; his face is round, chubby, topped with bright orange hair. He is perhaps a gas-station attendant, a shipping clerk. But here, lounging against the balcony guardrail, his back to the ice, Red is king. He knows everything you always wanted to know about the Rangers—and if you are afraid to ask, he will tell you.

When Red holds court, novices and apprentices group around him from neighboring sections, firing their tentative opinions at him two or three at a time, ready to change their minds immediately if Red should disagree. It sounds like children on a beach, imploring their slumbering parents to watch them, *really watch* them.

"Red! Red! Did you see Carr poke check—"

"Red! Hey, Red! That Gilbert stunk up the ice tonight, didn't—"

"Hey, Red! Pretty good checking by Tkaczuk—"

Like a chess master taking on twelve opponents at the same time, Red turns from one to the other, scornfully dismissing one, magnanimously assenting to another.

"Unbelievable," he says. "Unbe*lie*vable! *Three* power plays and we get *four* shots on goal. *Four!* If that—Gilbert? How the hell can you blame Gilbert, did you see—get out of here with that crap. *Seiling.* Neilson and Seiling *together* can't—hitting? *Hitting?* Where did you see hitting? Damn right. I tell you . . ."

His audience is rapturous. It's so hard to get Red's attention that it is something of a privilege to be attacked as an idiot. At least he listened.

Driven by such passion, torn between joy and fury at the performance of his team, the Ranger fan cannot be expected to spare compassion on the foe. And he does not. In common with hockey fans across the continent, the Ranger rooter is one of the most unsportsmanlike sports buffs in existence.

In baseball or football, an opponent's injury brings a hush to the most partisan crowd. The trainer rushes onto the field. After a few moments of ministrations, the enemy combatant struggles to his feet and gamely hobbles off the field to the cheers of the fans.

With Ranger fans . . . well, take the case of Ted Green, a former Boston Bruin defenseman now with the New England Whalers of the WHA, a feared player who seemed to regard hockey as an unfortunate interruption between brawls. In the fall of 1969, in the midst of a fight, a stick crashed down on Green's skull and fractured it. After hanging between life and death for days, Green returned to hockey with a steel plate embedded in his head.

In any other sport, Green's courage would have earned him respectful cheers. But last season, at the Garden, Green was met by a chorus of jeers and boos.

"Come on, Green, get off the ice, you're all washed up," one fan yelled over and over. "Go home you has-been." And then, as a lull settled over the crowd and the steel-plated Green skated into position for a face-off, a voice came booming out of the balcony:

"Come on, Ironhead, get off the ice!"

This gleeful and absolute hatred of the enemy blossoms during a fight. There is, in hockey, no idiotic propaganda that violence is only incidental to the game. When you put strong men on skates and arm them with sticks, people will hit each other. Almost no one gets hurt in a fight—skates don't give much traction—so most fights start and end with arm-wrestling, pulling a jersey over a rival's head, and falling on the ice.

But when a real brawl erupts—with fists flying all over the ice—the fans forgive anything, including a losing game, to roar out the blood lust. (It is, indeed, something of a tradition for a losing hockey team to stage a wild fight in the last period of play to inspire its rooters.) During the Stanley Cup opening round a few years ago, the Rangers were losing to the Toronto Maple Leafs when an all-out Pier 6 brawl erupted. In the fracas Toronto goalie Bernie Parent left his net to join in, a severe breach of etiquette, which holds that goalies—valuable and vulnerable players—are neither aggressors nor victims in a fight.

Suddenly, to the astonished roars of the crowd, Ranger goalie Ed Giacomin skated the length of the ice and crashed into his opposite number. After fifteen minutes of mayhem, order was restored—and Toronto goalie Parent found himself without his $200 customized face mask. Ranger Vic Hadfield had yanked it from his head and thrown it into the crowd, where it mysteriously disappeared.

"Keep it! Keep it!" the fans started chanting when they realized what had happened. "Don't give it back! Don't give it back!" They didn't, and Toronto was forced to put in a new goalie. (Incredibly, another fight broke out thirty-four seconds later, and the substitute Toronto goalie started throwing punches, and Ranger Giacomin *again* skated the length of the ice to crash into his rival. This time the face mask was securely anchored to the goalie's face.)

Given the willingness of Ranger fans to pour abuse on their heroes and villains, they are beyond hope when it comes to judging the fairness of referees. It is often hard to distinguish between legal and illegal moves in hockey because the game is so fast and so violent even when it is played according to Hoyle. But after thirty years of frustration, New York's hockey maniacs are convinced that *somebody* must be out to get them. And just as it is easier to persuade unemployed workers about powerful conspiracies of Eastern bankers than it is to convince affluent middle-class people, so the very record of futility is proof that the referees are in league against the Rangers. Learning this Truth—learning to yell, "Get the ref! Get the ref!" whenever he calls a penalty against Us—is something like a rite of passage.

Here is an eight-year-old boy attending his first hockey game, far back in the second promenade, sitting with his father, who has paid a scalper $20 each for two $7.50 tickets. The father has the look of a perpetual victim, the kind of man who works for a combination of Scrooge and Mr. Dithers, the kind of man who is insulted by bus drivers and snubbed by Sabrett hot-dog vendors.

But tonight, the father is part of the Crowd. As the game begins, the referee is introduced.

"Boooo! Booo!" the father shouts. "You're a bum! Go home!" His son watches with fascination.

As the game progresses, the father's indignation mounts. Every time a Ranger player is penalized, he is out of his seat.

"Ref, you stink! You Communist!" His voice breaks, sweat pours down his face. He draws on an inexhaustible wellspring of rage: every syrup-voiced politician, every creditor, is down there on the ice, disguised as the referee.

The son learns quickly. By the time the first period ends, he is standing on his seat, hands cupped to his mouth, echoing his father's anger:

"You . . . rotten, lousy louse! You bum!" There is no generation gap at Madison Square Garden.

Father and son also possess another abiding characteristic of New York hockey fans: they love not wisely but too well. Unlike their Canadian counterparts, New Yorkers do not grow up with hockey; few of them play the game as children, or even watch it frequently. It is, unlike baseball, football, or basketball, an acquired taste. It is also, at first glance, a ridiculously simple game. Once a fan learns about offsides (the puck must precede an attaching player across the blue line) and icing (you can't counter an attack by shooting the puck all the way down the ice) he knows enough to follow the play of the game. No self-respecting football fan would dare to offer advice without couching it in jargon: red dogs, crack-back, blitz, zig-out, passing planes, moving pockets, flares, and loops. In the Garden, the advice tends to be simpler.

"Shoot!" the father yells as the Rangers set up a play. "Shoot!" he yells as they regroup behind their own goal. The arsenal of offensive weapons—swift passing, feints to draw defensemen out of position, faked shots—he has no truck with these. "Come on, shoot, shoot, for Christ's sake, sho-o-o-ot!" It is rather like listening to Al Capp advise the National Guard on how to cope with student dissent.

At its most intense the fervor of a Ranger communicant transcends normal modes of communication. Iris, the queen of section 320, has reached that height. She is an anomaly—a hard-core Ranger fan who is a black woman. Most hockey fans are men, largely drawn from the white working class. But Iris is more than a token. She comes to the games armed with a large wicker basket: in it is a portable radio, so she can listen to a broadcast of the game she is attending; binoculars; a Ranger yearbook; and score sheets on which she records every goal and every penalty of every game.

So completely is Iris taken with the sport that she no longer cheers in English; she speaks instead in the language of tongues.

"Yaaahhh, yaaaahhh, c'moooonnnn!" she cries, as a Ranger flies down the ice.

"Whhaaat?" she screams as a Ranger power play is nullified by an offside call. "You—what—aaaaaggghhh!"

A Ranger trips an opponent, and a penalty is called.

"You cra—arrgh—faaaghhhh!"

For all of us—Wanda, Red, Iris, the father—the 1970–71 season was going to be Our Year. It was only logical: the Jets and Mets in 1969, the Knicks in 1970, and 1971 was the Rangers' turn. And after the Rangers won the first round for the first time in twenty years, it seemed indeed that this time the fates would be on our side. And so, in the sixth game of the semi-final round, we gathered to watch the Rangers battle the Chicago Blackhawks and their fate.

The Blackhawks were ahead in the series, three games to two. A loss would eliminate New York; a win would send the teams to Chicago for a decisive seventh game. When the Rangers fell behind 2–0, it seemed that the inevitable tragic end was in sight. But the fates were playing subtler games this time.

By the third period, the Rangers had tied the score at 2–2. By the end of the period, the score was the same. But there are no ties in Stanley Cup playoffs; the teams keep playing twenty-minute periods until somebody scores—and whoever scores first wins the game.

As the first overtime began, the tension became ridiculous. Even Mike the Usher, gray-haired, iron-faced, horn-rimmed, imperturbable, was perched on a stair, watching intensely.

The opening minute of play. Both the Rangers and the Blackhawks come within inches of scoring the decisive goal.

"Jeez," Mike says. "I haven't bitten my nails in thirty years."

"Keep bitin' 'em," a spectator growls. "That's the last time we won the goddamn Cup."

The first overtime period ends with the score still 2–2.

"I can't look," Mike the Usher moans. "The only way I can take a game like this is if I'm half in the bag."

The second overtime period begins, with Chicago attacking mercilessly. A shot hits the right post of the goal. Two inches over and it would have won the game and the series for the Blackhawks. Another Chicago shot—and this one hits the left post.

"They're trying' to kill me," Mike yells. "The bastards are tryin' to kill me."

The second overtime period ends. Between the mass rush to the men's rooms, and the queue for frantic telephone calls to wives and babysitters, some of the exhausted fans doze in their seats.

The *third* overtime period begins. It's been forty years since the Rangers played a triple overtime game. The crowd is silent, half from tension, half from exhaustion. Then, two minutes into the period, a Ranger shot is blocked but rebounds out in front of the net. Peter

Stemkowski slams the puck past the Chicago goalie. The red light flashed on. The Rangers have won.

For a full two seconds the bone-weary crowd, hypnotized by four hours of hockey, sit stunned. Then the roof gently lifts off and the Garden goes up for grabs. Mike stands up solemnly and begins shaking hands with men and kissing the women. Iris is dancing, hugging everyone within reach.

"You know," Mike says, "I *know* we're gonna lose that seventh game, but at least I can die happy."

"Lose?" yells a bystander. "Lose? You're outta your mind. We're going all the way. All the way!" Three days later in Chicago the Rangers lost 4–2.

This winter of 1973–74 the witnesses have returned. The scalpers shuffle back and forth in front of the Garden, surreptitiously hawking their wares in front of the uniformed police. "Who's selling?" "Who's buying?" "Who needs two?" "Who's got one?"

The fans pour abuse on the Rangers, they revile every official, they cheer every goal. By now, they are telling themselves, this year, this time, all the way. And by April or March, or perhaps by May, if the torture is extended, the Rangers will lose—gallantly or foolishly or heroically, but they will lose, and we will tell ourselves, well, *next* year. . . .

Damage Control

BY GARE JOYCE

When Wayne Gretzky read *Damage Control* in June 2003, he was reportedly moved to tears. As far as this editor is concerned, that is hockey's equivalent of the Nobel Prize, and so, if for no other reason, this piece is included. It's a hard look at what happens when one father essentially puts all his chips on his son's shoulders.

The hero of the story, Patrick O'Sullivan, was expected to go early in the first round in the 2003 draft. He was finally chosen in the second round, the fifty-seventh pick, by the Minnesota Wild. Most analysts suspected that it had to do with the team's reservations about O'Sullivan's violent and overbearing father, who, against the wishes of the family and the son, showed up at the arena. Gretzky, who had read the story a month before, made sure to meet Patrick and to speak with him for a while. In an interview with the CBC afterward, Gretzky said he told O'Sullivan, "You know, what you're doing is better than anyone else. You've stood up not only for other kids who are being physically and mentally abused, but you've stood up for yourself. . . . And not only is it a great story for him to tell, but hopefully it's going to help other kids."

A few months later, at the World Junior Championships, O'Sullivan scored two goals in the final game, helping the U.S. defeat Canada.

★   ★   ★   ★   ★

Patrick O'Sullivan always looks for his father in the stands. He's done it since he was a 2-year-old skating in Winston-Salem, N.C. He still caught himself doing it this season when, at age 18, he was the leading scorer for the Mississauga

IceDogs of the Ontario junior league. And at the NHL draft in Nashville before he even takes a seat, O'Sullivan will look around the arena, searching for his father. But this isn't Jim Craig trying to find his father after the *Miracle on Ice* in Lake Placid. On draft day, Patrick O'Sullivan won't be the only one looking for John O'Sullivan. So will Patrick's mother, Cathie, and a ready-for-anything team from NHL security. "I hope he won't be there," Patrick says, sounding more weary than angry. "I hope he'd know not to come with everyone looking for him, and with me not wanting him there. A perfect day would be getting picked by a team that wants me, and knowing my father is not in the arena."

Scouts rate Patrick, a 5'11", 193-pound center, as a top-five talent in the draft. There's no better finisher in the pool. In the time it takes most players to recognize a scoring chance, Patrick's already wired the puck into the net. He has the rare combination of near-psychic anticipation and surgeon's nerve. Mike Bossy had it. Brett Hull, too. It's the kind of gift that starts a father dreaming big dreams for his son. Dreams that can get out of control.

For the past year and a half, the teen hasn't worried much about his father being around. That's because after years of emotional and physical torment, Patrick stood up to him. He filed assault charges that landed John O'Sullivan in jail. By the time he was released, a judge had issued a temporary restraining order against him.

The team selecting Patrick will also want John O'Sullivan to stay out of the picture. To scouts and general managers, a dysfunctional family is as much of an impediment to a draftee as weak ankles. John O'Sullivan believed he was Patrick's greatest asset in the boy's pursuit of a pro hockey career. But according to more than one scouting director, he might be his son's greatest liability. And another scout puts it this way: "Kids from a troubled family hardly ever pan out."

So Patrick will sit beside Cathie and his sisters, Kelley, 15, and Shannon, 8, on draft day. He will wait to hear his name called—and hope that his father is in another area code.

Hockey fans know Wayne Gretzky's story starts with his father, Walter, a former minor leaguer, flooding a backyard rink in Brantford, Ontario, nurturing his son's talent with homespun wisdom.

John O'Sullivan wanted his story to turn out the same. Like Walter, John had played the game. Raised in Toronto, he figured he'd make it to the NHL if he worked harder than anybody else. He practically lived at the rink and the gym. When guys would knock off for a beer after a game, John would be doing push-ups and sit-ups, knocking back milk and protein powder. But his dedication didn't translate into stardom. Although John played a few games for junior clubs in Quebec and Saskatchewan, no NHL team drafted him. He was invited to the Winnipeg Jet's training camp one year and the Penguins' the next, but that's as good as it got in his brief career.

John landed in the Atlantic Coast Hockey League, but even in the minorest of the minors, he was a scrub, a forward who scored seven goals in his best season. "He was a loner who fought a bit," says Panthers general manager Rick Dudley, who coached John with the Winston-Salem Thunderbirds. "He didn't hang out with the other players." He did find a girl to hang out with: Cathie Martin, from Winston-Salem. They married in 1982, and three years later John left the game for good when Cathie gave birth to a son. As soon as Patrick learned to walk, John put a toy hockey stick in his hands—and swore he saw a special gift.

It's not clear when John O'Sullivan's support for his son's hockey career crossed the line—when, as Patrick says, "He started to live his dream through me." It may have been when he moved his family to Toronto so his 5-year-old son could play against better competition. Or when John insisted that Patrick play against boys at least a couple of years older. Or when he quit jobs because they clashed with Patrick's practice schedule.

To Patrick, John crossed the line when he made his 8-year-old son get out of the car a mile from home and run the rest of the way carrying his gear, his punishment for a subpar game. Or when John moved his family to Sterling Heights, Mich., to find better coaching for 12-year-old Patrick and his sister Kelley, then 9 and a budding tennis star. Or when Patrick was 13 and John was driving him across the Canadian border five or six times a week, an hour each way, to play against men as old as 21.

That season, Patrick played with a winger who was married and the father of a newborn. John O'Sullivan saw nothing wrong with that picture. After all, Wayne Gretzky had been a boy among men. But nobody was mistaking John O'Sullivan for Walter Gretzky, although word of this prodigy got around.

The USA Hockey development program in Ann Arbor recruited Patrick, and at 15 he spent a year playing with the best American talent his age. That was Patrick's most enjoyable season, and not just because of the wins in international age-group tournaments. He finally felt like part of a team, going to the same high school as the rest of the players. For once, he had friends, not just wingers. "I played with John at training camp in Winnipeg," says Moe Mantha, who coached Patrick for USA Hockey. "I told him to trust us. I think he did most of the time."

Still, John pushed his son relentlessly. Nothing was good enough. When Patrick scored, he seemed more relieved than happy. Teammates knew why. Some of them allowed referees to give credit for a fuzzy goal or assist to Patrick, to spare him John's wrath. A few times Mantha asked Patrick if he should go with him to the parking lot after a game to "talk John down." Patrick declined, fearing it would just provoke his father. Says Mantha, "I told John if he didn't change, his kid was eventually going to tell him to screw off."

At 16, Patrick was selected by Mississauga with the No. 1 pick in the Ontario Hockey League draft. To play in the OHL, Patrick would have to forgo his NCAA eligibility. He'd hoped to play college hockey with friends in the USA Hockey program. But John had never been able to cut it in the OHL. This was his chance for sweet retribution, and his son's chance to hit the NHL jackpot.

So Patrick became a Mississauga IceDog. As it happened, the coach and part-owner was Don Cherry, the legendary *Hockey Night in Canada* commentator. "John was wound real tight all the time," says Cherry. "I was worried something was up when Patrick came to the rink once with cuts and bruises that weren't from games." Says another team official: "By midseason Patrick thought it was either going to be his father killing him or him killing his father, whichever came first."

It didn't come to that. But it came close. Patrick O'Sullivan didn't have to look for his father in the stands at the game against the Ottawa 67's on January 4, 2002. He was the guy leaning over the glass behind the

IceDogs' bench. The one screaming at Patrick. "You're f—ing finished. You should have gone to f—ing college. You're going f—ing home."

The tension had been building all day. John and Cathie had driven 10 hours from Michigan to Ottawa for the game. They'd dropped Kelley and their other daughter, 8-year-old Shannon, at John's parents' in Toronto. The drive gave John time to simmer: Patrick was screwing up. He was soft. By the time they made it to the arena, John was seething.

On the bench, Patrick stared straight ahead. Without turning around, he yelled at his father to "F— off." After the game, Patrick was about to get on the team bus when, according to teammates, John grabbed him and shoved him into his van. John told Patrick he'd played his last game, and then drove from Ottawa to his parents' house in Toronto, ranting for the entire four-hour trip. Cathie was terrified, but Patrick was defiant: "I'd had enough. So many times I wanted to quit just to get back at him. But not now. I was going to play. It was my life, after all. I was even laughing at him."

When the van pulled up to John's parents' house before dawn, he went to collect Kelley and Shannon. Patrick got out of the van, too, telling his father that he wasn't coming home. He was making a stand for himself. It had to end now, he said, knowing exactly what was coming. On the lawn, with his parents and John's younger brother, Barry, looking on in horror, O'Sullivan started punching and kicking his 16-year-old-son. Fighting was John's game. He had more than 30 pounds on Patrick. It was the ACHL all over again. He left Patrick in a heap on the grass, bruised and cut.

John got in the car and drove off alone before Patrick got up off his knees. Cathie called the police. That afternoon, a judge issued a warrant for John's arrest. The next day, Cathie and Patrick visited Ice-Dogs GM Trevor Whiffen and told him what had happened. He was sympathetic. Assistant coach Joe Washkurak was not surprised. He'd seen it all too often in his day job as a social worker specializing in domestic crisis cases. "The red flags were out there," Washkurak says. "Everyone saw his obsessiveness. But in a lot of abuse relationships, the abuse goes on out of sight."

John was at large for a week. For the first time, Patrick would look in the stands and his father wouldn't be there. The IceDogs put in new team rules: Patrick wasn't to be left alone on road trips or at the arena, before or after a game. John gave police the slip until he was arrested near the IceDogs arena. He pled guilty to assault and spent 22 days in a Toronto jail. Cathie and the girls moved back to Winston-Salem. She talked to a lawyer about divorce. Patrick got a restraining order that barred his father from any close contact with him. John was barred from any hockey arena in Ontario. But he was still spotted at several games.

It's hard to think of a 17-year-old as being made young again. But the court order did just that for Patrick, who began playing better than ever and was named the top rookie in all of the Canadian junior leagues.

In April 2002 he went to the World Under-18 Championship in Slovakia and was reunited with many of his friends from the USA Hockey development program. "He seemed much happier," says Mike Eaves, who coached the American Under-18s. "One day I had the guys jog a couple of laps around a track to loosen up. Patrick is so competitive, he made it into a race and pushed other guys into running harder. And it was fun. You got a sense that he was breaking free."

And in the tournament Patrick did break free. Going into the final game, the U.S. needed a two-goal victory over Russia for the gold. On the ice was Nikolai Zherdev, now the top European prospect in the 2003 NHL draft. But he was overshadowed by Patrick. In the last minute, Patrick quarterbacked a power play that gave the U.S. a 3+1 victory and the gold. The American team's youngest member, he was also its leading scorer.

"It's simple," say one NHL scout. "O'Sullivan was the best player on the best team in a tournament against players a full year older than him." Cherry wasn't surprised. "He's a tough kid," he says. "By age 16 he had to go through more than most adults ever have to. Scouts may worry about his family. But he managed to score 40 goals this season with all this other stuff going on. That tells you what he's made of."

As of now, though, reports from the NHL's scouting service rate Patrick as No. 14 among this year's crop of North American draft hopefuls. If that's accurate, he'll be a late first-round pick. What's happened in the year since his triumph overseas has dragged down his stock.

To begin with, NHL scouts were disappointed by Patrick's play in the World Under-20 championship in Nova Scotia this winter. They had hoped to see the same player who tore up the Under-18 tournament. But Patrick didn't see much ice time and pressed too hard on the shifts he got.

And then there was the John O'Sullivan factor. The American Under-20 squad was accompanied to the tournament by a U.S. marshall, in case John, restraining order or not, made an appearance. Which he did. Patrick had no trouble spotting him in the stands. His only trouble was getting away. "He called my room at the hotel and we saw him around," Patrick said. "After the medal-round games, he tried to get down to the dressing room."

There was no violent incident, but NHL scouts knew about the intrigue. It's an NHL rule of thumb that the scouting of a player isn't complete until you've scouted the parents. To scouts, John O'Sullivan is more than a nuisance.

It takes a while to find John O'Sullivan, who's been on the move lately. He has no visitation rights to his children—Cathie is seeking a permanent restraining order in the U.S.—but John recently moved to Winston-Salem, a couple of blocks away from Kelley's school. No listed phone number. No return address on the unopened letters to Patrick and the girls. There's only one way to reach him: a call to his attorney: "I've had to use lawyers a lot lately," says John.

It's just a phone conversation. So you have to draw your own picture of someone who sees most everything in his life differently than his family. Does he have a thousand-yard stare on his face, or is he anxiously fidgeting? Is he in denial, or does he really believe?

John professes to still love his ex-wife and his kids. He hopes "that everything can be worked out." He says his family was taken from him by "agents and lawyers [who] have had too much influence over my wife and Patrick." He thinks he wasn't just a good father, but a very good father, better than his own. He says he wanted only the best for his kids. "Cathie and I might have done more if we had had more support," he says. "I was totally committed to doing anything for Patrick and my daughters. Kelley is top-10 in the state in tennis. She should get a scholarship." There no point in telling John that Kelley has not picked up a racket for months and has no plans to: that she's studying theater and film.

And while his assault on Patrick landed him in jail, John is un-repentant. "No regrets," he says. "I wouldn't do anything different." He also suggests that the brawl wasn't an assault, or even a fight. "We're best friends," he says. "We'd always wrestle and scrap a bit, like friends. I only wish Patrick were more like me as a player, a tougher guy."

When asked if he planned to attend the draft, and if Patrick would acknowledge him there, John's voice starts to break. "You're start-ing to push my buttons," he says, then nothing more. Click.

On the last Friday and Saturday in May, Patrick and the other top 99 players eligible for the 2003 NHL draft gather at a Toronto hotel near the IceDogs' rink for a scouting combine that's one part physical evaluation and one part personnel interview.

Almost all the players opt for a conservative look: dark suit, Cole Haan shoes. Patrick wears a baby blue shirt and metallic blue tie—not quite casual but not too slick, just the look of an 18-year-old who's more comfortable in jeans, biting the bullet at least halfway. He has 14 interviews on this Friday. The shortest is over in 20 minutes, the longest lasts an hour. It's hard to tell if the interviews end when the execs hear what they want to hear, or what they don't want to hear.

Patrick hears questions like this: How would you characterize your relationship with your father? What's the difference between your game now and five years ago? Do you drink? Have you ever been in trouble with the law? Ever been in jail. Nobody asks him if his father will be at the draft. But here's what he would have told them: that there's only a faint hope that his father will one day accept that their relation-ship is over. That for as long as he plays, everything he does on the ice will remind his father of other times, what John thinks were better times. That his father will always believe his son should have been bet-ter, tougher, more like he was. He would have told them that, yes, he'll scan the stands in Nashville searching for his father.

That he always has. Always will.

An Innocent at Rinkside

BY WILLIAM FAULKNER

William Faulkner didn't know a thing about hockey, but I include his "An Innocent at Rinkside" for the same inarguable reason *Sports Illustrated* chose to publish it in 1955: because he is William Faulkner. What's more, as far as this anthologist knows, this is the only article on the sport written by a Nobel Prize winner, and when it comes to ruminations about the game by the big guns of literature, hockey fans must take what they can get. Not that it's a disappointment. Faulkner's enigmatic prize-winning style is in full evidence in "An Innocent at Rinkside," in which a game at Madison Square Garden between the Canadiens and the Rangers is dissected like a watch, the pieces held up to the loupe to reveal thoughts about youth, the domestication of sport, American insecurity, and even a little hockey. Still and all, it was probably a good thing that he stuck mainly to matters Mississippian.

★　★　★　★　★

The vacant ice looked tired, though it shouldn't have. They told him it had been put down only ten minutes ago following a basketball game, and ten minutes after the hockey match it would be taken up again to make room for something else. But it looked not expectant but resigned, like the mirror simulating ice in the Xmas store window, not before the miniature fir trees and reindeer and cozy lamplit cottage were arranged upon it, but after they had been dismantled and cleared away.

Then it was filled with motion, speed. To the innocent, who had never seen it before, it seemed discorded and inconsequent, bizarre and paradoxical like the frantic darting of the weightless bugs which run on the surface of stagnant pools. Then it would break, coalesce through a kind of kaleidoscopic whirl like a child's toy, into a pattern, a design almost beautiful, as if an inspired choreographer had drilled a willing and patient and hardworking troupe of dancers—a pattern, design which was trying to tell him something, say something to him urgent and important and true in that second before, already bulging with the motion and the speed, it began to disintegrate and dissolve.

Then he learned to find the puck and follow it. Then the individual players would emerge. They would not emerge like the sweating barehanded behemoths from the troglodyte mass of football, but instead as fluid and fast and effortless as rapier-thrusts or lightning—Richard with something of the passionate glittering fatal alien quality of snakes, Geoffrion like an agile ruthless precocious boy who maybe couldn't do anything else but then he didn't need to; and others—the veteran Laprade, still with the know-how and the grace. But he had time too now, or rather time had him, and what remained was no longer expendable that recklessly, successfully; not enough of it left now to buy fresh passion and fresh triumph with.

Excitement: men in rapid hard close physical conflict, not just with bare hands, but armed with the knife-blades of skates and the hard fast deft sticks which could break bones when used right. He had noticed how many women were among the spectators, and for just a moment he thought that perhaps this was why—that here actual male blood could flow, not from the crude impact of a heavier fist but from the rapid and delicate stroke of weapons, which like the European rapier or the Frontier pistol, reduced mere size and brawn to its proper perspective to the passion and the will. But only for a moment because he, the innocent, didn't like that idea either. It was the excitement of speed and grace, with the puck for catalyst, to give it reason, meaning.

He watched it—the figure-darted glare of ice, the concentric tiers rising in sections stipulated by the hand-lettered names of the individual fan-club idols, vanishing upward into the pall of tobacco smoke trapped by the roof—the roof which stopped and trapped all that intent and tense watching, and concentrated it downward upon the glare of ice frantic and frenetic with motion; until the by-product of the speed and the motion—their violence—had no chance to exhaust itself upward into space and so leave on the ice only the swift glittering changing pattern. And he thought how perhaps something is happening to sport in America (assuming that by definition sport is something you do yourself, in solitude or not, because it is fun), and that something is the roof we are putting over it and them. Skating, basketball, tennis, track meets and even steeplechasing have moved indoors; football and baseball function beneath covers of arc lights and in time will be rain- and cold-proofed, too. There still remain the proper working of a fly over trout water or the taking of a rise of birds in front of a dog or the right placing of a bullet in a deer or even a bigger animal which will hurt you if you don't. But not for long: in time that will be indoors too beneath lights and the trapped pall of spectator tobacco, the concentric sections bearing the name and device of the lion or the fish as well as that of the Richard or Geoffrion of the scoped rifle or 4-ounce rod.

But (to repeat) not for long, because the innocent did not quite believe that either. We—Americans—like to watch; we like the adrenalic discharge of vicarious excitement or triumph or success. But we like to do also: the discharge of the personal excitement of the triumph and the fear to be had from actually setting the horse at the stone wall or pointing the overcanvassed sloop or finding by actual test if you can line up two sights and one buffalo in time. There must have been little boys in that throng, too, frantic with the slow excruciating passage of time, panting for the hour when they would be Richard or Geoffrion or Laprade—the same little Negro boys whom the innocent has seen shadowboxing in front of a photograph of Joe Louis in his own Mississippi town—the same little Norwegian boys he watched staring up the snowless slope of the Holmenkollen jump one July day in the hills above Oslo.

Only he (the innocent) did wonder just what a professional hockey-match, whose purpose is to make a decent and reasonable profit for its owners, had to do with our National Anthem. What are we afraid of? Is it our national character of which we are so in doubt, so fearful that it might not hold up in the clutch, that we not only dare not open a professional athletic contest or a beauty-pageant or a real-estate auction, but we must even use a Chamber of Commerce race for Miss Sewage Disposal or a wildcat land-sale, to remind us that liberty gained without honor and sacrifice and held without constant vigilance and undiminished honor and complete willingness to sacrifice again at need, was not worth having to begin with? Or, by blaring or chanting it at ourselves every time ten or twelve or eighteen or twenty-two young men engage formally for the possession of a puck or a ball, or just one young woman walks across a lighted platform in a bathing suit, do we hope to so dull and eviscerate the words and tune with repetition, that when we do hear it we will not be disturbed from that dream-like state in which "honor" is a break and "truth" an angle.

Toe

BY RED FISHER

Red Fisher has covered the Canadiens since 1954, and is still at it. He is in the Hockey Hall of Fame for writing, at least as far as the Hall is concerned. Fisher thinks otherwise. He "withdrew" his membership in 2003 over the fact that writers and broadcasters were not considered "honored" members, a technicality that probably would not matter to less contentious writers than Fisher, whose surliness sticks out in the piece below. It is about Toe Blake, the most celebrated of Canadiens' coaches, whom Fisher knew intimately. It is an honest remembrance of a friend as he fades into the sunset. Toe Blake died in 1995.

★   ★   ★   ★   ★

I t was cold, the man on the car radio was saying. Snow was on the way later that December day, he said. Five to ten centimeters, maybe, so bundle up warm.

The snow that had fallen in the Montreal region several days earlier had formed soft, white pillows on the short driveway leading to the nursing home. A white, lined face peered out of a second-floor window, then quickly disappeared.

Inside, Toe Blake sat in a hallway wheelchair, his head on his chest, hands crossed and eyes closed. It was 1991. Almost two years had passed since Blake had been brought to this place, twenty-three since he had retired as coach of the Montreal Canadiens. The top of the exercise suit he wore was as gray as the weather outside. The only small splash of color on it was the CH. The words "Montreal Canadiens," in red, were below it. The bottoms were blue. He sat there, dozing, locked in the terrible vise that is Alzheimer's yet, remarkably, still looking like the big bear of a man he always was.

"Hi, Toe," said Floyd Curry, who had played for Blake's Canadiens for the first three of an NHL-record five consecutive Stanley Cup-winning seasons in the last half of the 1950s. Hardly a week passed without a visit from Curry, who had become Blake's closest friend over the years. "Look who's here, Toe," said Curry.

Blake's eyes remained closed.

"Don't wake him, Floyd, he needs the rest," a guy said.

Curry tugged at his fedora. "Toe, we've brought you some cookies. Wake up, Toe."

A slim, black man named Andrew placed a hand on Blake's shoulder and shook him gently. "Wake up, Toe," he said. "Let's get you up. You've got visitors, Toe." Then he reached for the man who had been the very best of the NHL's coaches for thirteen uplifting seasons. He shook Blake again . . . gently. This time, Blake's eyes opened. An angry yell burst from his throat.

"That's it, Toe," said Andrew, his voice rising. "Let's get you out of the chair."

Andrew was on one side of Blake, holding and steering him into the bright, spacious dining room filled with empty tables. Curry supported him carefully on the other side. "There you go," said Andrew, easing Toe into a chair. "There, isn't that good? Look what we have for you," he said, lifting a cookie toward Blake's mouth. "Eat, Toe, it's good."

Toe Blake, winner of eight Stanley Cups during his glorious seasons behind the Canadiens' bench stared straight ahead, apparently hearing nothing, seeing less. On the other hand, would anybody have really known what he was hearing or seeing?

Once, everybody knew what Blake stood for, how he felt, what he thought, liked, loved, and hated. What he loved was to win. Losing was what he hated.

He was rough, gruff, intimidating, wise, compassionate, unforgiving, scheming, and hardworking—all of it dedicated to winning those eight Stanley Cups as a coach, including the five in a row. Winning wasn't merely a worthwhile target for Hector Blake, born August 21, 1912, in Victoria Miens, Ontario. It was everything. It was life itself—first as a player for two seasons with the Montreal Maroons, then thirteen with the Canadiens. Blake produced 235 goals and 292 assists, and won three Stanley Cups—the first with the Maroons, the last two with the Canadiens, where the Punch Line of Blake, Elmer Lach, and Maurice Richard was hockey's finest.

Left-winger Frank Mahovlich, an eighteen-season veteran of the NHL, was one of Blake's greatest admirers, even though he never played for him. He felt Blake was responsible for fifty percent of what was needed to win.

"I've always felt that a good coach is the one who wins," Blake agreed. "But fifty percent? If that had been the case with me, my teams would have won a lot more games."

Goaltender Gump Worsley was once asked what made Blake special as a coach. "There are twenty guys in that dressing room," replied Worsley, "and it's seldom you find even two of them alike. Toe knew each individual—the ones who worked from the needles, the ones who needed another approach. Between periods, he never blasted an individual. He'd say some guys aren't pulling their weight. The guys who weren't knew who he was talking about and you'd see the heads drop. But he'd never embarrass anyone in front of everyone. His ability to handle players—I guess that's what made him great."

Was Toe thinking about Gump or Frank this day, as he sat at the table, a plate of cookies in front of him? Once, he was full of life and laughs and mischief and blessed with a thirst for victory. His eyes snapped and crackled with the joy of competition. Now, at seventy-nine, his hair was white and his cheeks sunken. On this day, though, there was color in them.

"He looks good," said Curry quietly. "That's the best I've seen him lately. I was here a couple of weeks ago and he really looked terrible. I couldn't believe that was Toe."

Blake sat at the table, staring. He didn't open his mouth until Andrew gently brought a cookie up to it.

"It's good, Toe," he said.

"Eat, Toe, it's good," said Curry, now sixty-nine, who has devoted the last few years to taking care of the man who took such good care of Curry, the player. "Why wouldn't I?" asked Curry. "Toe was such a good guy."

Toe reached for a second cookie, then a third and fourth. On and on.

"He wants something to drink now," said Andrew. He lifted a small glass of cranberry juice to Blake's mouth.

"Have a sip, Toe," he said. "Wash it down."

Toe drew on the juice.

"*Merci*," he said.

Andrew looked through his gold-rimmed glasses and smiled. So did Curry.

"His appetite is fantastic," said Andrew. "He won't refuse food. He'll finish all of this," he said, with a wave of his hand at the cookie plate. "Most of the time, this is what he likes to do—eat. Your haven't seen anything yet."

He placed an arm around Blake's shoulder.

"C'mon, eat . . . there you are, Toe," said Andrew.

"Does he watch hockey games on television?" Curry asked.

"Does he know what he's watching?" a guy asked.

"I would say yes, to a certain degree," said Andrew. "My belief is he knows. My own opinion is he knows."

Curry left to make a telephone call to his wife. Toe, who always wore a fedora during his years behind the Canadiens' bench, reached for the brown one Curry had left on the table. In his left hand, he held what was left of the plate of cookies. With the other he pulled the fedora toward him. Then he ran his fingers over it—lovingly, almost— again and again.

"He seems to like your hat," Curry was told when he returned to the table. "It's almost as if he remembers what a fedora meant to him."

Curry blinked hard. "It's a damned shame, isn't it?" he said. "Look at his hands. He still has hands like a bear. Geez, he was strong. Look, he's finished the cookies."

Blake stared at the empty plate. Then he lifted it with both hands, tilted it toward him, and let the crumbs fall into his open mouth.

"Good, eh, Toe?" said Curry. "Very good. Remember me, Toe?"

Everybody remembers Toe. Everybody, that is, who developed a passion for hockey in the 1930s, the '40s, the '50s, and the '60s. As a coach, he was simply the very best. It's true that he had the National Hockey League's best talent during the five consecutive seasons, starting in 1955–56, that his teams won Stanley Cups. What made him the best was the way, somehow, he made the best teams better.

Indeed, getting the most out of the best was what Blake did best, which is what coaches in any sport are all about. Vince Lombardi is best remembered because he got the most out of his Green Bay Packers football teams. Well, Lombardi was football's Blake.

Blake's players respected, yet feared him. He was supremely loyal to them, and they to him. He had an uncanny talent of knowing when to raise and lower the volume. He produced winners, because he had no time to waste on losers. The only thing he hated more than losing was the unexpected.

Toe Blake was a complex man, which doesn't make him unique among coaches.

I remember one evening when Toe and I had been playing gin rummy for no more than an hour in my hotel room in Toronto. As usual, he was winning the low-stakes game, so watching him fling his cards on the table in disgust was something of a surprise.

"That's it," he snapped. "I'm leaving."

"What's the rush? We've only just started. It's early. Anyway, you can't just walk out of here after taking my money."

"Those guys have been fooling around," he said. "I'm going to check their rooms."

"What do you mean, fooling around? Hell, Toe, you've got a win and a tie in your two road games. What's wrong with that? Anyway, you've never done a room check before. It doesn't make much sense to start now."

"I'm checking their rooms," he insisted. Then he left.

"What about my money?"

"You'll have a chance to get it back tomorrow," he grunted.

Five minutes later, there was a soft knock on the door. Blake stood there, wearing a weak smile.

"That was a fast room check," he was told.

"Aw," he said, "I checked the first room, and both players were there. I think I woke them up. I was so damned embarrassed I decided not to check any of the other rooms. Get the cards. I need more of your money."

Ah yes, money . . .

Sports departments now spend a substantial percentage of their budgets sending reporters on the road. Today, for example, the Canadiens are accompanied on the road by twenty media people during the regular season, and more during the playoffs. It wasn't always that way, however. When I joined the *Montreal Star* in March 1954, reporters, with few exception, went on the road with the Canadiens only during the playoffs. What's more, the Canadiens paid for the transportation and hotels. They even provided the beat writers with a ten-dollar per diem. Hard, cold cash. Nobody questioned the practice—not the people who owned the newspapers, not the sports editors, not the team owners, not even the coaches and players. The few among us who did travel consistently didn't give the set-up a second thought. If our newspapers thought it was all right, it was fine with us. Case closed.

The Canadiens were in Detroit on this night in 1963, and, as usual, there were a few reporters in the dressing room before the game. Blake was deep in conversation with two Detroit reporters. I stayed off to one side waiting for the reporters to finish with Blake.

After several minutes, Blake turned and noticed me waiting there. He reached into his pocket for a wad of money. "Is this what you're waiting for?" he asked, peeling off a ten-dollar bill.

Both Detroit reporters laughed uncomfortably.

"Here," said Blake. "Take it."

"Stick it," I snapped, and stormed out of the dressing room.

Blake was nonplussed for a moment, then he stammered: "Hey, wait a minute, I was only kidding . . ."

Of course, he was kidding. What he was really doing was getting a laugh from the Detroit reporters at my expense, but this one wasn't even remotely amusing. I was still fuming the next day when I stormed into sports editor Harold Atkins's office. I explained what had happened the night before. "That's the last time I'm going on the road," I told Atkins, "unless this newspaper pays its own way."

"I'll have to check it out with the publisher," Atkins sighed.

John McConnell was stunned when the story was repeated to him. "Do you mean the Canadiens have been paying our expenses all this time!" he asked. "I had no idea we weren't paying our way," Mc-Connell said. "Make certain we pay our way from now on."

Blake was properly embarrassed over the incident—after thinking about it. His problem was that he often had a problem determining the fine line between amusement and humiliation. For instance, he didn't find anything funny in a story I once wrote—even though that was the idea when I wrote it. This was in December 1965.

"Toe there?" I asked the Forum's secretary.

"One moment," she said. She was heard talking to Blake.

"Who's calling?" she asked.

"Red Fisher," she was told.

The message was passed along. A voice sounding suspiciously like Blake's could be heard replying.

"He just left," she said.

"Thank you."

The story in the next day's newspaper detailed that brief conversation. It also mentioned that if Blake had been available, he would have been asked the following series of questions, but since he wasn't there, these are the answers he would have given me if he had been there. Great material, folks. Trust me. What I didn't know was the reason he didn't have time to talk to me on the telephone: he was driving his wife to an appointment with her doctor. She hadn't been feeling well for a while and Toe was worried.

The next night, while his team warmed up before the game, he charged into the press room, which was located down the hall from the Canadiens' dressing room. His face was beet-red with anger. About thirty people watched him stride to where I was sitting, shouting profanities along the way.

He stopped in front of me, clenching and unclenching his fists. "I should biff you one," he yelled. A Toe Blake about to lose control was not a comforting sight in those days. It never has been. The situation needed a strong and, I hoped, brave response.

I rose, adjusted my horn-rimmed glasses, and said: "Go ahead, you son of a bitch, I can use the money." Then I sat down—quickly.

Now he was so angry his lips moved but no sounds came out. His fists, however, continued to clench and unclench. Finally, he blurted: "You're so goddamn cheap, you probably *would* sue!" Then he turned, tore open the door and slammed it behind him.

Whew!

The next day, broadcaster Doug Smith started his sports report: "Toe Blake lost his cool again last night. . . ."

These things happen in this business now and then. Blake wasn't really angry about the story. Mostly, it was a case of feeling a lot of concern, as he should have, for his wife and best friend, Betty. He lost his cool, as Smith pointed out, which wasn't the first time a coach had lashed out at a hockey writer. Nobody died.

His mistake, though, was to strike out at a friend in front of a roomful of people. For more than a decade, we had spent a lot of time together on the road. Hardly a day went by when Blake, *Montréal-Matin* hockey writer Jacques Beauchamp, and I didn't have dinner together. If either Beauchamp or I reached for the bill, except on Christmas Day, each ran the risk of having our wrists snapped. Then, there were the card games in Blake's suite on trains and in hotels. Sure, occasionally, our voices would be raised in disagreement, but this time was different. "I should biff you one," he had threatened.

We stopped talking that night in 1965. Days passed. Then weeks.

Betty Blake telephoned one day: "Why don't you talk to Toe?" she asked.

"He tried to humiliate me in front of a roomful of people," I said. "I'll talk to him when he apologizes."

"You know how stubborn he is," she said. "He won't apologize."

"I'm just as stubborn as he is," she was told.

Mrs. Blake tried to act the role of the peacemaker several times during the weeks and months which followed. So did mutual friends.

"No problem," I would tell them. "He knows my number. He knows where he can find me."

The months came and went. The Canadiens lost the first two games of their Stanley Cup final to the Detroit Red Wings, then won the next four, giving Blake his seventh Cup in eleven seasons, a record which is likely to stand forever. Still, not a word passed between us. It was embarrassing. Childish, too. We would be the only two individuals on an elevator, and neither would say a word. Not a look was exchanged. Nothing. It wasn't easy. In almost every way it was a terribly difficult and sad situation. Try going through more than one half of a season and the entire playoffs without once interviewing the coach of the team you are being paid to cover. The people who saved me were the players, who were aware of the situation. They kept me fully informed of what was going on in the Canadiens' family. So did my colleague, Beauchamp, who knew everything there was to know about the Canadiens.

Eight months after Blake had blown his cool, my wife, Tillie, and son, Ian, were injured when a cab they were in was involved in a collision. Ian had suffered cuts and bruises. My wife's shoulder was broken.

Early the next morning, the telephone rang in my home.

"It's Toe."

"Yes, Toe."

"How's your wife and kid? I just found out they were in an accident yesterday."

"They'll be fine, Toe. My wife has a pin in her shoulder, but she'll be up and around in a few days."

"That's good," he said. "Uh . . ."

"I'll tell my wife you called."

"Give her my best," said Blake.

"Toe?"

"What?"

"It was nice of you to call."

★   ★   ★   ★   ★

Jacques Plante peered into the mirror in the Canadiens' dressing room and ran his fingers lightly alongside the fresh stitches. Seven had been needed to close a savage cut that ran from the corner of his mouth, along his cheek, and through his nostril.

"Looks pretty ugly," I told the Canadiens' netminder.

"Not bad. I've seen worse. This was gonna happen sooner or later." He shrugged.

The day was November 1, the year 1959. A little more than three minutes into the first period of this Canadiens-Rangers game in New York, Andy Bathgate had moved in on Plante and backhanded a puck which struck the goalie in the face. The Canadiens star promptly sprawled on his stomach, his head cushioned in an ugly pool of blood. Bathgate raced to the fallen goalie and lifted his head. Blood poured from the wound onto the New York player's fingers. Bathgate shook his head and skated away.

A moment later, Plante struggled to his feet. A towel was placed over his face, but still the blood dribbled down his sweater and fell in droplets on the ice. Plante swallowed some blood as helping hands guided him to the medical room, but once inside the area, he shook off the supporting arms.

"Lie down on the table," he was told.

Plante shook his head. Instead he moved in front of the mirror.

"Before you do anything," he told the doctor, "I want to see what it looks like."

The doctor scraped away bits of loose flesh from the wound before inserting the stitches. Plante lay there, soundless, his fingers locked, as the needle knifed through the raw flesh.

Twenty minutes later, Plante left the room and skated back onto the ice to the sound of thunderous cheers and a lively rendition of "For He's a Jolly Good Fellow" from the Garden organist. He went directly to the Canadiens' room, where coach Toe Blake was waiting.

"How bad is it?" Blake asked.

"It's sore," Plante replied.

"Why don't you wear your mask for the rest of the game?" suggested Blake.

For some weeks, Plante had been making small noises about doing precisely that. Why not, he argued. Was it really necessary for goaltenders to stand there while pucks came at them through thickets of players? Players were shooting harder. Curves were starting to appear on the blades of sticks. Deflections were becoming more and more dangerous. Who needs it?

He had spent a lot of time with equipment manufacturers, throwing ideas at them. Why not a face-fitting mask? Yes, maybe it would be difficult to see a puck lying at his feet, but why not? Wasn't that better than no mask at all?

"I don't think I can go back in without it," Plante told Blake. So wear the mask he did. Prior to his injury, Plante had stopped three shots. After donning the mask, he was beaten only once on twenty-five shots. Now, at game's end, he sat in the dressing room, fresh blood dibbling from under the patch that covered his wound. Another patch, caked with dried blood, covered a five-stitch cut on his chin, a souvenir of a Canadiens game against Chicago a week earlier.

"After the puck hit me," he told the throng of reporters, "I didn't think any bones were broken. But what bothered me most of all was that I swallowed some blood. I didn't feel too good and my teeth felt numb."

What about the mask? Could he see properly with it? Did he feel more confident with it?

"I wouldn't have played without it," said Plante. Then he added: "Well . . . maybe I would have."

Toe Blake wasn't an instant convert to the cause. He knew Plante had been experimenting with masks. "He can practice with one, if he wants," he had snapped earlier, "but no goaltender of mine is gonna wear one in a game. We're here to win."

Plante didn't wear the mask in the Canadiens' next game. But he wore it in the game after that, and, once he did, goaltending and the game were changed forever.

Jacques Plante was different. He wasn't intimidated easily. He had firm ideas about what was good for his game and for him. The puck stopped with him, and nobody else. He would do what he felt was right for him—on and off the ice. What was good for him, he insisted, was right for the Canadiens. If Canadiens management didn't think so, well, there were other teams.

On their seven regular-season visits to Toronto in the six-team era, the Canadiens always stayed at the Royal York Hotel. Nice place. Bright, clean rooms. A superb location in downtown Toronto, just a brief subway ride to Maple Leaf Gardens and only a short walk from favorite bars and restaurants.

Plante, however, was not an enthusiast.

"I can't stay in this hotel anymore," he told Blake one day.

"Why not?"

"My asthma. I get an attack every time I come to this place. I'm sure it's the bedsheets. I'll stay at the Westbury. It's right next door to the Gardens."

Blake reluctantly agreed.

Later that season, Blake and the Canadiens were in Toronto for another game. That morning, Blake invited me to go with him by subway to the Leaf's practice in the Gardens.

The ride is only six or seven minutes. There's a short walk along the platform, up a short flight of steps to Carlton Street, and a two-minute walk east to the Gardens.

Blake and I started up the steps, turned a corner—and there was Plante walking toward us, a lady friend on each arm. We passed on the steps.

"Well, good morning, Mr. Plante," boomed Blake. "Nice day, isn't it?"

"Ah, good morning," muttered Plante, who continued to walk down the steps toward the subway platform. He turned the corner, and disappeared from view.

Blake started to laugh. "How d'you like that?" he grunted. "Asthma. Bedsheets. I should never have let him change hotels in the first place, but he's gonna make one more move the next time we're in town."

That night, after the game, Plante visited Blake on the train.

"Uh, Toe, about this morning. They're my cousins, you know."

"Sure they were," said Blake.

"I have cousins in every city," argued Plante.

"Sure you do."

"My asthma . . ."

Blake broke in, "The next time we're in Toronto, you're gonna have to get used to the bedsheets at the Royal York."

Case closed.

Blake loved Plante, the goaltender, but didn't like him as a person. The Canadiens coach didn't like surprises, and Plante was full of them. On some nights. Blake would arrive at the arena to find Plante waiting for him. "I don't think I can play tonight," Blake would be told.

"What's the problem?"

"Asthma."

Later, Blake would fume. "That son of a bitch is driving me nuts. I never can be sure when he's playing, but he always ends up playing. I don't know how much more of this I can take."

At the same time, Blake always insisted Plante was the best goaltender he'd ever seen. "Especially those five years we won the Cup, eh? I played with [Bill] Durnan, and he was the best I'd seen up to that time. Plante was better during those five years."

Blake knew it. So did Plante. So did his teammates, even though he stretched their patience from time to time. It's true he played behind many of hockey's best players, starting with Doug Harvey on defense. There were nights when the Canadiens were so dominant, his workload was minimal. But he always made the big stops when the Canadiens needed them. No goaltender I have known had as much confidence in his own ability.

Take the 1961–62 season. Harvey had won his sixth Norris Trophy as the NHL's top defenseman in 1961. Plante, however, had missed the Vezina (fewest goals against during the regular season) for the first time in six seasons. Yet despite his dominance at his position, Harvey, the NHL's best defenseman, was traded to the New York Rangers for Lou Fontinato. It was a trade which didn't make any sense at all. Was it because the Canadiens had failed to win the Stanley Cup for the first time in six seasons? That's unlikely. Was it, as I've suggested elsewhere, Canadiens management's way of finally getting back at Harvey for the role he had played in the formation of the short-lived Players' Association in 1958? Probably. Was it the first shot in the breakup of the dynasty? Definitely.

"How much is this team going to miss Doug?" I asked Plante on the first day of training camp.

"I figured that would be the first question I'd be asked in training camp," he said with a grin. "Listen to this: Doug Harvey is the greatest defenseman in the National Hockey League. All of us, and especially me, owe him a lot. He helped me win five Vezinas in a row. But now I'm going to show you how good Jacques Plante is. I'm going to win the Vezina without him."

"Do you really think you can?"

"Watch me."

Despite the absence of Harvey, the Canadiens allowed only 166 pucks to pass the goal line that season, twenty-two fewer than the previous year. They finished in first place with 98 points, six more than the previous year and thirteen ahead of the second-place Toronto Maple Leafs. Plante played seventy games, enjoyed a modest goals-against average of 2.37—and won his sixth Vezina. He also won the Hart Trophy, which goes to the NHL's most valuable player.

Two years later, though, Blake had had enough of his star goaltender and Plante was traded to the Rangers. Blake stayed with the Canadiens where he won three more Stanley Cups in the next five years—but only after going four seasons without one. That empty streak had started with a semi-final loss to the Chicago Blackhawks, where the best left-winger in NHL history was making good things happen.

Yeah, Bobby Hull, like Plante, another guy with firm ideas about what was good for him and good for hockey.

Not surprisingly, people occasionally ask me to name my favorite game or games. Of course, there have been good games and bad ones, great and only acceptable ones. Then there are those which have stirred the soul and remained locked in my mind forever.

Game eight, of course, in the 1972 Team Canada-Soviet Union series, was one of those. I know I'm not alone in that. Millions of Canadians have memories of Paul Henderson's historic goal which provided Team Canada with a 6–5 victory after they had entered the third period trailing, 5–3. The Goal also provided Team Canada with a 4–3–1 series victory, sending most of Canada on an emotional roller coaster the likes of which has not been seen before or since.

As good and as emotional as that game was, it's not the best I've ever seen. That accolade goes to game three of the 1961 Stanley Cup semi-final between the Chicago Blackhawks and the Montreal Canadiens. It started at 8:00 p.m. on Sunday, March 26, and ended almost six shirt-twisting hours later on Monday, March 27.

There is no hockey crowd anywhere quite like the one in Chicago Stadium. There are no individual sounds in the arena. Instead, there is a sort of white noise, a steady kind of roaring hum which engulfs them, and on this night there was a good reason for it. This, after all, was the Canadiens team which had won a record five consecutive Stanley Cups, and there was no real reason to believe that the torch would finally be passed. The Canadiens had finished the regular season in first place with 92 points, Chicago in third, with 75. The Canadiens had scored 254 goals, the Blackhawks, 198. The Canadiens had allowed 188, the Blackhawks, 180.

Here they were, after splitting the first two games of their best-of-seven series in Montreal, where visiting teams almost never win in the playoffs. Jacques Plante versus Glenn Hall, Jean Béliveau versus Stan Mikita, Bobby Hull, and Dickie Moore. The rocket had retired during training camp, but his brother Henri was there.

What occurred that night in Chicago was, arguably, the greatest performances by two goaltenders in NHL history. From the start, the game belonged to Plante and Hall. Breakaways, long shots, slapshots, close-in shots—they saw them all and stopped them all for the entire first period and most of the second. Then, with less than two minutes remaining in that period, a gritty, hard-nosed left-winger named Murray Balfour, who had been "sold" to the Blackhawks by the Canadiens in June 1959, scored the game's first goal. The crowd erupted.

Could Hall do it? Could he hold on? Could the Blackhawks do it? Hell, could the Canadiens do it?

The third period was a clone of the first two. Scoring chances on both sides. First Plante. Then, Plante again. Hall. Hall again. As the teams approached the final minute of regulation time, Balfour's goal continued to stand straight and tall, like a sentinel. Would it be enough?

After all, these were the Canadiens. There was Béliveau. There was Richard. Yes, Bernard Geoffrion had been injured and was out of the game, but there were Moore and Doug Harvey.

There were only forty seconds left in regulation time when Toe Blake motioned to Plante to head for the bench. The Canadiens' net stood empty as the teams awaited a face-off in the circle to Hall's right. Richard was there, lightly scuffing the blades of his skates on the ice, waiting for the puck to drop. If Henry lost the face-off, the game would be over. If he won, there was still a chance.

The puck dropped, Henri got control of it, and, in one motion, lashed a short shot past a stunned Hall. The crowd, which had been on its feet for longer than a minute, was stilled. How could this have happened? How could the Blackhawks hold off the Canadiens for more than fifty-nine minutes, yet now, with only thirty-six seconds left, overtime was looming. How? Why?

Early in the first overtime, Béliveau went in alone on Hall, and shot wide. Ralph Backstrom swept in and lost the puck at the last moment. Bill Hay, who's now the president of the Calgary Flames, shook himself loose and skated in alone on Plante. The puck hurtled toward an open, upper corner, but Plante lunged desperately and deflected the puck with the shaft of his stick. Hall stopped Moore. Minutes later, the puck is twisting and turning in the Canadiens' crease, but referee Dalton McArthur whistles the play to a halt when several Canadiens fall on it. At the end of the first overtime, Plante had made eight stops and so had Hall.

There were more scoring opportunities by both teams in the second overtime. Once, Donnie Marshall slapped a puck out of the air and watched it drop behind Hall, but referee McArthur promptly ruled that Marshall's stick was above his shoulder when he made contact with the puck. No goal. In fact, no goal was scored in the second overtime period.

Early in the third overtime, Chicago's Ron Murphy was penalized. Seconds later, Béliveau swept in on Hall, but the Blackhawks' goaltender made yet another one of what would be fifty-three stops. Seconds later, Chicago's Tod Sloan had an open net—and missed. Then, Hall stopped Marcel Bonin and Junior Langlois. Richard, the hero of regulation time, broke in alone, but a split-second lunge by Hall at the last possible moment stopped him. Claude Provost had an open net, but shot wide.

As the clock neared the twelve-minute mark of the third over-time, referee McArthur whistled down the Canadiens' Moore with a minor penalty. Borderline stuff, particularly considering the time, the game's tempo, and the game's importance. Put it this way: there had been occasions earlier in the game when far more obvious penalties could have been called—against either team. Twenty-eight seconds later, at 12:12, Murray Balfour put the puck behind Jacques Plante from a scramble in front of the net. It was all over—except for the bedlam which followed.

The instant Balfour scored, twenty thousand fans leaped to their feet, their wild cries sweeping the arena. Strangers hugged and kissed. The ice was littered with debris. The Canadiens, who had reached a spe-cial high when Richard scored the tying goal with only thirty-six sec-onds remaining in regulation time, and a low when Marshall's apparent winning goal was disallowed in the second overtime, stormed after ref-eree McArthur. Why the penalty? How could he call a penalty at that stage of the game?

Behind the Canadiens' bench, Toe Blake had another protest in mind, something a little stronger than words. He reached for the gate leading onto the ice, shrugged off the restraining hands of several play-ers and took off in a slow, uneven trot toward McArthur, who was lean-ing over the official scorer's bench on the opposite side of the rink.

McArthur still had his back to Blake when the Canadiens' coach flung a punch which struck the referee on the shoulder and de-flected onto his jaw. It was only then that McArthur turned, his eyes widening in surprise at the sight of Blake. That was also the moment when several Canadiens players wrapped their arms around their coach and led him from the ice.

It was a wild finish to one of hockey's greatest games, and cer-tainly my greatest. It was also, as it developed, the start of the end of the Canadiens' dynasty. Sure, they won the next game in Chicago, but then Hall shut out the Canadiens in game five in Montreal, and held them scoreless again in game six at Chicago. The Blackhawks went on from there to meet the Detroit Red Wings and won their first—and as it turned out, only—Stanley Cup since 1938. The Canadiens, meanwhile, didn't see another Stanley Cup until May 1, 1965, when they beat, yes, the Blackhawks in seven.

After the game, I approached NHL president Clarence Campbell in the referee's room. "What happens now?" I asked.

"I don't know," said Campbell. "I really don't know. I'll have to go by the book. Rule 67B says that if a coach or manager holds or strikes an official, that coach or manager will be immediately suspended for the balance of the game and fined substantially. He will also be ordered to the room. It happened at the end of the game . . ."

"Does that mean Blake won't be suspended from the next game?"

"The rule applies only to this game," said Campbell. "The incident has nothing to do with other games, but frankly, I don't know . . ."

The next afternoon Blake was still fuming over the incident. He was also worried—or at least he should have been. It's one thing to protest a controversial loss, and he had a good case for one, but coaches don't go around punching officials, or they shouldn't. In short, there was some explaining he had to do. For that matter, Blake didn't have far to go: Campbell's room was just down the hall from Blake's.

"How could you do something like that?" Betty Blake asked her husband. "That was stupid."

"Yeah, pretty damned stupid," I seconded.

"He doesn't allow a goal in the second overtime, and Moore's in the penalty box for what—hooking—when they get their goal," Blake snapped back. "That's what's stupid."

Blake wondered what would happen to him. I said a suspension was unlikely, but a fine was a definite possibility. "Just pay the money, whatever it is," I told him.

"Yeah? How much?"

"Two thousand." (Blake's annual salary at this time was $18,000.)

"Well, it better not be more than five hundred dollars," snorted Blake.

"Pay," he was told.

Moments later, there was a knock on the door. "Mr. Campbell wants to see you," Blake was told.

"I'll be there soon," said Blake.

"He wants to see you right away."

Blake left for Campbell's room, but was back in a matter of minutes. A flush suffused his cheeks.

"Suspended?"

"No."

"Fined?"

"Yeah."

"How much?"

"Two thousand."

Blake, of course, went on to coach for another seven seasons and three more Stanley Cups. Dalton McArthur wasn't that lucky. He was fired before the start of the 1961–62 season.

I haven't gone back to see Toe since that day in late December 1991. Why? I've convinced myself that that visit was too painful. I sat with him for nearly two hours, and he didn't look at me once. His "*merci*" to Andrew was the only word he spoke. Too painful? Does that make sense? Was that reason enough not to go back? Probably not.

Blake missed coaching terribly after leading the Canadiens to his eighth Stanley Cup as a coach in 1968. He mourned long and hard after his wife lost a five-year battle with cancer. He joined the Canadiens' front office and had a desk there for years, but he never really liked the idea of sitting behind one. The onset of Alzheimer's was painfully slow, but people noticed. His friends, starting with Floyd Curry, feared for him and looked after him—looked after him as much as a proud man would allow. Eventually, Toe needed the constant care only a nursing home could provide.

He was one of a kind, particularly during the hockey season when every practice was a joy and every game an adventure. Now, the leaves turn red and yellow and die, the snow falls and I see him again and again the way I once knew him and I tell myself that's the only way I want to remember him. It's the only way he would want to be remembered.

Does that make sense? I think so.

Hockey Nights: The Tough Skate Through Junior-League Life

Guy Lawson's "Hockey Nights" appeared in *Harper's Magazine* in 1998, and, true to the magazine's somewhat grim persona, it is a dour portrait of the minor-hockey-league system, peering in on the seamy realities of life on the junior-hockey circuit. The young players, looking for a break into the big leagues, which will probably never come, endure isolation in far-flung towns, which pin their pride on the success of their junior team. It is a world dominated by clannishness and outright fear, as seventeen-year-olds are expected to start, and win, brawls in front of what might literally be described as "angry villagers." Lawson's piece is a meditation about violence, and yet, the piece sings with those details that only a die-hard fan would notice. Despite everything, Lawson, clearly, is in love with the game.

★   ★   ★   ★   ★

In September the streets of Flin Flon, Manitoba, are deserted at twilight. The town has no bookshop, no record store, no movie theater, no pool hall. Main Street is a three-block strip of banks, video shops, and Bargain! outlets. The 825-foot smokestack of the Hudson Bay Mining and Smelting Company rises from one end of the street, and the Precambrian shelf stretches out from the other. In the Royal Hotel, gamblers forlornly drop quarters into the video slot machines. Farther up the street at the Flin Flon Hotel, the front door has been broken in a fight, and inside strangers are met by suspicious glances from miners wearing baseball caps with slogans like YA WANNA

GO? and T-shirts that read, with the letters increasingly blurry, DRINK, DRANK, DRUNK. Susie, who works behind the counter at the Donut King, says a major shipment of LSD has arrived in town and half the students at the local high school, Hapnot Collegiate, have been stoned out of their minds for weeks.

Described by *Canada: The Rough Guide* as an "ugly blotch on a barren rocky landscape," Flin Flon, population 7,500, straddles the border between Manitoba and Saskatchewan, 90 miles north of its nearest neighbor, The Pas, 500 miles up from Winnipeg, and a thirteen-hour drive due north of Minot, North Dakota. In this part of the world, Flin Flon is literally the end of the line: the two-lane highway that connects it to the rest of North America circles the perimeter of town and then, as if shocked to its senses, rejoins itself and hightails it back south.

But Flin Flon is also the heartland of Canada's national game. In a country where every settlement of consequence has a hockey arena and a representative team made up of players twenty years old and younger, the Saskatchewan Junior Hockey League is one of the grandest, oldest competitions. And Flin Flon is one of the grandest, oldest hockey towns. I had played hockey in towns like Flin Flon—in a league one level below the juniors—before I went to college. Many of my teammates had gone on to play junior hockey; some became professionals.

One hot day in August, seventeen years after I'd left western Canada, I flew north, arriving from Toronto in a twin-prop plane, to spend the first month of the new season with Flin Flon's junior hockey team. Hockey, as I remembered it from my own teams, was an untold story. It was also the path I had chosen not to take.

At the airport, I was greeted by the Flin Flon Junior Bombers' coach and general manager. Razor (like everyone else in hockey, he goes by a nickname) was in his early forties, solidly built, with a deep raspy voice and the confident, slightly pigeon-toed stride of a former athlete. He had grown up in Flin Flon and had been a defenseman for the Bombers. He had gone on to play a long career in minor-league professional hockey as well as some games—"a cup of coffee here, a cup of coffee there"—with the Boston Bruins in the National Hockey League. As we drove into town, Razor told me that the previous year, his first full season as coach, the Bombers had finished with the second-worst record in the SJHL's northern division. This year, he said, was going to be different. He had big tough forwards, speed, and two of the best goalies in the league.

A blast of cold air hit me as I walked out of the 90-degree heat and into the Whitney forum's simulated winter for the first time. Meeks, a veteran Bomber left-winger, was alone on the ice practicing his signature trick: tilt the puck on its side with the stick, sweep it up, then nonchalantly cradle it on the blade. Lean and large and slope-shouldered, he was one of the toughest players in the league. As he left the ice, I heard him say to Hildy, the team trainer, "Tell Razor I'm not fighting this year. This is my last year of hockey, and I'm not missing any games." He was twenty years old. He had sat out a third of last season because he had broken his hand twice in fights. His thumb was still out of place, the joint distended and gnarled.

In the Bombers' dressing room, Meeks's sticks were piled next to his locker stall, the shafts wrapped in white tape and covered with messages to himself written in black Magic Marker. One note read MEGHAN, the name of his girlfriend; another said HOCKEY GOD; and a third, WHAT TO DO? While he took off his shoulder pads and loosened his skates, other players, hometown kids like Meeks or early arrivals from out of town returning from last season's team, drifted in. Boys with peach fuzz and pimples—Rodge, Quinny, Woody, Airsy, Skills, Dodger—they seemed to transform into men as they pulled on their pads and laced up their skates. I went to the stands to watch them play.

The Forum is a squat, dark, tin-roofed building on the shores of what used to be Lake Flin Flon but is now a drained and arid wasteland of tailings from HBM&S's smelter. Dozens of tasseled maroon-and-white championship banners hang from the rafters. Photographs of nearly every Flin Flon Bomber team since the 1920s look down from the walls. And there is a pasty-faced portrait of Queen Elizabeth in her tiara at the rink's north end.

With no coaches and no fans, nobody but me around, the rink echoed with hoots and laughter. Scrub hockey, like school-yard basketball, is a free-form improvisation on the structures and cadences of the real game. Passes were made between legs and behind backs. The puck dipsy-doodled and dangled, preternaturally joined to the stick, the hand, the arm, the whole body, as players deked left, then right, and buried a shot in the top corner of the net. In those moments, the Forum seemed an uncomplicated place where the game was played purely for its own sake: *Le hockey pour le hockey*.

The Bombers, like virtually every team in the SJHL, are owned by the community; the team's president and board of directors are elected officials, like the mayor and the town council; and the team is financed by bingo nights, raffles, and local business sponsorship. HBM&S once gave the Bombers jobs at the mine—with light duties, time off to practice, and full pay even when the team was on the road, an arrangement that was a powerful recruiting tool for prairie farm boys—but these days there are no jobs at HBM&S and there's little part-time work in town. Some of the players do odd jobs to earn spending money. Like junior-hockey players across Canada, most Bombers move away from home by the time they're sixteen. Long road trips, practices, and team meetings leave little time for anything but hockey. For decades, players were expected either to quit school or slack their way through it; now the Junior A leagues advertise hockey as the path to a college scholarship in the United States.

The Bombers' training camp began the morning after my arrival. Eighty-four teenagers turned up for tryouts at the Forum, most driven from prairie towns across western Canada by their fathers. Razor, dressed in a Bombers' track suit, maroon with slashes of white and black, positioned himself at center ice. His seventy-three-year-old father, Wild Bill, stood in the broadcast booth above, scouting the players. When Razor blew his whistle, the hopefuls skated at full speed; when Razor blew the whistle again, they slowed to a coast. At the scrimmages that weekend, Flin Floners drinking coffee from Styrofoam cups wandered in and out of the arena, their ebb and flow marking the beginning and end of shifts at HBM&S. Like contestants in a beauty pageant, the players had only a fleeting chance to catch the eye of Razor and his coaching staff; unlike beauty contestants, these hopefuls were allowed full body contact and fights. Three, six, eleven—I lost count. The fights seemed to come out of nowhere, with nothing that could sanely be described as provocation but, for all that, with a certain unity of form: the stare-off, the twitching of a gloved hand, and the unmistakable message "Ya wanna go?" then striptease-like, the stick was dropped, gloves fell, elbow pads were thrown aside, helmets were taken off—a bravura gesture shunning any effete protection—and two players circled each other, fists cocked.

On Saturday morning, Sides arrived in Flin Flon from Moose Jaw. He was seventeen, skinny, shy; he wore a Christian Athlete Hockey Camps windbreaker. Razor and Wild Bill were excited that Sides, a late cut by the Warriors of the elite Western Hockey League, was in town. Rodge and Meeks, twenty-year-old veterans and leaders on the team, had heard about Sides, too, and decided to put the rookie arriviste to the test. Sides had played only a couple of shifts in an intrasquad match before Meeks was yammering at him, challenging him to a fight. Looking both terrified and afraid to look terrified, Sides skated away from Meeks. "Leave him alone," Razor called down from the press box. "Keep in touch with yourself."

"Meeks isn't the right guy. He's too good a fighter," Razor said to me. "We'll send someone else, and if the kid answers the bell and stands up for himself, he'll be accepted by the team. If he doesn't, we'll go from there." Sides scored three goals that session. The next afternoon he fought Ferlie, a man-child six inches shorter than Sides but an absurdly eager and able fighter. Skate-to-skate, lefts and rights were thrown in flurries. Sides's head bounced off the Plexiglas as he and Ferlie wrestled each other to the ice. The players on the benches stood and slapped their sticks against the boards in applause. Sides and Ferlie checked their lips for blood, shook hands, exchanged a grin.

Northern Exposure—An Exciting Kickoff Tournament of Junior A Hockey started the following Friday when the Bombers played the North Battleford North Stars. A few hundred miners stood along the guardrails, among them Meeks's father in a T-shirt that said TOUGH SIMBA and featured a lion cub chewing on a piece of steel. The Forum's southwest corner was dotted with students from Hapnot Collegiate, the boys near the top and the girls closer to the ice. Security guards in Dadson Funeral Home jackets circled the arena. The Bombers skated out to cheers; the crowd stood, baseball caps off; a taped version of "O Canada" played; then, with sudden ferocity, Flin Flon's preseason hockey began. Players swarmed off the bench, bodies slammed into boards, the puck flew from end to end. Less than two minutes into the game, the North Stars scored on Dodger, the Bombers' first-string goalie, in a scramble in front of the net. Thirty seconds later, Ferlie was sent off for roughing. Less than ten seconds after that, a teenage girl in the stands was hit in the face by an errant puck; she casually threw the puck back on the ice. Four minutes and ten seconds into the opening period, Dodger let in a second goal, a wrist shot from the top of the slot. During the playoffs the previous season, Dodger had made sixty-two saves in an overtime loss in Watrous, a feat his team-mates spoke of with hushed awe, but today Dodger couldn't stop a thing. Two minutes and fifty-three seconds later Meeks got a penalty for slash-ing. Fourteen seconds later Rodge scored for Flin Flon. Air horns sounded and Bachman-Turner Overdrive's "Takin' Care of Business" blared over the speakers. And on it went: sticks whacked across legs, gloves rubbed into faces after the whistle, the game a relentless Hobbesian cartoon of taliation and retaliation, misconduct, inciting misconduct, and gross misconduct. Rodge, the most gifted player on the Bombers, stopped on the way to the dressing room at the end of the first period to sign au-tographs for children calling out his name. "It's a *Gong Show* out there," he said to me. "It's always the same in exhibition season."

Between periods, I followed a crowd to the bar in the curling club next door to the arena. A dozen men were sitting at a table drink-ing rye whiskey. What did they think of their team this year? I asked. "Pussies," they said. What did they think of Razor? "Pussy." A former Bomber, slurring drunk, reminisced about his glory days—when Flin Flon, he boasted, was the toughest town anywhere. Picking up on the theme, a burly man who called himself Big Eyes and whose son had captained the Bombers a few years earlier, told a story about an all-you-can-eat-and-drink charity fund-raiser a few years back at which a brawl broke out. Big Eyes couldn't remember why or how the fight started; he did remember, he said with a glint in his eye, that the raffle tickets he was supposed to sell the next morning were covered in blood.

I stepped outside for a breath of fresh air. Aurora borealis was out in the northern sky. A few feet away a little boy pushed another lit-tle boy onto the gravel in the parking lot. "Faggot," he said. The other little boy got to his feet and shoved back: "Faggot."

* * * * *

In the gazebo in front of Razor's cottage near Amisk Lake a few miles out of Flin Flon, the swarming mosquitoes and no-see-ums kept out by the screen, a red cooler stocked with beer, steaks ready for the barbecue, Razor and Wild Bill and the assistant coaches held a long debate, complete with diagrams, about the dressing room: Who should sit where? Who had earned a prime spot? Who needed to be sent a message? There was also the matter of the tampering dispute with the Opaskwayak Cree National Blizzard of The Pas, who, Razor said, had had a Bomber player practice with their team. Razor angrily had demanded $30,000 and the big defenseman or two he needed to round out his roster; the Blizzard were offering a forward they had imported from Sweden. The merits of a player from Thunder Bay on the verge of making the team were also discussed: he had the quickness to wrong-foot the defense, but he had a long mane of coiffed blond hair and wore an earring off the ice.

Razor wanted the Bombers to attack. On offense, in the grand banal tradition of Canadian hockey, the Bombers would "dump and chase": shoot the puck into the opposition's end, skate like hell after it, then crash bodies and hope to create a scoring chance. On defense they would "build a house": each player would be a pillar, spreading to the four corners of the defense zone, supporting one another, and moving the foundations of the house as one. Razor's team would forgo the flourishes of brilliance, the graceful swoop across the blue line, the geometrically improbable pass, the inspired end-to-end rush. They would play the man, not the puck. They would play what Razor called "ugly hockey." "You've got to play with balls, big balls," Razor had told the Bombers in the dressing room between periods in one of the Northern Exposure games. "Look at yourself in the mirror before you go back on the ice. Look in the mirror and ask yourself if you've got balls."

The Bomber players were very good, but two or three ingredients short of the strange brew that makes a professional athlete. Rodge lacked all-consuming desire. Woody was too thin, Quinny too plump, Reags too small. Meeks and Dodger were not dexterous enough in handling the puck. When I skated with them at morning practices, though, instead of seeing what they weren't, I saw what they were. They were fast and skilled and courageous: Rodge, with a low center of gravity, calm and anticipating the play; Woody grinning as he flew smoothly past a stumbling defenseman; Quinny letting go a slap shot and boom, a split second later, there's the satisfying report from the wooden boards; Dodger flicking a glove hand out to stop a wrist shot; Meeks trundling down the wing like a locomotive, upright, his legs spread wide, his face blank with pure joy.

Scrimmaging with the Bombers, the pace and sway of the game came back to me. Watching out for me—"Heads up, Scoop," "Man on, Scoop"—the Bombers hurled one another into the boards with abandon, the arena sounding with the explosive thud of compressed plastic colliding with compressed plastic. The speed of the game reduces the rink to the size of a basketball court. Things that are impossible to do on your feet—go twenty miles an hour, glide, turn on a dime—become possible. The body and mind are acutely aware of physical detail and, at the same time, are separated from the earth.

After Northern Exposure, Razor held the year's first team meeting in the Bombers' dressing room. Two dozen pairs of high-top sneakers were piled on the mats beside Beastie's Blades, the skate-sharpening concession next to the dressing room; Razor had recarpeted during the off-season, and no one except Hildy was allowed in without taking off his shoes. This season Razor had also put the team logo—the letter "B" exploding into fragments, a design donated by the company that had supplied HBM&S with its dynamite in the 1930s—on the floor under a two-foot-square piece of Plexiglas, as the Boston Bruins had done with their logo when Razor played for them. The dressing room was a dank cavern at the southeast corner of the arena, rich with the smells of decades of stale sweat. Its ceiling was marked with the autographs of Bombers of seasons past.

In front of their newly assigned stalls, Rodge rubbed Lester's ear with the blade of his stick and Reags rested his hand on Meeks's back. Dodger sat in a corner with his head in his hands. In their final game of the Northern Exposure tournament against the Dauphin Kings, with the bombers trailing 4–1 in the fist period, Ferlie had started a line brawl; in an orgiastic outbreak of violence, all the players on the ice had begun to fight at the same time. Now Razor addressed the topic of fighting. Because of the SJHL's penalty of compulsory ejection from the rest of the game for fighting, Razor, said, other teams would send mediocre players out to try and goad Flin Flon's best players into scraps. "I know things are going to happen out on the ice. It's the nature of the game," Razor said as he paced the room. "But Rodge, Lester, Schultzie, the goal scorers, you can't fight unless you take an equally talented player with you. If we lose one of our best, we need them to lose one of their best."

"You told Ferlie to fight against Dauphin," Rodge said.

"No," Razor explained, "I didn't tell Ferlie to fight. We were getting beaten and I said, 'If you want to start something, now would be a good time.'"

The Bombers all laughed.

Razor turned to Meeks. "Meeks, I don't want you to fight. The other team plays two inches taller when they don't have to worry about you. We need the intimidation factor of you out there banging and crashing." Razor said he wanted to change Meeks's role. He wanted Meeks to be a grinder, not an enforcer. He wanted Meeks to skate up and down his wing, using his size to open up space on the ice.

At the barbecue in Razor's gazebo, Meeks had been a topic of concern. The coaches were worried that Meeks was under too much pressure at home. Meeks's father and brother wanted Meeks to ask for a trade; at practice one morning, Meeks's father had told me he didn't think the Bombers had a chance this season because they had too many rookies on the team. Maybe, one of the coaches had suggested, Meeks should move out of his family's house ten miles out of town and billet with another family in Flin Flon. "I want to give the kid the world," Razor said. "He deserves it. If I ask him to do anything, he'll do it. He's vulnerable, though."

The rhythms of the hockey season set in quickly; practice at eight in the morning so that the players still in high school could get to class on time, lunch at Subway, long empty afternoons, fund-raising appearances to sell Share of the Wealth and Pic-A-Pot cards to chain-smoking bingo players. Paul Royter, a hypnotist, came to town for a three-night stand at the R. H. Channing Auditorium, and a half dozen Bombers went up onstage to fall under Royter's spell, which, it turned out, meant lip-synching to Madonna and Garth Brooks. The legal drinking age in Manitoba is eighteen, and most of the players on the team were old enough to go to bars, but Razor had banned the Bombers from Flin Flon's beverage rooms, a rule he waived only once so that some of the boys could go to a matinee performance by Miss Nude Winnipeg. Nineteen of twenty-three Bombers were not from Flin Flon, and Razor told me that resentful locals would try to beat up the Bombers if they went into a bar.

On the second Saturday in September, Razor lifted the Bombers' eleven o'clock curfew to let the team watch the final game of the World Cup between Canada and the United States. Late that afternoon, carrying the twelve-pack of pilsner I had been advised to bring along, I went to Ev's place. Ev was one of the locals playing for Flin Flon, and his parents had taken in Bombers from out of town as billets for years. This season Rodge and Dodger were staying in Ev's parents' basement. With hockey posters and the autographs of the Bombers who had passed through their doors written on the basement walls, Ev's place was a fantasyland for a teenager living away from home: pool table, beer fridge, a couple of mattresses on the floor beside the furnace, a hot tub on the patio.

At twilight, Bornie, Reags, and I piled into a car and drove past houses, searching for the party. We found that Funk, who had played for Flin Flon a few years ago, was having a shake at his house. Rodge and Woody were sitting on the floor of the den playing a drinking game with Holly, Melanie, and Deanna, the girls who arrived fashionably late for the hockey games and sat slightly apart from the rest of the Hapnot section—the girls whom the players, and the town, called Pucks or Bikes.

"You want to play, Scoop?" Rodge asked me.

I looked down at a salad bowl filled with beer.

"No, no thanks," I said.

We got back into Bornie's car and went to Hildy's billet, a few blocks away. More than half the Bombers were there, some sipping Coke, most with a twelve-pack of Molson Canadian or Labatt Blue between their legs. It had been front-page news that in the semifinal match between Russia and America, played in Ottawa, the Canadian crowd had cheered for the Russians and booed the Americans. Now Canada was playing the United States.

"All the guys who treat women with respect are here," Meeks said as the game started.

"Who's going to get on the phone and find the chicks?" Schultzie asked.

"Skulls knows where they are," Ev said.

"I do not," Skulls said.

"Don't hold out on us," Schultzie said.

"I don't know where they are," Skulls said. "I swear on hockey."

The game between Canada and America was played at an astonishing pace. Both teams were dumping and chasing, cycling the puck against the boards, relying as much on muscle and force as on skill. The majority of players in the NHL are Canadian, but because franchises in Quebec and Winnipeg have relocated to major-market cities in the United States in recent years and because the economics of hockey are changing and growing vastly more expensive and lucrative, it is a common complaint that the game is being Americanized. Still, three of the players on the Canadian team had played in the Saskatchewan Junior Hockey League, and some of the Americans had played junior hockey in western Canada as their apprenticeship for the NHL. The SJHL influence on the style of play was obvious. This World Cup game was, in its way, ugly hockey.

"Gretzky sucks," Skulls said in the middle of the second period. "He's a pussy."

"You're full of shit," Quinny said. "He's the greatest player of all time."

"He's a floater," Skulls said. "He doesn't go into the corners. He's not a team player."

Lester turned to Dodger. "That Swede Razor might get from The Pas is gay, eh."

In the next second Canada scored to take a 2–1 lead. We leapt to our feet and let out a huge cheer. Chief, a big defenseman from Patuanka, a native community in the far north of Saskatchewan, stayed sitting.

"I want the Americans to win," Chief said. "They're playing the same way as Canadians and they're playing better."

"Yankee lover," Bornie said.

In the third period the Americans scored to tie the game and then scored again to take the lead. Canada came back with increased desperation. The faces of the Team Canada players were drawn, anxious: Canada's destiny and national pride were at stake. But the Americans withstood the onslaught. In the dying seconds, a pass came to Wayne Gretzky in front of an open net. Gretzky, so many times the hero, missed the puck as it flitted off the ice and went over his stick. Canada had lost.

"I wouldn't mind losing to the Russians," Reags said on the ride back to my apartment. "But not the fucking Americans—always bragging all the time, so cocky. It's not fair. It's our game."

"Fishy fishy in the lake,
Come and bite my piece of bait. . . .
Fishy fishy in the brook,
Come and bite my juicy hook."

Meeks repeated his good-luck mantra as we trolled for pickerel on the southern shore of Amisk Lake. It was the morning after the Canada–U.S. game, and Razor had organized a team fishing trip. Meeks and I were in a small boat, the outboard motor chugging, a cool breeze creasing the black water. At a Bombers meeting a few days earlier, Razor had announced that Lester would be the captain; Rodge, Airsy, and Woody, the assistant captains. Meeks had hung his head in disappointment. Razor told me he didn't want to put too much strain on Meeks. "I'm still a leader on this team," Meeks said to me. During the exhibition season, he had often played doubled up in pain, his face contorted into a grimace. He had, he told me, ulcerative colitis, an extremely painful stomach disease brought on by stress, and he had forgotten to take his medication. He had moved out of his family's home and was living in town now with Reags's family.

I asked Meeks what it was like growing up in Flin Flon. "It was different," he said. "There were a lot of rock fights. Guys'd get hit in the head all the time. Once you got hit, everyone would come running and start apologizing. It was a good time."

When Meeks was thirteen, his father and brother had taught him how to fight in the garage after school. "I'd put the hockey helmet on, and they'd show me how to pull the jersey over a guy's head, to keep your head up, when to switch hands." Listening to Meeks, I couldn't help but remember when I was thirteen. My father had made it a rule that if I fought in a hockey game he would not allow me to keep playing. The first time he missed a game, I fought. After the game, the father of the player I fought tried to attack me. The fathers of my teammates had to escort me from the arena. It was terrifying.

A few of the Bombers had told me about the present that Meeks's older brother—a giant of a man and an ex-Bomber, with 30 points and 390 penalty minutes in one season—had given Meeks for his eighteenth birthday: a beating. "Yeah, he did, Scoop," Meeks said sheepishly. "My brother would say, 'I can't wait until you turn eighteen, because I'm going to lay a licking on you.' The day of my birthday he saw me and started coming after me. I grabbed a hockey stick and started swinging, nailing him in the back, just cracking him. It didn't even faze him. Next thing you know, my jersey's over my head and he's beating the crap out of me. My mom and one of my brother's friends hopped in and broke her up."

"Why did your brother do that?" I asked.

Meeks shrugged. "I turned eighteen."

He expertly teased his line. "I just want to turn into a professional fisherman," he said. "Stay out on the water and think about life."

Most days Dodger wandered the parking lots and streets of Flin Flon in search of empty pop cans, nonrefundable in Manitoba but worth a nickel across the border in Saskatchewan. Because his billet at Ev's place was at the other end of town, Dodger had taken to storing his jumbo plastic bags filled with crushed cans in the front yard of the apartment I had rented for the month. During training camp I had met Dodger's father, an anxious, eager-to-please man. "He's hard on himself," Dodger's father said of his son. "I tell him to relax, let life take its part."

Dodger, like many goalies, was probably the most skilled athlete on the team, agile and fast and alert. He was in his fourth season in the SJHL but had played poorly in the exhibition games and practices. He had let in soft goals and had even pulled himself from a game against the

Nipawin Hawks after they had scored six times by the beginning of the second period. He had seemed to disappear into his equipment, his face hidden behind his mask, and the slow, ponderous way he had of moving off the ice had been replaced by nervous twitching. It is a hockey cliché that goalies, who stand alone in their net, are the game's eccentrics, and Dodger, who would sit quietly staring at the floor in team meetings and didn't much go for "the rah-rah and all that," was allowed that latitude. Still, Don, one of Razor's assistant coaches, was angry that Dodger wasn't taking the games seriously enough. "He's going around saying it's only exhibition season. I don't like that. That kid's got to be focused from day one."

But there was a reason for Dodger's lack of focus. "I've got a real story for you, Scoop," he said to me one morning after practice. "It's got nothing to do with hockey, though." Dodger's real story, the one that had been playing on his mind constantly, and which he told me in pieces over a few days when I passed the time helping him look for pop cans, began the Easter weekend of 1995, when Dodger was back home in Regina, Saskatchewan. He and Al, his best friend and an old hockey buddy, had been on a jag, hitting bars, going to parties, the same sort of things I did when I was around his age and living in the same city. On Sunday night, after drinking beer and Southern Comfort in the parking lot beside a hockey arena, Dodger was too ill to carry on. Al borrowed Dodger's fleece hockey jacket, took Dodger's bottle of Southern Comfort, and went downtown with another friend, Steve, to pick up a hooker. Unable to coax a prostitute into the car, Al hid in the trunk until they found a woman willing to get in with Steve. She was a Saulteau woman from the Sakinay Reserve named Pamela Jean George.

"I was watching the news the next night with another friend," Dodger said, "and a story came on about the murder of Pamela Jean George, and my friend said, 'Can you keep a secret?' I go, 'Sure.' He goes, 'They killed her.'" Al and Steve, white boys from the well-to-do south end of the city, both athletes, popular, good-looking, had, according to Dodger's friend, taken Pamela Jean George to the outskirts of town, where she had given them oral sex. Al and Steve then took her out of the car, brutally beat her, and left her for dead, facedown in a ditch. Al split for British Columbia the next day without saying good-bye to Dodger.

Steve stuck around. One week passed. Another week. Dodger was constantly sick to his stomach. He thought it was only a matter of time before they would be caught. He didn't know about Betty Osborne, a Cree girl from The Pas, who was pulled off the street and killed by local white boys in 1971. In Betty Osborne's case, the open secret of who had done it was kept for nearly sixteen years until, at last, in 1987, three men were charged and one was convicted of second-degree murder.

Finally, with no news of the investigation and the growing prospect that Al and Steve would never be caught, Dodger felt that he was going to crack. At a friend's wedding reception, he told someone who he knew would tell the police. A couple of days later, while Dodger was watching an NHL playoff game, the police called him. "The cops wouldn't have had a fucking clue," Dodger said to me. "They were looking for pimps, prostitutes, lower-class people." Dodger was, he told me, scheduled to testify against Al and Steve in a few weeks, and he was finding it difficult to concentrate on hockey.

"I'll tell you what I'm really bitter about: people hinting that it's all my fault. The guy who told me about it in the first place came up to me at a party and said, 'I know this may sound harsh, but I'm going to have a tough time feeling sorry for you because I know it got out at the wedding reception.' And I was like, 'Who the fuck are you to talk to me? Show a little nuts.' This guy tries to play the role, like it's been really tough for him. I heard girls were calling him and saying, 'I feel so sorry for you, losing your friends. If you need someone to talk to I'm always here.' If girls called me I'd say, 'Fuck you. Don't feel sorry for me, feel sorry for Pamela Jean George.'"

Ever since I had arrived in Flin Flon and had heard about the Pucks and Bikes, I had wanted to meet them. Ev, one of the Bombers who was still going to Hapnot Collegiate, convinced the girls to meet and talk with me at twilight at the Donut King.

"I don't understand why anyone would write about Flin Flon," Susie said to me from behind the counter as I waited for the Pucks and Bikes. Because I had no telephone in my apartment, the Donut King had become a kind of makeshift office, and for weeks, with increasing bemusement, Susie had watched me shouting over the howling northern wind into the pay phone in the lobby. "There's nothing to write about," she smiled. I asked Susie if she ever went to Bombers' games. "I went this year to see if any of them were cute," she said. "They might look okay, but once you get up close they have zits or their teeth are crooked. I guess I went to see them lose, because they suck and I want to see them get killed."

"Would you date a Bomber?" I asked. "I'm not allowed to," she said. "My sister says, 'As if I'm going to let you walk around town and have people say, "There's your Bike sister." '"

Just then the Bikes pulled up in a blue Mustang and I took my leave of Susie. The car smelled of perfume and tobacco and chewing gum. We drove out to the town dump, where we sat and watched fifteen or so brown and black bears pick through the garbage and stare at the car's headlights. Holly, who had had a long plume of blonde hair when I had seen her at the Bombers' games and who now had a pixie haircut—the plume had been hair extensions, it turned out—was the femme fatale of Flin Flon: du Maurier cigarette, bare midriff. She told me that when she was dating Rodge last season her ex-boyfriend, a local she had dumped in favor of Rodge, had jumped up on the Plexiglas at the end of a game and screamed at Rodge, "I'm going to kill you!" This year, though, Holly said she wasn't interested in any of the players. "I don't have a crush. I wish I did. I'm guy crazy like hell, but I'm not even attracted to any of them."

Deanna, who was driving the car and had a pierced eyebrow, purple hair, and an inner-city hipster's Adidas sweat top on, allowed she had a crush on one of the Bombers. Melanie, quiet in the backseat with cherry-colored lipstick and a sweater around her waist, told me she had one real crush and another crush she was faking so that an awkward, shy Bomber wouldn't feel left out.

"The players say we're Pucks," Holly said, "but they're the ones who phone us. We don't even give them the time of day and they're asking, 'What're you doing tonight? You want to come over?' Without us they wouldn't have any friends in Flin Flon."

The spectacle of the bears began to wear thin. The girls suggested we drive to the sandpit on the other side of what used to be Lake Flin Flon and watch the nightly pouring of the slag at the HBM&S

smelter. The slag pouring was a disappointment: a thin line of lava red barely visible against pitch black, steam rising and joining the sulphur dioxide chugging out of the company smoke-stack. Afterward, over strawberry milkshakes at the A&W, the girls told me about teen culture in Flin Flon: cruising around looking for house parties, driving to hang-outs in the forest outside town—the Hoop, the Curve, the Toss Off—lighting a fire and drinking beer until the police chased them. Deanna said, "Flin Flon was in *The Guinness Book of World Records* for the most beer bought per capita in a weekend, or something like that."

"I hate rye," Holly announced. "I get into fights when I drink rye." She told me about the Boxing Day social last year. "This girl pissed me off, so me and a friend tag-teamed her. My friend slapped her and I threw my drink on her and she started blabbing at me so I grabbed her and kicked her in the head and ripped all her hair out. She was bald when I was done." The girl had to go to the hospital to have her bro-ken nose set, Holly said, now speaking in quiet tones because she had noticed the girl's aunt a few tables down from us. "And then she went to the cop shop and filed charges, even though she was four years older than me."

Melanie and Deanna exchanged a furtive glance. They had never been in a fight; Holly had never lost a fight.

Saturday night was hockey night in Flin Flon. Game-day notice in the store windows along Main Street advertised that evening's match against the Humboldt Broncos. The night before, in the opening game of the regular season, the Bombers had defeated Humboldt 2–1. Beastie, who drove the tractor that cleans the ice at the forum, toked on an Old Port cigarillo. "Pretty tame last night," he said. On the ice, the Stittco flames were practicing before the main event. A dozen girls, including Razor's eleven-year-old daughter, who had recently given herself the nickname Maloots, skated lengths of the ice and worked on passing and shooting the puck. At the end of the session one of the girls dropped her gloves as if she wanted to fight and then, in full hockey uniform, turned and did a graceful lutz.

It had been payday at the company the day before, and 700 fans, nearly a tenth of Flin Flon's population, came to watch the game. In the

Bombers' dressing room, the players sat and listened to Razor, their fore-
heads beaded with sweat from the pre-game skate. The new jerseys had arrived, and the pants and gloves the bombers had bought secondhand from
the Peterborough Petes of the elite Ontario Hockey League, the only
other team in Canada with maroon-and-white colors, had been passed
out. Norm Johnston, the coach of the Broncos, had coached in Flin Flon
in the early 1990s, and his teams had a reputation for fighting and intimidation. Razor, in his game attire of shirt and tie, black sports coat, and tan
cowboy boots, paced the room and told the Bombers that Johnson would
try to set the tone of play but that they should not allow themselves to be
provoked. What did Razor want to see from his players? He wrote the
homilies on his Coach's Mate as Bombers called them out rapid-fire:

HARD WORK

INTENSITY

INTELLIGENCE

UGLINESS

"How about the Whitney Forum?" Razor asked. The Bombers began to
chatter: "C'mon boys!" "It's our barn!" "Fucking rights!"

"We're going to own the building," Razor said. "We're going
to rock the Whitney fucking Forum! We're going to take the fucking
roof off!"

Two and a half minutes into the first period Rodge and
Schultzie had scored, and twice "Takin' Care of Business" had played on
the loudspeakers. Razor's ugly hockey had the Broncos disoriented and
backing off by half a step. I sat with Meghan and her friends in the Hapnot section as they tried, with little success, to start a wave. Meghan was
a senior, a mousy blonde, petite and pretty in a woolly-sweater, Sandra
Dee kind of way. She was the daughter of an HBM&S geologist; Meeks
was the son of a union man. Most afternoons I would see Meghan and
Meeks walking down Main Street holding hands. In the stands, she told
me she had never seen Meeks fight. "I didn't come to the games last
year, before we started dating. I tell him not to fight, because he's not
like that. He's really gentle. He should write on his stick: LOVER NOT A
FIGHTER."

By the second period, the Bombers were leading 4–1 and completely outplaying the Broncos, but the Flin Flon fans had turned on their own team. Johnston, as Razor had predicted, had seen to it that the Broncos were slashing and shoving and trying to pick fights. And the Bombers weren't fighting back. Humboldt would get penalties, Razor had told the Bombers, and Flin Flon could take advantage of power plays. "Homo!" Flin Flonners screamed at the Bombers. "Pussy!" Woody, the Bombers' best defenseman, fell to the ice and covered his head as a Humboldt player tried to pummel him. A minute later, Turkey, another Bomber defenseman, did the same thing, but the referee, who had lost control of the game by now, gave Turkey a penalty anyway. Ev was sticked in the stomach by a Bronco but didn't retaliate.

"You're a fucking woman!" Meeks's older brother shouted at Ev from the railing. In a scrum in front of the Bombers' net, Meeks was punched in the head, but he, too, followed Razor's instructions and didn't fight. It didn't matter though: both Meeks and the Bronco got kicked out of the game. Meeks was jeered as he skated off.

A chubby twenty-one-year-old sitting near me, dressed in a leather jacket with the Canadian flag on the sleeve and unwilling to give his name in case the players read this article, explained why he was hurling abuse at Flin Flon: "It's embarrassing to the fans, to the team, the town. You look at all the banners hanging from the rafters, all the tough guys who have played here. The Bombers should have the balls to drop their gloves."

In the dressing room between the second and third period, the faces of the Bombers' coaching staff were pale: Flin Flon was easily winning the game, but they were also, absurdly, losing. The Whitney Forum, territory, pride, tradition, manliness were being attacked. The game was, as Razor had told the Bombers repeatedly, war; it was, in the Clausewitzian sense, the continuation of hockey by other means.

At the start of the third period, after a quick shower, Meeks came and sat with Meghan and me. "I talked to my dad and my brother," he said. "My brother told me to fight. Fuck him." Meeks and Meghan held hands as we watched twenty minutes of mega-violence. When number twenty-two for the Broncos skated to center ice and dropped his gloves, challenging someone, anyone, to a fight, Bornie took him on. There was a loud cheer. Lester fought at the drop of the puck. Airsy beat up a Humboldt player and winked to the Hapnot section as he was led to the dressing room for the compulsory penalty. Schultzie ran his fingers through his peroxided hair before he swapped blows with a Bronco. "People are getting scared to play now," Meeks said. At the final siren, with both benches nearly empty because of all the players ejected from the game, a Bronco was still chasing Skulls around the ice.

The Bombers' dressing room was a riot of whoops and hollers. Flin Flon had won the game. Flin Flon had won the fights. "That's the way a weekend of hockey should be in Flin Flon!" Razor bellowed.

In the midst of the celebration the head of the local Royal Canadian Mounted Police knocked on the door and brought a little redheaded boy with a broken arm in to meet the Bombers. "All right guys, watch the swearing," Razor said. The tiny Flin Flonner went around and shook the players' hands.

Six days later, in the middle of a five-night, four-game road trip, the Bombers' bus barreled south through the narrow rutted back road of Saskatchewan toward the prairie town of Weyburn. Razor and Wild Bill and Blackie, the radio announcer who broadcast the games back to Flin Flon, sat at the front of the bus, Razor thumbing through the copy of *Men Are From Mars, Women Are From Venus* that his wife had asked him to pick up while he was on the road. Behind them, the twenty-three Bombers were splayed in their seats. The dress code most of the boys follow for official team functions—shirt and tie, Bombers' jacket or suit jacket, baseball cap—eased as ties were loosened and gangly limbs stretched across the aisle. It was quiet on the bus; after losing to the York-ton Terriers in the first game of the trip, Razor had told the team that he wanted them to visualize that night's upcoming game against the Red Wings. Razor had also told Dodger that he would be the starting goalie for the first time in the regular season. There had been a mistrial in Al and Steve's case, and Dodger's testimony had been postponed in-definitely; Razor hoped that, with the pressure off, Dodger would begin to play up to his abilities. A few rows behind Dodger, Meeks leaned his head against the window. He was growing his whiskers in a wild, slanted way, with seemingly random slashes of the razor across his face. He had

had a terrible dream the night before. He couldn't remember what it was, but it was terrible. And his medication wasn't working, so his stomach was giving him awful pain.

In the back row of the bus, where I had been assigned a seat, I sat with a few of the players and watched the harvest prairie roll by. "I think it's brutal if people say you can't play hockey and be a Christian," Bornie said to me. "I just watch my mouth, try not to swear, and do my job. If you have to fight, you fight."

"It's not up to Christians to judge others for swearing," said Schrades, the other Bomber goalie. "We don't judge them for *not* swearing."

"They can do whatever the fuck they want," Ev said.

"You'll go to hell," Sides said to Ev. "That's the truth."

"Judgment Day is so hypocritical," Ev said. "Christians are supposed to be forgiving, and then they say anyone who doesn't believe can't come into heaven even if they're a good person."

"It's hard not to sin out on the ice," Airsy said.

"I'll probably go to heaven," Schultzie said.

When we arrived in Weyburn and walked into the Colosseum I had a shock of recognition. The last time I had been in the Colosseum was in the late 1970s, just before I "got a letter" offering me a tryout with the Regina Silver Foxes, a now-defunct franchise in the Saskatchewan Junior Hockey League. Everything about the Colosseum had seemed huge then, the stands and ice surface and the red-and-white banners hanging from the rafters. I didn't want to take road trips and miss school, I had a bad knee, I wanted to drink beer and chase after girls. That's what I told my teammates, Boner and Dirt and Cement. I had lost touch with them long ago, but I knew they had all gone on to play professional hockey. The real reason I quit playing, though, what I didn't tell my friends, was that at the time, I had grown to hate hockey. It was in rinks like the Colosseum that I realized I had become, as they would say in Flin Flon, a pussy.

By game time, the Colosseum was nearly full. Many of the people in the stands were parents of Flin Flon players from farms and towns in southern Saskatchewan. Weyburn had won the league championship two of the last three years and had a team stacked with imports from Quebec and northern California and Latvia. When the Bombers skated out to a chorus of boos, Meeks, following his pre-game ritual, went straight to the bench and took off his helmet and gloves and lowered his head and prayed. In minutes the Red Wings were all over the Bombers. Dodger's play, unlike his nervous, uneven play in the exhibition season, was sensational—diving, sprawling, kicking shots away with his leg pads. On a clean break-away for Weyburn, Dodger made an acrobatic save. A few seconds later he gloved a slap shot from the point. I stood and whooped. The bombers began to come back. Rodge swooping past the Weyburn blue line with the puck and raking a wrist shot from ten feet out. Frustrated, the momentum now with Flin Flon, the Red Wings started to hack at the Bombers. With only seconds left in the first period, number seventeen for Weyburn hit Woody in the face with his stick.

In the second period, the score still 0–0, Seventeen skated past Sides and whipped his feet out from underneath him. Called for a penalty, Seventeen shot the puck at the linesman. It was, I thought, a familiar script: ripples become waves and rise rhythmically, climax-like, toward the fight. But then, suddenly and unpredictably, the Red Wings scored three quick goals on Dodger. "Sieve! Sieve!" the crowd taunted Dodger. Meeks skated out to take a shift. The puck was dropped, and Skulls, who was playing center, went into the corner after it. Seventeen followed Skulls and slammed him into the boards. Skulls's helmet came off, and Seventeen, seemingly twice Skulls's size, kept shoving, ramming Skulls's face into the Plexiglas. Across the rink, Meeks had dropped his gloves. He skated toward Seventeen, throwing off his helmet and tossing his elbow pads aside.

Meeks had explained his fighting technique to me back in Flin Flon: "I can't punch the other guy first," he said. "That's why I've got a lot of stitches. The other guy always gets the first punch and then I get mad." Meeks took the first punch from Seventeen square in the jaw. Meeks's head jerked back. He grabbed Seventeen by the collar and threw a long, looping, overhand right. He pulled Seventeen's jersey over his head. Another shot, a right jab, an uppercut; switched hands, a combination of lefts. A strange sound came from the audience, a mounting, feverish cry: Seventeen was crumpling, arms flailing, as the linesmen stepped in and separated the two. Meeks waved to his teammates as he was led off the ice by the officials to the screams of the Weyburn fans. The Bombers scored four minutes later. Between periods in the dressing room Razor shook Meeks's hand. "Great job."

Two days later we crossed the border into the United States, heading for Minot, North Dakota, and an encounter with the Top Guns, the only American franchise in the Saskatchewan Junior Hockey League. The flat of the prairies became the dun-colored hills and valleys of the North Dakota Badlands, the face of each rise marked by massive stones arranged to spell "class of 19—" for each year of the past five decades.

Ev, who had never been to the United States before, chanted every thirty seconds, "This is the furthest south I've ever been. This is the furthest south I've ever been."

"I don't like it here," Rodge said. "It's too far from home."

"People aren't as nice in the States," Bornie said.

"Look at that shitty little American town," Lester said as we drove through a roadside village. "It sucks cock compared to a little Canadian town." Lester and a couple of the Bombers began to hum the Guess Who song "American Woman."

When we arrived at the All Seasons Arena, Liberace's version of "Blue Tango" was echoing through the building as the Magic Blades, Minot's nationally ranked precision skating team, worked on their routine. The rink was in the middle of the fairground, a modern complex, new and brightly lit, with no banners hanging from the rafters and no memorabilia on display. Joey, a Minot player from southern Manitoba and a friend of Meeks and Woody and Ferlie, joked with the Bombers before the game. "They play the American anthem," Joey said, "and we have to stand there and listen, and we're, like, we couldn't give a shit."

For local high school hockey games, one of the Magic Blades told me, the place was packed with more than 3,000 fans, the crowd led by cheerleaders with pom-poms and fight songs, but only 452 turned up to watch the Bombers and the Top Guns.

"Let's get ready to rumble!" the announcer yelled over the loud-speaker as the Top Guns and Bombers skated out for the game.

In the stands, eating french fries covered with ketchup and vine-gar, Meeks told me about the Weyburn game and his fight. He showed me his hands. The knuckles were badly swollen and cut. "Seventeen stuck Woody in the face in the first period," he said. "I wasn't on the ice then, but the whole game he was slashing and punching people, going after Sides and Skulls. Between periods, Razor came into the room and said to wait until the third period and someone's going to take care of Seventeen. He looked at me but he didn't say anything. I knew my role. I'd be the one taking care of it."

Meeks couldn't play and wasn't sure when he would be able to play again.

"I called Meghan and told her I broke my hand," he said. "She said, 'You did not.' I said I did, I had to fight. She said I shouldn't fight. She said that I always have a choice."

There was a long silence. On the first day of the road trip, less than an hour out of Flin Flon, Meeks had asked me how to write a love poem. Should it rhyme? he asked. What should a love poem say? For almost a week he had scribbled notes in the blue spiral notebook that he used to write to Meghan. For now, though, Meeks had given up on writing poetry; he could barely bend his fingers, and he thought his thumb was dislocated again.

After the game, driving through the fairground, it was quiet on the Bombers' bus. The Bombers had played four games on the road and had lost four very close games. Cokes and the chocolate chip cookies Sides's mother had baked for the team were passed around. Ahead there was a thirteen-hour ride north through the ancient rock of the Precam-brian shield, through swales of muskeg, endless stands of jack pine and spruce and trembling aspen, the bus swerving occasionally to miss caribou and wolves that had strayed onto the road.

The next day, before I left Flin Flon, I went to skate with the Bombers one last time. At the Forum, Beastie told me about Blackie's broadcast of Meeks's fight in Weyburn. "Blackie pretty near creamed his jeans," Beastie said. "He's describing the bout, all the shots Meeks is getting in, and he's yelling, 'There's a good old home-town Bomber beating!'"

In the dressing room, Reags came and sat beside me. He was upset that I was leaving with the Bombers on a losing skid. I should stay until

Friday, he said, when they were sure to defeat the Melville Millionaires. I pulled on my jock pad, shin pads, shoulder pads, elbow pads, jersey; wrapped tape around pads, and fastened Velcro tags—a sequence I had repeated since I was scarcely old enough for kindergarten. I tightened the laces of my skates and stood and walked out of the Bombers' dressing room, past a sign with one of those sports clichés on it—IT'S MORE THAN A GAME—and glided onto a clean sheet of ice, the smack of pucks against the boards echoing around the empty stands.

After I left town, Flin Flon would suffer another losing streak, and, after a dispute with the team's board of directors over trading Schultzie for a defenseman, Razor would be fired. Dodger would testify against Al and Steve in the murder trial. The killers, relying for their defense on their intoxication and diminished responsibility, would be convicted of manslaughter and given sentences of six and a half years each, with parole possible in only three and a half years. Dodger would be traded to a team in another junior league. The Bombers' new coach would ask Meeks to fight all the time; Meeks would lose confidence and would have a screaming argument with the coach. Two games before the end of the season, he would get kicked off the team. He would not be allowed in the team photograph. The Bombers would finish last in their division.

On my last day in Flin Flon, after practice, Dodger stopped by my place to pick up the enormous plastic bags filled with crushed pop cans that he had collected in the past month. As he gathered his cans from the yard, Dodger showed me the letter he had drafted to send to Harvard, Brown, Cornell, and a bunch of other American schools, to inquire about playing for them next season. It was still September, but it had snowed in Flin Flon and the cold of the coming winter was in the air. Shifts were changing at the company, and Main Street was lined with pickup trucks. Dodger zipped up his fleece Bombers' jacket. Maybe he would try to play professionally in Europe, he said. He was in his final year of eligibility for junior hockey, but he wanted to keep playing.

Building a Rink of Your Own

BY JACK FALLA

Jack Falla lives in the suburbs of Boston, where his backyard rink, which he has grandly dubbed the Bacon Street Omni, has been a wintertime attraction for skate rats throughout the neighborhood since he first built it in 1982.

Falla is currently an adjunct professor at Boston University's College of Communication, but, for many years, he was a staff writer at *Sports Illustrated*. In 1984, he wrote a cover story on the Oilers' winning their first cup. He also contributed a backpage piece on the Omni. The latter generated far more letters than the former, and Falla became, in a way, the dean of the backyard rink, and is regularly called upon, in winter at least, to dispense rink-building wisdom.

In "Building a Rink of Your Own," Falla really gets down to the nitty gritty, covering everything from what color plastic sheeting to purchase, to exactly which weather pattern you should be watching for on the Weather Channel.

★ ★ ★ ★ ★

I don't understand the exact triggering mechanism, but I get the urge for digging every October when low gray clouds come scudding in on a northwest wind, the frost-blackened tomato plants hang limp on their hockey stick poles and the leaves of our two maple trees turn red and orange in that final leap of arboreal flame as summer burns itself out before the relentless advance of the long, dark New England winter.

That said, there is nothing especially lyrical about digging twenty-three postholes while trying to angle the northeast corner of the rink around the southeast corner of an abandoned septic tank, the concrete cover of which will not permit posthole digging. It does, however, make a very interesting configuration in that corner of our rink, where a sideboard suddenly juts out at about a thirty-five-degree angle, a board I credit with teaching a generation of young hockey players the game's oldest rule—keep your head up.

But before we go too far with the digging, nailing and flooding, let me make a couple of disclaimers:

What I'm about to describe is not the *only* way to build a rink. It probably isn't even the best way. Indeed, there are as many ways of building a backyard rink as there are rink owners. But this is the way that has worked for me for seventeen years. If you can improve on it—and you probably can—I wish you well. As for me? I'm going to stick with what I know works.

The Basic Idea

Our backyard rink is essentially a corral of plywood boards lined with a sheet of plastic and filled with water to an average depth of roughly ten inches (i.e., four or five inches at the shallow end and fourteen to sixteen inches at the deep end). To this we've added a few features like screening above the boards to keep the pucks in play, floodlights, a real hockey net, flags of various hockey-playing nations and our own banner—a custom-made flag with our rink's name in red letters on a white background: *The Bacon Street Omni*.

I know of a few people—Wayne Gretzky's father Walter among them—who simply flooded natural depressions in their yards and, aided by deeply frozen ground or tamped-down snow, were able to create a rink without using a plastic liner. But if you live south of Canada or the USA's northern tier states you're better off using plastic to keep the water from seeping into the ground or leaking away during what, in recent years, have been all too many mid-winter warming spells.

One caveat: Don't try building a rink unless you have a relatively flat backyard. We have about a one-foot variance from the highest to the lowest points in our yard. What's the maximum variance you can get away with? I don't think anyone can say with certainty but my best estimate—based on the way the water pressure bends our plywood boards—is in the vicinity of sixteen inches.

Building Materials

Your main start-up cost will be for plywood, studs and plastic. You can build a rink without any power tools. A posthole digger or an auger would help, but I still dig my postholes with a long-handled garden spade and a spud and that works just fine. A saw, a claw hammer and a staple gun will be the only other tools you should need.

I made my rink boards by buying fourteen sheets of four-by-eight-foot three-quarter-inch plywood. I then had the building supply store cut seven of the boards in half length-wise, thus giving me fourteen two-by-eight-foot boards in addition to the other seven uncut four-by-eight boards. I use the big boards at the deep end, or what we call the "shooting end" of the rink, and the low boards around the rest of the rink. If you plan to play hockey end-to-end—instead of the kind of "half-court" game we play—then obviously you'd want high boards at both ends of the rink.

You'll also need about thirty ten-foot studs. Twenty-one of those studs will serve as the "legs" of the large boards. I nail one stud at each end and one in the middle of each four-by-eight sheet of plywood so that two feet of the stud extend below the board (this will be the leg that goes into the ground) and four feet extend above the board (I later nail garden wire to these studs to keep pucks from flying out of the rink).

Cut the remaining studs into three-foot lengths (you'll get three from each stud) to be used as the legs on the low boards. I use one leg at each end of the low boards, nailing the stud so that its top is flush with the top of the board, and the one foot of stud extending below the board is the leg that will go into the ground to hold the board in place.

The boards will be a one-time expense and a one-time labor. We still have a few boards from our first rink built in 1982, and even the ones that we had to replace lasted at least eight to ten years. It's also a lot easier to replace one or two boards each season than to build all of them from scratch.

For my plastic liner I buy a seamless sheet of six-mil clear plastic in a standard size of forty feet wide and one hundred feet long. That forty-foot width is commonly available, although I recently learned it is possible to order sixty-foot-wide sheets. Assuming you use the typical forty-foot-wide sheet, you won't want your rink to be more than about thirty-five feet wide at its widest point because you'll need the extra five feet of plastic to extend up the boards to hold in the water.

The plastic is, for me, an annual expense because it gets ripped from skates, pucks, shovels and the industrial staples that hold it to the boards. I get clear plastic instead of the easier-to-find green because the darker color will absorb more heat from the sun and that's something I don't want.

A tip: I skip what would otherwise be the final lawn mowing of the year in my backyard. I like to let the grass grow long to serve as a natural cushion for the plastic and to protect it from sharp pebbles or old staples or whatever else might puncture the liner. Likewise, I'm happy to let a few autumn leaves build up where the boards go into the ground. These also serve as a natural cushion (but it's a miserable job to rake them out in the spring when they're waterlogged and half-rotted).

Can You Dig It?

The hardest part of building a rink is digging the postholes and putting up the boards. You've got to get this done before the ground freezes, which here in southern New England can be late November to mid-December. My target date for having all the boards in place is Thanksgiving, and I haven't been frozen out yet.

The holes for the big boards are about two feet deep and the holes for the lower boards are a little more than one foot deep. By now I've dug through the same ground so often that the soil is cleared of heavy rocks and the job gets easier from year to year. On the other hand, posthole digging is unpleasant work, so I make it palatable by doing it in short bursts. Indeed, I can—and often do—dig a two-foot-deep hole during halftime of an NFL or NCAA football telecast. And before Daylight Savings Time ends I'll often use the late afternoon to get a little exercise by digging a hole and putting a board in place.

If your soil is especially rocky you may want to get a spud—a four-foot metal rod with a chisel-like point—to serve as a kind of pick axe, loosening the soil and making it easy to shovel. A hatchet or small saw is also useful if you have to cut through tree roots. *A tip:* Pile up the dirt *behind* the hole (i.e., outside the skating area) so sharp pebbles that bury themselves in the grass won't pose a threat to your plastic liner.

Obviously, one posthole can accommodate two board legs. The ends of each board should be touching each other to create the smoothest seam possible. Not every seam will be perfect (we'll deal with that problem in a few more paragraphs) but you want the boards as close together as you can get them. As you lower each board into its hole and refill the hole with dirt, make sure you tamp down the ground firmly to hold the board in place.

There are probably easier ways to do this. A friend of mine who is in the building trades and is far more adept with power tools than I am has affixed three-quarter-inch pipe as legs on his low boards and has sunk one-inch pipes into the ground to serve as sleeves. He can pop his low boards into place in a few minutes. And when he removes them in the spring he simply caps the tops of the pipes that remain in the ground. However, the system doesn't work as well on the larger boards and for those he uses the same system I use.

Sealing the Seams

When all the boards are in place you will have completed your "corral." But because the seams—the places where two boards meet—rarely will be perfectly flush, you'll want to cover them with a soft, strong material to prevent the plastic from ripping on the rough, sometimes splintery end of a board or from being pushed out through a gap in the boards and rupturing under the accumulating pressure of the water. At various times I've used canvas from an old tent, strips of carpeting, pieces of artificial turf and strips cut from an old leather jacket. I secure the strips over the seams with five-eighths-inch tacks. If I have a large opening—say anything more than a half inch—at the deep end of the rink I sometimes nail a piece of wood over the gap and then cover the wood with a soft fabric.

Besides sealing the vertical seams you also have to pay attention to the horizontal seams—the places where the bottoms of boards meet the ground. Since your yard is probably uneven, there will be gaps where the bottom of a board is not perfectly flush with the ground. I fill these gaps with old sheets or rags collectively known in our house as "rink rags." About a dozen times in the course of a year Barbara will hold up an old coat or curtain or blanket she plans on throwing out and ask, "You want this for a rink rag?" The answer is invariably yes.

Put the rink rags inside the boards where they will also help to cushion the plastic liner and prevent it from being pushed out under the boards by the pressure of the water.

Warning: Don't install the plastic liner until the day you're ready to flood. The longer the plastic is exposed the greater the danger it will get torn. And even if it doesn't get torn it will collect leaves, most of which will rise to the top when you flood, thus temporarily ruining the ice surface.

Fence Me In

When the boards are in place I nail a long strip of garden wire (*Note:* Chicken wire isn't strong enough to stop a puck unless your shot's even weaker than mine) to the studs above the high boards on the "shooting end" of the rink, thus raising the total height of the backstop (boards and fencing combined) to about seven feet, high enough to keep most shots from sailing out of the rink. In recent years I've taken to nailing the heavier garden fencing to the inside of the studs, then nailing a roll of chicken wire to the outside of the studs, thus giving me a double wall of fencing inches apart. What happens is that a hard shot (hey, don't look at me) that forces its way through the inner garden wire will have lost all of its power by the time it hits the chicken wire and, thus, will drop straight to the ground inches behind the boards. Pucks are a lot easier to recover when they're all in the same place instead of sprayed all over the yard. We call this the Bacon Street Omni Automatic Puck Recovery System. But we haven't patented it so you can use it.

Flooding

Timing is everything when it comes to flooding. Don't get fooled by those first few frosty days of late fall or early winter. What you need is about a three-day stretch of serious cold wherein night temperatures drop to the teens or single digits on the Fahrenheit scale and daytime temperatures don't rise above freezing. The colder the better.

But you also want to flood a day *ahead* of an arriving cold front. In December I become the Weather Channel's biggest fan as I watch for a sustained blast of cold Canadian air slamming down out of Alberta and heading for New England. Approximately twelve to twenty-four hours before the cold front's arrival I'm ready to put in the plastic liner and start flooding.

Rolling Out the Plastic

Roll out your plastic and staple it to the sides of your rink boards. Make sure the plastic liner extends far enough up the boards to be above the water level. We staple ours all the way up on the low boards and about three feet high on the high boards. You can always trim away extra plastic, but if the water rises so high that it flows out of the rink you've got trouble.

As soon as the plastic is in place, turn on the hose and start flooding. Using one standard garden hose it takes us between eighteen and twenty-six hours to fill our rink. If your outdoor faucet is frozen—and if it isn't frozen on the day you flood you can be sure it will be during the heart of the skating season—simply pour warm water on it. Even on the coldest day, two saucepans of warm water will thaw out a faucet.

Check your rink frequently while you're flooding. The rising water exerts so much pressure on the plastic that it often pulls it off the boards, in which case you have to go out and re-staple. It's easy to re-staple the plastic to the low boards, but the high boards—the place where our plastic is most likely to pull away—are another matter. Twice I've had to wade out in frigid water to re-staple the plastic. But that was before I fig- ured out that if I left the wire fencing loose at the bottom I'd have enough room to reach under the fencing and over the boards to re- staple. Once we have ice—and before the pucks start flying around— take a few finish nails and complete the fastening of the fencing.

You also want to keep an eye on all of your seams—vertical and horizontal—to make sure there's no leakage. Even at night I go out with a flashlight every three or four hours, checking for problems. You won't get much sleep on the night of the first flooding.

Making Ice

Ice makes itself, so this is the easy part.

When you think you have enough water in the rink—as a rough guide I'd say you want at least three inches at the shallowest point—simply put the hose back in the cellar (it will freeze if you don't) and wait for nature to do its winter's work. But wait patiently.

The water will skim over quickly—usually while the hose is still running—but it could be two to four days, or even longer, before your ice is thick enough to skate on.

I have a series of tests for my ice, beginning with a few taps on the surface with the blade of a hockey stick. If the ice can withstand that, then I usually butt-end it with the stick, the resulting hole giving me a good idea of the thickness of the ice.

When I can't drive the butt end of the hockey stick through the ice, then I step over the low boards and—holding onto the board—I gradually transfer my weight onto the ice until I hear a crack. If the ice doesn't crack, then I put my entire weight on it and shuffle around a lit- tle bit. If the ice cracks I get off it immediately. But if I can walk around the entire rink without hearing any ominous crackings then I can be fairly certain that the ice is ready for skating.

Warning: Don't go checking the thickness of your ice while wearing skates. If you should break through the ice the blade of the skate will probably rip your plastic liner and, to the best of my knowl- edge, that's an impossible repair job.

Resurfacing

Thou shalt not skate if thou hast not shoveled. That's the first commandment of rink ownership as it applies to any skater ten years old or older. A backyard rink is a lot of fun, but first you have to pay your dues.

After the rink has been skated on for a while, snow will begin to build up to a point where it interferes with stick-handling and passing the puck, and if it builds up deep enough, it will interfere with skating. If you're not through skating for the day then all you have to do is scrape the snow off the ice and keep on playing. We scrape our ice with plastic shovels, which seem to do a better job and to snag on the ice less than aluminum ones, though I don't know why that is.

Do not put water on the ice if you plan to use the rink again that day. It is amazing how long it takes a sprayed rink to freeze up, especially when compared to the almost instant freezing you see when a machine resurfaces an indoor rink. But even when outdoor temperatures have been in the teens and twenties I've made the mistake of trying to resurface the ice only to have to wait hours—sometimes half a day—before the ice is ready to skate on.

But when you're finished with the rink for the day, then you'll want to resurface it completely. Here's how:

1. *Take the goal off the rink.* We slide ours over to the low sideboards and simply tip it upside down and out of the rink so that the crossbar is lying on the ground. It's easy to tilt it back the next day. If you leave the goal—especially a metal-framed goal—on the ice, the water you put down will build up around the goal frame and will freeze the goal into the ice, a dangerous situation if and when someone crashes into the goalpost. Also, a warm, sunny day during a mid-winter thaw will see the goalposts warm up and melt their way into the ice, again making the goal immovable and dangerous for any player who crashes into it.
2. *Scrape the rink.* I said that when I reached fifty years of age I'd buy a snowblower for the rink, but as I write this, I'm fifty-five and I still clear the ice with a plastic shovel. I rationalize this as

having some cardiovascular benefit, though I think there might be some macho taint to my thought process.

3. *Drag out the hose and begin spraying.* I start at the high boards and work from sideboard to sideboard back toward the shallow end, where I step over the low boards and am standing outside of the rink when I spray the last few square feet of ice.

4. *Throw the hose back in the cellar and have a good night's sleep.* Your ice will be as good as new in the morning.

Tip: Have both ends of the hose facing **up** when carrying the hose to the cellar or bulkhead. If either end is facing down, water can run onto your porch or your bulkhead steps, freeze and present a safety hazard. I try to drain out most of the water when I disconnect the hose, but I don't mind if a quart or so stays in the hose and runs out on my cellar floor. Better there, where it will evaporate quickly than on the porch or stairs where it might stay frozen for weeks.

Lights

Floodlights will let you get added hours of enjoyment from your rink. We have four 150-watt adjustable floodlights mounted on a garage beside the rink and another mounted on the porch roof. Together they light up almost the entire ice surface and allow us to skate at night. Just make sure the lights are far enough away from the rink so that they won't be hit by a deflected puck.

And one word of warning about night hockey. We have what we call a "Six O'clock Rule" which says that after six o'clock at night, all hockey will be played with tennis balls, not pucks. This is to keep the noise down and not intrude upon neighbors.

Taking Down Your Rink

Sometime between Valentine's Day at the earliest and St. Patrick's Day at the latest a rising sun and gradually warming temperatures will begin melting our ice and evaporating some of the water, thus rendering the rink unusable. It's obvious when it's time to drain the rink and store the boards. It's not my favorite job, but as the years go on, it's become part of the ritual of spring—which is to say I deal with it better when I think of rink removal less as the end of the skating season and more as the earliest harbinger of summer.

Drain It Slowly

When the ice in the north or shallow end begins to melt, I use a dandelion picker to poke holes in the plastic. But be careful. If your rink is near your house—as ours is—you don't want to poke so many holes that the escaping water saturates the ground and floods your cellar. I got greedy one year and jabbed about fifty holes in the plastic liner. Six hours later I had the beginnings of an indoor swimming pool in my cellar. Now I poke ten or a dozen holes in the shallowest part of the rink and when the water recedes, I step out onto the plastic and poke a dozen more holes. The effect is like the tide going out on a plastic beach.

When the plastic is exposed I take a pair of shears and cut it sideways (that is along its forty-foot width) into strips roughly four to six feet wide. Then I fold each strip in half lengthwise, roll it up and tie it with a string preparatory to stacking it up like so much plastic cordwood to await the arrival of the trash collectors or a trip to the dump.

After the plastic is out, I take a claw hammer and pull the tacks out of all the strips of fabric that I used to seal the vertical seams. Be careful removing these tacks. You don't want to lose one in the grass where it could pierce your liner next year, or worse someone could step on it. I save these pieces of fabric and reuse them from year to year.

I then take down the fencing and transfer it immediately into the garden where it does summer duty as a trellis for peas.

It's easy to pull out the low boards and store them in the garage. But the big boards—the four-by-eight-footers with the ten-foot studs nailed to them—are another and more difficult matter. Removing them is a two-person job. We use two long-handled shovels as levers. Run the blade of the shovel under the board, then step on the handle and the board will begin to come out of the ground, whereupon you and your partner can lift it out completely and carry it to its summer storage area, which in our case is against the back and sides of our garage.

Fill in the postholes and throw some grass seed on the dirt around them. After a few mowings you'll hardly be able to see where your rink has been.

One of the questions I've been asked most frequently is: Doesn't the rink kill the grass? No. The plastic liner actually serves as a kind of greenhouse so that the grass that has been under the plastic (and under the ice) usually begins to turn green before the grass in the rest of the yard.

I'm not going to sugarcoat it. Building and maintaining a rink is hard work in cold weather. But worth it? It is when I go out for an early morning skate, when Barbara, leaving the rink lights off, skates beneath a spray of winter stars, and when, in winters past, we watched our children and their friends lose themselves in the joy of impromptu hockey games. In two or three years we hope to see our first grandchild—born a few weeks before this chapter was written—take his first wobbly skating strides here at the Bacon Street Omni.

Worth it? As Barbara said: "Anyone can love summer, but to love winter you have to carry your sunshine around with you."

Our rink lights up our life.

My Career with the Leafs

BY BRIAN FAWCETT

There are only two stories that are complete lies in this anthology, and this is one of them. That said, if a poet did join a team in the NHL, this is probably exactly how things would unfold. Fawcett actually is a poet, in addition to being a sometime columnist for Canada's *Globe and Mail*.

★   ★   ★   ★   ★

I'll explain how I came to play hockey for the Toronto Maple Leafs. It was surprisingly easy, and other people with similar ambitions to play in the Big Leagues might be able to pick up some valuable tips. I'm a poet, you see, and one of the things we do as part of our job is an occasional public reading. I had a reading to do in Toronto, and one of the first things I did when I got there was to drop down to Maple Leaf Gardens. The day I went, the Leafs happened to be practicing.

As I sat in the stands watching the Leafs skate around the rink I got an idea. I walked down to the equipment room, and politely asked a man who turned out to be the trainer if it would be okay if I joined the practice.

"Sure thing," he told me, just like that.

I asked if I could have a uniform to wear.

"Sure," he said. "What number would you like?"

"How about number 15?" I said innocently.

The number belonged to Pat Boutette at the time, but he was injured and I knew he wouldn't be around. I felt a surge of ambition— maybe I could beat him out of the job! Minutes later I was out on the ice with the Toronto Maple Leafs.

I skated around for a while, carefully declining any involvement in the passing and shooting drills while I tried to get my floppy ankles to cooperate. Instead of cooperating they were beginning to hurt, so I drifted in the direction of the coach, Red Kelly, who was yelling instructions at the players. I leaned casually on my stick the way I'd seen Ken Dryden do on television, and looked down at my skates. I watched the drills for two or three minutes until the ache in my ankles started to fade, then edged closer to Kelly.

"Mind if I take a turn?" I asked as evenly as I could.

"Not at all," he replied. "Let's see what you can do."

Somebody pushed a puck in front of me and as I reached for it I tripped on the tip of my left skate and fell flat on my face. What to that point had almost been a dream turned abruptly into a nightmare. I lay on the ice for a second, peering at the puck as if it had tripped me, and wondered why I couldn't wake up. I thought about quitting right then and there.

I had nothing to lose, so I didn't quit. I got up, picked up my stick, and looked Red Kelly in the eye. He didn't move a muscle—didn't laugh or anything. I pushed the puck forward and skated after it in the direction of the goalie—it was Gord McRae I think—slowly gathering speed. About fifteen feet from the net I deked to my left without the customary deke to the right. The deke took McRae with it, and I cut to the right. The net was wide open and I shoveled the puck into it on my backhand.

All of this is incredibly difficult for a left-shooting skater to do. In fact, the whole maneuver is an impossible one, and everyone who saw it knew it, including Kelly, who was staring at me with his mouth open. For my part, I had no idea how I'd done it, except that it had been awful easy.

"Not bad," Kelly shouted. "Not bad at all."

If scoring that first goal had been easy, the rest of the practice wasn't. I'm not a great skater at the best of times, and I wasn't in shape. I seemed able to score goals almost at will, but I had difficulty with the defensive drills, particularly the ones that involved things like skating backward. I fell several times, and one time I went into the boards so hard that Kelly skated over and told me to take it easy.

As the practice ended, he asked me if I could drop by his office after I showered. I told him I'd be pleased to, and after a shower I can't remember at all, I was sitting in a stuffed red Naugahyde chair staring across a big desk at Red Kelly and Jim Gregory, the General Manager of the Leafs.

Kelly was writing something on a pad of yellow foolscap. Gregory did the talking.

"You've got some interesting moves out there," he said. "I caught the whole thing from up in the box. Where'd you learn your hockey?"

I decided to tell them the truth.

"Well," I replied, "I really haven't played organized hockey since I was about twelve. I watch Hockey Night in Canada, of course, and I guess I've learned a lot from that."

"Where do you come from?" he asked.

"That's kind of a hard question," I replied, trying to figure out what the truth was. "I'm from the West Coast. Well, not the coast, actually. I'm from up north."

"What brings you to Toronto?"

"I'm a poet," I said, "here on business, doing a public reading."

"No kidding," he said, looking reasonably satisfied with my answer. "I guess you know Rota. He's from up there."

I was stumped. I didn't know any writer from up north named Rota. Kelly saw my confusion.

"New kid," he said. "Plays for Chicago."

"I've heard of him"—I shrugged—"but I never played with him. He's a bit younger than I am."

There was a silence, as if the two of them were trying to decide which of them should speak. Finally, Gregory stood up and cleared his throat.

"How would you like to play hockey for the Toronto Maple Leafs?" he said.

"I'd really like that," I said quickly. "I'd prefer to play just the home games, though. I hate traveling."

Gregory seemed puzzled by my request, but he agreed to it, probably because I didn't ask for anything else.

"We play Boston on Monday night," he said. "We'll see you at the rink at 6 p.m." He paused. "Make that 5:30, and you can get in an extra half hour of skating."

I stood up. "I can probably use it." I smiled.

Kelly grunted, and then grinned, and I followed him out of the office and down the long concrete corridors of Maple Leaf Gardens to the players' entrance. He shook my hand.

"Good to have you with us," he said, with a lot of sincerity.

"It's good to be part of an organization that takes chances," I said, with even more sincerity. "Toronto treats its visitors well."

Kelly smiled and waved good-bye as I stepped through the open door into a fine early winter blizzard.

The next thing I knew I was sitting in the Leafs' dressing room beside George Ferguson, suiting up for the game. Kelly came in and announced the player assignments.

"Fawcett here is going to be playing home games for us," he shouted, pointing vaguely in my direction. "He'll play on the wing with Ferguson, and Hammarstrom for a while, and we'll see how things go. Any questions?"

To my surprise, a fair number of the players knew who I was, and it turned out that some of them had even read my work. Out of the corner of my eye I saw the two Swedes, Hammarstrom and Salming, exchange glances. Maybe they thought having a poet on the team might take some of the heat off them. They were still relatively new in the league, and they were taking a lot of physical and verbal abuse from the rednecks and goons who were worried about foreigners changing the game and taking their jobs. The rap on the Swedes was that they were chicken, particular Hammarstrom, who the papers were saying was allergic to the boards. Personally, I thought his skating more than made up for those faults.

I wondered a little at Kelly putting me on a line with him, but decided that he was trying to compensate for my poor skating. Every team in the league would stick their goons on our line, that was certain. Kelly probably figured Hammarstrom would skate his way out of trouble, and I would talk my way out.

We'd see soon enough. It was nice to be able to play with Ferguson, who I thought was one of the smarter centers to come into the league in a while. I planned to do what any rookie should—keep my head up and my mouth shut. It would be a new way of working, that was for sure.

The first period of that game was nothing to remember. My check, predictably, was Wayne Cashman, probably the dirtiest player in the league. I went up and down my wing without incident, partly because Cashman wasn't much of a skater either. He cut me with his stick several times, but I didn't bleed much, and I ignored it when he got me with the butt end just as the period ended. I waited until I could breathe again and skated off to the dressing room with the rest of the team.

Early in the second period Lanny McDonald and Don Marcotte were sent off for trying to remove one another's vital organs, and Kelly sent me out with Hammarstrom on a five-on-five. The Bruins sent out Greg Sheppard and Cashman. The face-off was in our end, and Hammarstrom won it, got the puck back to Ian Turnbull, and he banked it around on the boards to where I was waiting. I circled once, almost lost my balance, and headed up the ice. As I crossed the red line, I saw Cashman skating toward me with a gleam in his eye. I kept going toward Orr at the blueline, did the deke to my left as if to move between Orr and the boards, and then cut sharply right. Orr went for the first deke and so did Cashman, who by this time was right behind me prodding at my liver with his stick. When I deked to the right, Cashman ran into Orr and both of them went heavily to the ice. I had a two on one with Hammarstrom, and I slid the puck over to him. He drew Al Simms over, passed back, and I had only Cheevers to beat. I did it again; deked left, cut right, and plunked the puck over the bewildered netminder into the upper right corner of the net.

I stuck my stick up in the air the way I'd seen it done on television, and was trying to honk my leg when I ran into Hammarstrom and we both fell down. Turnbull came over to congratulate me and Salming skated over to dig the puck out of the net. He handed it to me, grinned, and said something in Swedish I didn't understand. Hammarstrom grinned at me the same way and pointed to Cashman, who was skating in small circles at center ice with his head down.

It was a tight-checking game, and the score was still 1–0 halfway through the third period. That was as far as I got that night. I skated into the corner for a Ferguson pass, Cashman went in behind me, and only Cashman came out.

Eventually I came *to*, but that was well after the game was over. The Leafs had won it 2–0. Cashman got a penalty for hammering me, and Sittler scored on the ensuing power play. That's what they told me, anyway.

I made it to the practice the next afternoon, none the worse for having spent the night in the hospital to make sure I didn't have a concussion. I didn't get much sleep because the interns kept coming in every half hour to see if I was going to go into a coma.

"Are you there?" they asked, and lifted my eyelids with one finger to flash their penlights at my pupils. About 4 a.m. a very young intern came in. He was a hockey fan.

"You're the new guy with the Leafs, eh?" he asked.

"Yeah," I croaked.

"Nice move you made on that goal you scored," he said. "Where'd you learn that?"

"Watching television," I answered, telling the truth.

"I hear you write poetry too," he said.

My head hurt, so I just grimaced.

"Pretty strange," he said. "Watch out for Cashman."

He checked my eyes so carefully I thought he was looking for poems, but he said I'd probably be able to leave in the morning.

At the practice the next day, Ferguson told me to watch out for Cashman too.

"You were lucky," he said. "Cashman spent two periods setting you up. We all knew it was coming, but I guess you had to pass the test like anyone else."

"Some test," I complained. "All I can remember about it is my bell ringing when it was over."

I played the three games in that home stand, scoring again in the last one against the Rangers, and setting up a goal by Ferguson. The team was away for the next three games, and then back for three more. While they were away I worked on my skating, circling the rink again and again until my ankles were too sore for me to move anymore. I tried skating without a stick, but found, as I had when I was a kid, that skating that way was beyond me. I needed the stick for balance and without it I could barely stand.

When the team came back, I confided to Ferguson that I couldn't skate without a stick.

"You're kidding," he said.

"No," I told him, "It's true. I only got skates every three years and the first year they were too big and the third year they were too small."

Ferguson had a good eye for details. "What about the second year?" he asked.

"I had weak ankles back then."

"You still have weak ankles," he said.

"I use the stick for balance," I said, as we went on circling the rink.

Ferguson was skating backward to tease me. "Skating is easy," he laughed. "For me it's like breathing."

"I feel that way about some other things," I replied, "but not about skating."

"You don't look as if breathing is very easy right now," he pointed out.

While we unlaced our skates after practice, he asked me cautiously what it was like to be a writer.

"It's my way of breathing," I said.

"How'd you get into it?" he asked with genuine curiosity.

"I guess I was about thirteen," I said. "Right after I quit playing minor league hockey."

Ferguson and I became friends. He taught me a lot of the basics of pro hockey and I gave him books to read in return. I was interested in Rilke and an American poet named Jack Spicer at the time, and he pored through everything I lent him. I always had books in my equipment bag, and he dug through it regularly to see what was there. He asked me if Canadian writers were as good as Americans.

"The old guys are pretty tame," I said, "but there's a few writers under forty who might turn out to be interesting."

"Jeez," he said, "how long does it take to get good at it?"

"Usually about fifteen years of hard work," I said. "A few get good earlier than that because they have special attentions or come from environments that encourage them," I went on. "But that's rare. Most of us have to learn pretty well everything about the culture twice, and that takes time. After that, there's the job of keeping on top of it as it changes. A lot of writers get one good review of their work and they have to please their public, or worse, they decide that they're geniuses, and don't have to listen to anything. So they imitate themselves until they lose their ability to learn. After that they just get drunk, or academic, or spend all their time trying to please the reviewers and filling out grant applications."

He wanted to know about the grants, so I explained to him the economics of trying to be a serious artist in a country that wants to have serious art without having to put up with the inconvenience and cost of paying the artists.

He looked skeptical. "Except for that, hockey is pretty much the same," he said after a moment's thought. "Only hockey players get screwed up more easily and a lot faster."

"That's because there's more people paying attention," I said, "and there's more money involved."

That home stand was a good one. I scored my third goal, drew assists on one of Ferguson's, and another on the power play, passing from behind the net to Sittler in the slot. Only four goals had been scored while I was on the ice, and after seven games I was plus five. Then the Leafs were off again on a five-game road trip and I went back to my solitary skating, circling the ice over and over again until slowly, very slowly, my skating began to improve. I skated clockwise first, and then counter-clockwise. Going counter-clockwise was easier, maybe because on the corners my stick was closer to the ice. But I couldn't quite master skating backward, and stopping remained a problem unless I was close to the boards. But I developed reasonable speed skating straight ahead, and during games I combined my lack of stopping skill with my speed to provide the team with some excellent bodychecking.

Ferguson and I went out on the town the night after the team flew in from Los Angeles. He showed me the important sights of

Toronto, like Rochdale and Don Mills, and later that night we walked down to Lake Ontario and threw rocks at all the empty cartons floating in the water. There had been a thaw, and it was like spring—dirty snow was piled up everywhere, abandoned cars were being towed off the street, and the curious sensation I'd had of being in Middle Earth began to dissipate. There were lovers everywhere, discussing Parliament, and kissing and fist-fighting as the fog rolled in from the lake to meld with the darkness coming up from the East.

We played our only other home date of the season with the Bruins several weeks later. As the game approached, I got a lot of good-natured ribbing from the guys about what to do with Cashman.

"Check him into the boards with a powerful metaphor," advised Sittler.

"And then slash him with an internal rhyme," someone else chimed in.

I laughed at the gags, but deeper down I was worried. The press had picked it up and were amusing themselves, mostly at my expense. Allen Able in *The Globe & Mail* wrote something about it being a test of whether the stick is mightier than the pen, and in an interview Cashman noised it around that he not only disliked my style, he detested poetry. Anybody who wrote poetry, he said, had to have something wrong with their hormones. That wasn't all he said, either. He told the interviewer he was going to show the fans that there was something fishy about me, promising to make fillets out of me *and* my poetry.

As I skated out for the pre-game warm-up, Cashman gave me the evil eye, so I gave the fans a demonstration of how fast I could skate through the center-ice zone. Kelly, out of kindness I guess, kept our line away from Cashman's as the game began, but on the second shift I saw the Bruin right-winger head for the bench right after the face-off, and Cashman came over the boards. Somebody froze the puck, and as we lined up for the face-off deep in Bruin territory, Cashman skated up to the circle, and around me once with his stick about a quarter of an inch from my nose.

"I hope you got a nice burial poem written for yourself," he sneered. "You skinned my behind and I'm gonna carve yours off and throw it to the crowd."

I looked him right in the eye and mustered up all my powers of language.

"Suck eggs," I said.

On the face-off Ferguson drew the puck back to Salming and I skated to the corner to wait for a pass. Cashman ignored the puck and followed me. I ducked an elbow. It missed me, but the ref didn't miss it, because I slid down the boards as if I'd been pole-axed. Cashman got whistled for an elbowing penalty, and then a misconduct penalty when he tried to chase me into the stands. I skated away from him and three of my teammates stayed between us to make sure I stayed alive. Kelly kept me on the power play and I banged Sittler's rebound past Gilles Gilbert to make it 1–0.

When I got to the bench, Kelly told me Howie Meeker wanted to interview me after the first period. It was Saturday, and the game was being televised nationally.

I'd forgotten it was Hockey Night in Canada. You get like that in the pro's—you forget everything that makes the world tick for real people. You also pay a price. The price I was going to have to pay for my forgetfulness was an awful one. I hadn't brought any poems in my equipment bag. I was being handed the largest audience any poet in this country ever dreamed of and I wouldn't have a thing to read.

A few minutes later I was sitting in front of several television cameras with the customary towel over my shoulder, watching Howie Meeker introduce me to the nation and thinking that the dream was going to turn into a nightmare if I couldn't think of something quickly. My mind was a blank.

"We've got Toronto left-winger Brian Fawcett here in the Hockey Night in Canada studios at Maple Leaf Gardens," Meeker announced in a voice that sounded more nasal in real life than on television.

He was hunched toward the cameras and I noticed he sat closer to them than I did. I hadn't seen a brush cut for years or, for that matter, as much makeup as he had on his face, and I was sorting through all that novelty without listening to what he was saying. Luckily, he was babbling as inanely as usual at the camera and ignoring me completely:

". . . nice to see a young player come up to the NHL with a good grasp of hockey fundamentals and play sound heads-up positional hockey the way you've been doing. Gee whiz, but I just get thrilled when I see a young kid with his mind on the game skate away from a player like Wayne Cashman. And it pays off, don't you see? It must have been less than a minute before you scored that beautiful goal like you were born with a stick in your hand and skates on your feet."

He hadn't actually asked me a question, but he seemed to have finished.

"Actually, Howie," I said, too nervous to do anything but tell the truth, "I haven't played much hockey since I was twelve or thirteen years old, and I'm thirty, so I'm not much of a kid anymore. I've been mainly concerned with language, and more specifically with disjunction in poetry, for the last few years. You might say I've been learning the tools of an extremely complex trade."

Meeker appeared not to have understood. Maybe he thought I was speaking French. He ignored everything I said, and went off in another rant.

"Well, Brian, how do you like being with a team like the Leafs, eh, with their tradition of ruggedness and hard work?"

"Well, Howie," I said, still not sure if he realized that I understood English, and pretty sure he didn't know I was a poet, "I find the ruggedness something of a problem. Northrop Frye and Margaret Atwood created a problem a few years ago by writing some books about the importance of Nature and the frontier, and a lot of similarly empty glamor nonsense about rugged Canadian pioneers, and as a result a lot of the writers in this country now go around wearing logging boots and punching people for no reason. I used to do it myself, actually."

Meeker was staring at me, his jaw somewhere down around his navel. I took this as a signal to continue.

"I mean, violence may be natural, but Nature isn't a very good model for behavior. It's really been overestimated."

I knew I was gesticulating too much, and starting to yap. I'd forgotten about the cameras—it was Howie Meeker I wanted to convince. I couldn't stop.

"Art is really about civilization," I said, "not about Nature. All Nature does is overproduce, then waste most of it, and then resort to violence when the garbage starts to stink. When human beings follow Nature, you get guys like Hitler."

I was really flying, so I went to Meeker's question about hard work next.

"Hard work, like you say, is really important, Howie. The more I know about this game, the more I begin to realize that the real secret is hard work. I guess that goes for hockey as well."

Meeker, for some reason, seemed to have lost his voice, so I went right on.

"If you'd given me a little more notice, I could have brought some work here to read, but I guess these interviews are a bit too short to give the folks at home any real idea of what's going on, let alone a sense of the breadth and skill and variety of good writing going on in this country today."

Meeker stuttered back to life.

"Ah, ahhh. . . .Yes, well. . . .Well, Brian, I wish you and the Leafs the best of luck in the upcoming second period," he said, regaining a measure of control that didn't show in his face.

"Back to you, Dave Hodge!" he said hoarsely.

I smiled politely at the camera until fade-out. I'd seen a few guys start to pick their noses when they thought they were off-camera, and I wanted people to remember what I'd said.

Meeker turned on me. "What was that all about, you crazy sonofabitch?"

I began to explain, but he walked out of the studio without listening to my answer.

The dressing room was oddly silent when I returned. I sat down next to Ferguson and pulled the towel from around my neck. He was sitting with his head between his knees, as if he were air-sick.

"Didn't you know about Meeker?" he asked incredulously.

"Know what?" I said, stuffing the towel into my equipment bag as a souvenir. "He seemed kind of ticked off when I talked about writing, but then he did ask those dumb questions, and he didn't stop me from answering them the way I wanted to."

"Geez, man, that's the unwritten law of hockey," Ferguson said. "You're supposed to pretend you're really dumb."

It was my turn to be incredulous.

"Darryl thinks there's some kind of agreement between the owners about it," he said. "When you get out of Junior Hockey, you're given a sheet of things you can say to the press. You talk dumb, talk about teamwork, and all that crap."

My head was reeling. When I was a kid I believed that the world was full of secret rules and conspiracies, but this was real life—the Big Leagues. I couldn't believe what I was hearing.

"I mean a few years ago," he continued, "when Kenny Dryden started getting interviewed, he used all kinds of literate words like 'tempo' and so on, pronounced all the words properly, and there was a terrific uproar. But he was in law school and they had to accept it. I dunno. They may get him yet—force him to retire."

Ferguson shrugged, and a note of hopelessness entered his voice. "Rumor is," he said, "that this whole business of us being stupid and inarticulate is an explicit policy of the Feds—right from the top."

I looked around me to see if he was kidding. A couple of guys just nodded and looked the other way, but most of them were glaring at me. Kelly looked really angry.

"Aw, come on, you guys," I said to no one in particular. "Why put up with this? I've seen what's really true. Look at the books lying around the dressing room."

Several players slipped large hardbound books into their equipment bags. Sittler, everyone knew, was a big Henry James fan—said it helped his passing game. And Tiger Williams had come up from Junior already heavily into Artaud. The league had its share of jerks, it was true, but unless you noised it around, you were left alone if you had intellectual interests. I guessed they were mad at me because they thought I might have let the cat out of the bag. Hockey, Kelly told me later, was in enough trouble.

There was a TV set in the dressing room, and we watched as Meeker came on the screen to do the highlights of the period. My goal wasn't one of them. A few of the guys exchanged significant looks, but everybody remained seated, as if they were watching something very sad.

When a commercial came on, I asked Ferguson who'd died.

"You did, dummy," he said.

"Aw, come on," I said. "Why? Is it that bad? All I did was to get Howie Meeker mad at me."

"It's a lot worse than you think. You'll be blacked out," he said, grimly. "No radio perks, no television interviews, and as little newspaper coverage as they can give you. What you *will* see will all be bad."

"That's okay," I said, philosophically. "I'm pretty used to that."

I scored the winning goal in the third period by going around the defense in the usual way, and I didn't even get third star. I went up and down my wing against Cashman, took his checks, many of which were flagrantly vicious and should have drawn penalties, and I threw a couple of my own in his direction. Cashman was given third star, actually, and Meeker said he was the one Bruin on the ice who had dominated his opponent.

Ferguson and I had a few beers after the game. I invited the rest of the guys, but nobody seemed interested. "You're really a goof," Ferguson said cheerfully. "Do you know that?"

"How was I supposed to know?" I said, irritably. It seemed like everybody knew the rules but me.

"Look," I said, "I didn't go through the system like you guys did. For me it was all watching the tube, and thinking about it. How was I supposed to know—I mean, I've never believed much of what I've seen on television, but I did think Hockey Night in Canada at least was for real."

Ferguson grunted. "Rules are rules," he said. "Nobody but you believes they're supposed to be just."

"I'd settle for knowing what they are," I said bitterly.

"Would you really?"

"I'm not sure," I admitted. "I guess I really want to know who the big shots are who make them."

I didn't find out who the big shots were, that night or on any of the ensuing nights that season. I played my hockey as well as I could, and I played it in more or less the kind of obscurity I had been warned to expect. I scored nine goals and built twelve assists in twenty-seven games, and I was invited back for training camp the following season even though I played increasingly less often toward the close of the season.

As I was packing up to go home, the two Swedes came over and mentioned how much they'd enjoyed my presence during the home games, and asked if I'd be able to visit them in Sweden during the summer.

"I've got a lot of writing to catch up on," I told them. "My season's really just starting now."

Salming grinned that same grin I'd seen in my first game.

"I understand this," he said. "No fun to go to Sweden if you're interested in the Pros in English language."

"Something close to that," I admitted.

He and Hammarstrom left the dressing room laughing. They sure weren't like the Scandinavians I knew from watching Ingmar Bergman movies. I wandered over to where Ferguson was packing his equipment, and said good-bye. His bag was full of books, and he was having a hard time getting them all in. Finally, he had to give up, and he left with a pile of them under one arm. He turned at the door.

"I'm going to try to write some stuff myself this summer," he said. "Mind if I send you some of it?"

"Do," I replied. "You've got my address?"

"Sure have." He smiled. "Well, see you. Stay in shape."

"You too," I said. But I was talking to his shadow. He'd disappeared.

That summer passed in a flash, and by mid-September I was back skating and shooting again with the Leafs. The season started, and by December I had four goals and as many assists, and I thought, I was doing okay.

But the team wasn't doing well at all. We were fourth in our division, and Ballard could be heard snorting and snuffling all the way to Buffalo.

Then, before a practice right after a road trip that had gone badly, King Clancy walked into the dressing room, announced that Kelly had been fired, and that John McLellan was the new coach. Two days later Ferguson was traded to Pittsburgh. The day after that, McLellan called me into his office.

"Brian," he said, "I talked things over with Jim, and we, uhhh. . . ."

He seemed to be stumbling for the right words.

"We don't think your heart is really in this game. You're not skating. . . ."

"I can't skate," I cut in, but he ignored that and went on.

"We want you to retire."

"I'm practically a rookie!" I spluttered.

"You're thirty-one," he said, "and you're not going to get any better. Meeker is still after your behind, and you're a target for every goon in the league. Both Jim and I spent some time over the summer reading your work. You're a better poet than a hockey player. You've got to go for that."

I fussed and fumed, but I ended up agreeing with him. I had two, maybe three years of good hockey in me. With poetry I had maybe forty years, and I would only get better. I'd miss the crowds and the attentiveness of the critics, even though they'd done a good job of ignoring me. But I wouldn't miss Toronto and its bars, and I wouldn't miss the poetics, which, try as I did to ignore them, are as venal and profit-oriented at Maple Leaf Gardens as they are in the English departments of the nation's universities. If more poets were to play pro hockey instead of pretending flowers or vacant lots are really interesting things might get better. But I wasn't going to hold my breath.

"You're right," I told McLellan. "I'll retire right now."

And I did. I walked out the way I had come in, gave back the blue on white and the number 15, and stepped out into the dull Toronto streets as if it were the next morning and not the next year I'd awakened to.

Three weeks later I got a letter from Ferguson, postmarked Atlanta. In it was this poem:

It's cold in Pittsburgh, colder still
in Philly. The north wind blows all night
from Canada, and these raucous crowds
that hoot and holler for our blood, Hey!
They're the coldest thing of all.
Skate and shoot, the coaches tell us

Skate and shoot. But masked men block the goals
and I am checked at every turn.

Each year more miles to go
More senseless contests of the will.
My heart is like the puck; often frozen
too often out of play, too often

stolen by the strangers
in the crowd.

The Style Is the Man

BY HUGH HOOD

While working on a biography of the legendary Canadien center, Jean
Béliveau, author Hugh Hood skated with him for an afternoon. The result is an up-close look at what separates a great hockey player from the
rest of us, right down to his thoughts on the backhand, and the fit of his
skates. Béliveau played with the Canadiens for eighteen seasons, winning ten cups with them, and was the team's captain for the last ten of
those years. In his career, he scored 507 goals.

Hugh Hood, who died in 2000, was one of Canada's most respected writers, and over a long career published more than thirty
books, including seventeen novels. He taught for nearly forty years at
the University of Montreal.

★   ★   ★   ★   ★

On a Sunday morning in June we arranged for some unin-
terrupted ice time at the Town of Mount Royal Arena.
The idea was that I would watch Jean closely as he
worked through the different phases of skating and play-
making, from the vantage point of the ice. Gerry Patterson, Jean's business advisor, came along too, and refereed for us. You don't get the same
view of Jean, even from a seat at rinkside, that you do when you're playing with him—it's a totally different impression.

We weren't wearing uniforms or equipment, just shirt and
trousers, so it didn't take much time to dress. I usually wear a pair of
heavy woolen sweat socks over a second, lighter pair, when I'm skating,
and I asked Jean what he uses.

"Just one pair, a light cotton sock. You've got the uniform socks too, remember. They don't have a whole foot in them, but they do have the strip that goes under the arch of your foot, so you've got a certain amount of bulk in your skate. I like to have my skates fit me like any other good-quality shoe—they've got to be flexible and comfortable, and I don't want my feet all muffled up in thick wool."

He finished lacing his skates and stood up. I noticed that he had to duck his head going through the dressing room door. Jean is six-three, and the skates add about two inches to his height. I was profoundly impressed by his height and speed when I got out on the ice beside him, and he didn't have game equipment on. With the shoulder and elbow pads and the rest of it, he must be a pretty overwhelming sight when he's coming at you and really putting out.

I pulled my skate laces tight, wondering if I should try to get along without those extra socks and then remembering that I'd likely have to buy another pair of skates a half-size smaller. Jean will use three or four pair a year sometimes, but I keep a pair of skates almost indefinitely (I'm apparently not giving them the same amount of wear). I decided to stay with the ones I've got, but I can see that he's right about the way the boot should fit, because he moves in skates as through they were attached to his feet by nature. When I came out to the ice, Jean was already skating around in the style of a pleasure-skater, somebody whom you might see at any city park on a winter afternoon for fun. It was plain how much he enjoys skating from the way he moved—everybody has seen a man like this at a neighborhood park, who simply loves skating for its own sake because he's good at it and because it's a tremendously pleasurable activity in itself. That's an element that even a keen analyst of hockey might miss—the sheer physical pleasure of the basic activity involved. Some other sports require such intense, painful, concentrated effort (often because the physical movements involved aren't natural to the human body) that whatever pleasure results comes mainly from the competition. But hockey is built on a physical action that is a delight in itself, and you could tell this by watching Jean that morning in the TMR Arena. He skates in a way that tells you at once that he just damn well *loves* to skate, enjoys it, would do it as much and as often as he could, even after twenty years of amateur and professional hockey. It was a treat to watch.

At first he wasn't making the hockey player's moves. He was turning from back to front, stretching his legs out far, relaxing and pleasing himself and looking more like a figure skater than I'd ever seen him. I realized, watching him in those first minutes, that if he hadn't been a hockey player he might have been the greatest of classical figure skaters. The whole rhythm and line of skating changes when you take away the hockey stick; plenty of hockey players lose their grace and balance without it. Jean simply looked, if anything, more stylish and graceful without the stick than with it. But the thing that really caught my eye was his joy in being out there, just skating.

I hadn't been on skates since the first week in April, so I proposed some warm-up skating—to give me a chance to calm down a bit, but also because I really needed to see what Jean does. If you come into the Montreal Forum at seven-thirty on the night of a game to watch the teams take their warm-up, even if you're in a box seat, you might be misled into thinking that the boys aren't moving too fast or putting out very much. They just seem to laze along, working out the kinks perhaps, loosening up the knees and thighs and hips, but not going very fast.

It would be a mistake to think that. I'm a reasonably good skater for a man of forty who has never been a professional hockey player and who is in moderately good physical shape. If I work out for forty minutes or so, I get to the point where I can get over the ice relatively fast. *Relatively fast*, that is.

I would say from close, direct observation that Jean can skate much faster backwards, without apparent effort, that I can skate forwards at top speed. Make no mistake about it, a skater like me and a skater like Béliveau—we aren't skaters in the same sense. I asked Jean to begin by taking those slow warm-up strides, going from right to left (counter-clockwise, which is his best turn and my bad one) and we skated along beside each other and talked. He was skating pretty upright, standing almost erect.

I said, "I thought you bent over a bit more, quite a lot more in fact."

"Not at the beginning of my warm-up. Watch, here's how you begin."

He was taking rather short strides, kinking the legs slightly at the knee and moving from both the knee and the thigh, quite loosely almost as if he were walking.

"If you come onto the ice," he said, "and start moving your fastest immediately, you're taking the risk of a muscle pull, in the groin or the calf. And you don't want to put too much strain on your knees at the start of a workout. Knee trouble has hurt more good hockey players than almost anything else. I like to move around slowly, and pretty upright, at the beginning. As a matter of fact, during the first three or four days of training camp, I'm likely to get soreness in the lower part of my back, over the kidney region, from the bending forward that you have to do when you're going full out."

I said, "I think of your skating stride as one that keeps you bent well over, with your head and shoulders out in front of your torso."

"Oh yes, I'll bend. But you have to remember not to get over too far forward because it can begin to cut off your breathing. A skater who's in a tight crouch will get winded much quicker than somebody who's more erect. So your first few minutes are like this, easy, not pushing too hard."

"Where does the power in your stride come from, from those big muscle groups up the back of the leg?"

"The push comes from there, but there's another element of your stride, a kicking or stepping action, from the knee. I think the power comes from your push, and the quickness from the knees and the muscles above the knees in front of the leg. I told you about the big muscle development on Yvan Cournoyer's legs, just above the knees. I think that's where he gets his quickness. The speed with which you can flex and unflex these knees, with that kicking action, is even more important than the strength of your push."

He began to skate a little faster, and I began to feel myself struggling and sweating. "O.K., Jean," I said, "let's see you let it out a bit."

He was gone. Like that!

I was now skating as fast as I can, and the gap between us widened and widened until Jean was moving at least twice as fast as I was. It was as though he'd pressed a switch or turned a key. He just moved his whole rib cage slightly forward and down, leaned a bit, and left me. What this change reminded me of most was the shifting action in an automatic transmission—there's a faint whir and bump and then you're in a new speed range. As Jean moved from the relaxed warm-up skating into something approximating game speed (approximating it, that is, at no time was he extending himself) there was a *qualitative* change in his motion—the difference between the professional and the amateur of modest ability. This is a real difference, not just one of degree; if what Jean does is skating, then what I do is not.

We'd started off counter-clockwise—Jean's good turn, and my awkward one, and I'd noticed that he was able to lean much further over as he turned, thus cutting a much sharper curve, than I could. It took me four or five extra strides to make the turn around the end of the rink. When we began to skate to my good side, clockwise, I could get a little further down toward Jean's turning angle, but not enough to save a single stride. I was still moving my legs in a flurry of waste motion, while he glided into and out of those big rink-wide turns in three to four strides. He got much more distance on each stride than I did; he could go much deeper into the corner areas than I could because of his sharper turns, and he was so wholly in control of his balance and his whole body, and so unconscious of the difficulty of skating that fast, that he could pay full attention to anything happening at any point on the ice surface.

An ordinary skater like me must always have in the back of his mind that, after all, he is positioned on a slippery surface and can easily fall. That obviously never crosses Jean's mind as he skates; he is so completely habituated to it that the possibility of losing his balance doesn't exist for him.

This is true of his skating backwards, just as much as the other way round. When we'd done about five minutes of warm-up, he began to show me some of the other aspects of his skating style. He swung around to skating backwards, then to the front again, then backwards. I noticed that whenever he turned around he did it with his weight on his left foot, and I pointed it out.

"Do you always do that?"

"I do it instinctively when I'm not in a game. And I think that I'd turn from forward to backward on the left foot in a game. But to move from backward to forward in a game—you've got to be able to do that on either foot. Just think about it! If you're trying to forecheck in front of the net, and the puck-carrier comes out to your right, you've got to be able to turn to that side, instinct or no instinct. I imagine that everybody feels more comfortable to one side or other. I'm not giving away any secrets when I tell you that I swing around easier with my weight to the left."

"Would that make any difference in actual play?"

"I think it may make some difference. It's easier to pick some players' weaknesses than it is others, and naturally you'll try to exploit them where you can. But you can't keep a 'book' on the players in hockey to the same extent you can in baseball, where the pitcher and catcher can confer and set up a whole sequence of pitches to try to take advantage of a batter's faults. Sometimes when I'm coming in on a defenseman I'll remember that he's weak to the outside and try to go there; but that might be impossible because of the position of my wings."

"That turnaround to skating backwards is pretty important, right?"

"Yes, a defenseman has to be able to do it without thinking about it. He'll find himself in a game skating backwards as fast as he can move, without remembering how he got into that position or when."

"Let's see you do it," I said.

Jean began to move backwards, crossing one foot behind the other in a rapid turn, and then switching to the defenseman's style, moving the hips from side to side in a crouch, and this was when I found out how much superior his backward skating was to my forward movement. He seemed to be aware of the precise dimensions of the rink, and to feel no need to look behind him to see where he was going.

He said, "I know where I am from what's in front of me. You get a sense after a while of how much space you've got to move in. And you know where the other players are supposed to be. You can move backwards pretty freely in a game."

"And you do that when you're forechecking?"

"Only occasionally. But a defenseman will skate backward almost as much as forward in a game, and it's much more important to him than to a center or a wing."

Watching him move like that, going around back to front at high speed and talking to me at the same time, began to make me feel slightly dizzy. "Why don't we pause for a minute?" I said. "You can show me the right way to stop, and I can use a stop right now."

He sent up a shower of ice with his skates, doing something I'd never noticed before, probably because I'd never seen him skate at this distance. Most ordinary skaters, braking while moving forward, will turn their knees to right or left, and brake with the blades of their skates parallel, so that their skates exert an equal braking force. The natural result of this is a dead stop, and a second motion is required to begin skating again. Jean doesn't do this. When he stops, the rear foot, almost always the left foot, exerts the braking force. He rocks the blade from toe to heel, almost like a dance stop, with the forward foot barely scraping on the ice. Doing it this way, he finishes up as though he were still in motion—poised with his weight in balance ready to swing off onto a new course. He doesn't seem to try to jam on his brakes, but rather to swing to a stop, such that the stop is only a minute pause before a new action begins. The rocking action of the rear skate lifts his weight, as though he were making an almost invisible jump from a springboard, at the end of the maneuver. This is because the actual game is played in that way—no time should elapse between a stop and a new start; they should flow right into each other.

"It all comes from that rear foot," Jean says, "and the forward foot is like a rudder or a wing, a guide more than anything else. Often you don't come to a full stop between whistles."

"I've been doing it wrong all my life," I said.

"No, what you're doing is correct if you want to stop dead. It's just that most of the time you have to go in a new direction at once. So you move right through your stop and push up and off."

He did it again and I watched carefully; the swinging, lifting motion was very evident and extremely graceful.

Jean said, "Doing what you do is a good exercise, stopping completely and starting up again. I don't do it during the pre-game warm-up, but in practice, I'll do plenty of stops and starts for my wind; they really take it out of you. Another exercise that I use all the time is to skate around the rink at the warm-up pace, then when I come to the blueline I'll go as hard as I can to the next blueline, then slow down and make my turn, then go hard from blueline to blueline. That simulates game conditions very closely. You're changing speeds without thinking about it during a game, and you need to be able to shift gears, so to speak, without having to think about it. Any change in speed should come as a surprise to your check, so you have to be able to change without giving any sign that you're going to do it. Watch me."

He skated around the rink a couple of times, changing pace at the bluelines, and again the fluidity of his style was striking. Approaching the blueline, he'd be moving easily, and suddenly as he crossed it his whole body would blur into the new speed without any warning.

"That's an excellent exercise," he said, skating back over to me. "I think the Rocket had the best change of pace I've ever seen. You'd think he'd be going all out, when all at once he'd burst over that blueline so fast you wouldn't believe it was the same man. It's something you simply have to be able to do without having to think about it."

That's perhaps the really remarkable thing about Jean's style; it's completely natural and apparently unconscious; he'll make adjustments in his pace and balance, and the way he holds his body, constantly as the demands of the situation dictate, without strain or effort. And he can do things that you have to see close up to believe, amazing feats of dexterity. Watching from the stands, you might think taking a face-off a pretty simple operation, where even a mediocre player might have an almost equal chance against Jean. It isn't so.

We took eight or ten face-offs together, with Gerry Paterson dropping the puck. As the centers come up to the point of the face-off, their sticks are about at the center of the red spot on the ice, with the tip of the stick as close to the edge of the spot as possible. You can't put the blade of the stick into the red area till the puck drops. A top center moves that stick blade in there like a knife blade—snick, snick, in, out—and it's hard to believe how fast Jean's stick moves. When that puck hits the ice, his blade comes in, zip, zip, and the puck is twenty feet away, just where he wants it. Taking these face-offs with him, I was astounded—it's the only word—at the speed of this movement, and I could understand how Yvan Cournoyer could score a crucial goal against the Rangers *six seconds* after a face-off outside the New York blueline.

Jean's stick action at the face-off is difficult to describe. When I watched it happen the comparison that immediately occurred to me was the motion of a small snake's tongue. Those little snakes are often seen around summer cottages, and they catch insects on the end of their tongues, with the tongue sliding in and out so fast that you can barely see it. That's the way Jean moves his stick; he must have wrists of incredible strength and sensitivity because he doesn't just get the puck, he can put it precisely where he wants it. On several of the face-offs we tried he sent it back to the point to his left, and for the life of me I still can't see how he directed the puck in that direction. I watched as hard as I could, trying to win one face-off, and I could not see any movement in his stick blade that would move the puck behind him. But that's where it went; the aiming motion was too fast for me to see it. And I didn't win any face-offs either.

The movement of his wrists and the blade of the stick is simply too fast to see. We took one after another, and Jean would call his shot, "Left wing. To the point. In front of the net. Shot on net." And he put the puck exactly where he called it every time. Not within a foot of where he intended; *exactly* where he intended, just like a billiards champion. The delicacy of the wrist and arm motion must be quite a lot like that used in handling a cue, infinitely accurate. I think this particular revelation was the thing that impressed me the most about our workout. Jean has been taking face-offs for twenty-five years, and I figured he'd be a master at it, but I hadn't expected that what he does would be such a different kind of thing from the very best, most concentrated attention I could bring to the play.

We would move into position and I'd be concentrating just as hard as I could on moving my stick as the puck fell, and I'd listen to Gerry Patterson's voice, only half hearing it.

"You guys ready?"

The puck would drop and I'd move my stick as fast as I could, really flicking my wrists, and it wouldn't be any use. The puck would be at the blueline where the point man would pick it up. Gerry and Jean would be grinning at me, and I'd come out of my fit of concentration and say, "I can't see how you did that."

It was the same with the passing game. A little exercise that players will use in a practice or before a house-league or minor-league game is to stand maybe ten feet apart and start passing the puck back and forth from one to another, gradually moving back so that the distance increases; the object is to make the pass as flat along the ice and as crisp, sharp, as possible. You try to get that good wrist action going for you so that the puck has some zap on it, and you try to put it right on the other guy's blade. You can practice receiving the puck as it comes back to you, cradling it carefully by inclining your stick blade over it as it comes in. The trick is to ease that puck back onto your blade with no hops or ricochets which might cause you to lose control. Standing more or less still like that, you can pass pretty precisely—better than you might in a game. It's fun to do and it's very good for the wrists.

When Jean and I tried this exercise, I had a little better luck than with those face-offs. The arena staff had given us beautiful ice—not a scratch on it when we arrived—and the puck wasn't flipping over deep cuts or chips on the ice. It slid smoothly, which meant I could propel the puck better than I usually do. So that was fine; but it didn't put me in Jean's league, or remotely near it, even on this simple exercise. His passes were beautiful—it's the only word—in their precision and their extraordinary force.

It was their force that really got me. Ordinarily when you get one of these warm-up passes from one of your friends, it'll come quickly all right, but you don't feel it all the way up the handle of your stick and right up your arms into your shoulders. With Béliveau passes, you do. He'd be standing there twenty feet away, plenty of light in the building, nobody getting in our way, and nevertheless I couldn't spot what he was doing that was so different from what I'm used to. He was doing something, though, because the puck was coming to me with the same minute accuracy as the face-offs. I never had to move my blade; it was as though the puck was attached to it the way a yo-yo is attached to your finger, or as if it were magnetized by my blade. Once or twice I'd swear that I moved my stick after Jean put the puck in motion and— I don't understand how exactly—the puck *still* landed right where it should on the stick blade, a little toward the tip. It felt extraordinarily comfortable, just right, and then I had a sudden wave of understanding. Just like he's done with so many real hockey players, he was *making me look and feel good.* I suddenly understood why Dick Duff says that everybody wants to play with Jean. As a hockey player I am not good, but Jean was making it possible for me to execute this simple play properly. I wasn't losing the puck; it wasn't nipping over the top of my stick; it was just right. And yet it came with great force. I felt my blade moved backwards by the force of the impact, and I could sense the shock in my fingers, in the muscles of my forearms, even in my shoulders; as they say in baseball, he was really putting something on it.

The same thing happened when we tried making pass plays while we were in motion. I'm a right-hand shot, so I asked Jean to feed me some passes as I was breaking up the right side. He positioned himself just outside the defensive zone on the left side, and I took a wind-up, then skated as hard as I could down the right side, trying to keep my stick well out in front of me on the ice as a target. Skating hard like that I tend to forget everything except trying for speed, and I wasn't anticipating the arrival of the puck the way a good player would. But every time we tried the play, it would come out of nowhere on a sharp angle, and lay itself on my stick bade, or where the blade would be if I hadn't gone off balance and lifted it, or hadn't veered slightly because of my uncertainty on skates at that speed.

When Yvan Cournoyer is executing this play, Jean knows that he'll have his stick where it's supposed to be, that he won't suddenly jerk his head to one side to keep his balance, or change course slightly. He can therefore lay that pass in there exactly. With an amateur of no particular skill taking the pass, he can't be sure that his wing will be in the right spot. And yet the puck was always well within my reach, in a spot where I could have completed the play if I'd been properly coordinated.

We tried this play four times. On the first try, I got so absorbed in trying to move my feet with decent speed that I didn't look for the pass, just concentrated on trying to hold my skating together. The puck passed in front of me and bounced off the right boards. Even at that, I was able to get my stick on it after it had taken a bounce.

"Pretty good," Jean hollered at me. "But you've got to look for the pass. Let's try it again."

I huffed and puffed for a minute, got my breath back, and gasped, "Yeah, nearly had it." I came back down the ice, turned and started down the boards again. This time the pass came in very tight, almost on my skates. Cournoyer would kick it ahead; I just let it bounce away from me.

"You're skating a little faster now," Jean said. "Again?"

"Wait till I get my breath. O.K., let's have that again."

Back around, wind-up for a good run at it—this time I was in the groove enough to be able to look for the puck and when I saw it come I made the mistake of sweeping my stick back to pick it up behind me. Instead it passed well out of reach and banged into the corner.

"You don't need to reach back for it," Jean said. "If you've got your head twisted around as you stab at the puck, you're going to get knocked down, because you won't be looking for the defenseman. You have to trust the man who's making the pass to get it well up there, so the puck is where you can see it and the defense at the same time. Now we'll do it again."

"O.K." Wind-up, rush, go go go . . . this time I completed the play, not perfectly but acceptably, taking the puck on the face of the stick blade just in the right place to get off a forehand wrist shot. "I'll quit while I'm ahead," I said to Jean. "I didn't think you could get me to make that play. I've never taken a pass right in my life."

"Well, it isn't an easy play," he said. "When it's done right it looks easy; the winger seems to put his stick on the puck without breaking stride and without changing the design of the play. He and the puck are moving very fast, and they've got to come together just exactly right. In the NHL you can't be close with your passes; you've got to be dead on. The first time you tried it, the puck was in front on you, and you picked it up off the boards. In a game, you couldn't do that, because it wouldn't be there; the defenseman would have moved it out to his center. Unless the pass is accurate, and the wing knows how to receive it, it'll turn into a loose puck and possession will change hands."

I was feeling winded, so I said, "Let's take a break, and then I'll play defense on you, is that O.K.?"

We ran through one-on-one defensive play next. (During this workout, Jean managed to cover every aspect of the game except goaltending.) I got into position, first at left, then at right defense, and he rushed the puck on me. I think that, next to those bewildering face-offs, the chance to watch Jean rush the puck was the most enlightening thing we did. I keep coming back to this idea that we might think a face-off was a face-off, or a fake a fake, no matter whether it was Béliveau doing it or an untalented amateur. Ha!

I used to think of fakes as a recognizable distinct series of moves—a drop of the shoulder, a feint in one direction or another, a look to right or left, a deke with the stick—separate and distinguishable movements. When Jean makes a series of fakes, they come so fast that they blur together, and you just don't know where the puck is. The whole series is so smooth it's incredible. I'd heard of defensemen "getting tangled in their skates" but never thought it was more than a metaphor. It isn't a metaphor; it's exactly what happened to me every time he rushed the puck on me. Just like during the face-offs, I'd be watching him come toward me as keenly as I could and then the funny business would start. As nearly as I can figure it, he'd do six or eight different things in *under two seconds*, and then he'd be behind me.

It seems to me that I'd have time to think one thing—go left, say, or go right—and by the time I'd started to do it I'd know that I was going the wrong way, try to reverse myself, and find one leg going left and the other right. That's when I began to get the feeling of getting tangled in my skates.

The first time it happened, I said to myself, "I should have tried a pokecheck." So the next time I held my stick in the left hand and shoved it way out to my left, at the same time getting down as low as I could, trying to cover as wide an area as possible. He put the puck between my legs that time.

"If you do that with your stick," he said, "there's nothing to prevent me from moving the puck through there. And I know you're not going to hit me."

"You can count on that," I said, laughing.

"Another thing," he said. "You're backing much too far in. You're screening your goalie. What you want to try to do is make the play as close to the defensive blueline as possible. Everybody knows that, I think, but sometimes it's hard to do."

"There's one other thing I'd like to try on defense," I said. "You know that play where you lean on the defenseman, and control the puck with your right hand as you go around him? Let's try that."

"You want me to lean on you?"

"Not exactly. I don't think you'll have to, but I want to see what that play looks like from here."

"All right," he said, a little doubtfully, I thought, and he went back to center-ice to start his rush.

The photographs of this particular play are famous; they always show Jean leaning over at an angle to his left, with his left arm crooked by his chest, with the other arm stretched way out so that the puck is out of the defenseman's area altogether. When you see the photograph, the action is still. I'd always wondered what it looked like to the defenseman in the middle of the play.

He started to come at me, and I got hypnotized. I knew what he was going to do, and considered making a move. But on skates Jean stands six-five, and seeing somebody that tall and heavy bearing down on you and preparing to lean on you is disconcerting. I suddenly remembered I had a wife and children, and thought to myself, "You'd better get out of the way before you get killed." He came by me just as he does in the pictures, down low to his left, and you can bet I wasn't doing anything to get in his way. I couldn't have got near that puck with a bulldozer. The idea of that much weight at that speed was the thing that persuaded me. Anyway, I got a good look as he went by in that familiar attitude, which looked just the way it does in the pictures except for the motion and its intimidating quality.

"I can see how you'd have a lot of success with that one," I said.

Jean said, "It's my best move," and chuckled.

After that it seemed to me safer to pack up the riskier parts of the session, so we finished with some shooting exercises, working in turn on each of the three fundamental shots; the slapshot from a distance, the wrist shot from closer in, and the backhand.

Jean began with his slapshot and I kept a close eye on him. Of the different shots, the slapshot is probably the most misunderstood by young players, who usually try for power at the expense of accuracy.

"It's no good at all if you can't put it on the net," Jean kept saying, underlining the point. "Plenty of players will get the blade up above their heads on the backswing, and then move it through the puck as hard as they can, like driving a golf ball or swinging for home runs. Now, even in golf or baseball a shorter and more controlled swing will give you greater accuracy, and you aren't on skates. It stands to reason that if you're moving fast on ice when you swing you'll need all the accuracy you can get. Otherwise your shot will be banging off the boards, ten feet from the net—which just means a loose puck and possession for the defending team. What you want to do with a slapshot is to combine power and accuracy. Here, I'll show you."

He shot several times with pinpoint accuracy, calling the target each time. "Upper left corner, upper right corner, left side low, right side low." He could put it anywhere he liked, and his backswing was very short. The blade of the stick was coming back maybe three feet, just about even with his hips, no higher. I spotted something else that was very interesting which you wouldn't be able to see from a seat in the arena. The blade of his stick wasn't sweeping through the puck completely uncontrolled. As the blade came down to the ice, the lower edge right on the ice surface, just before the point of impact Jean made a slight adjustment to the angle of the blade, like a golfer who is trying to get under the ball in a trap. There was the slightest little wiggle in there, just enough to put some additional control on the puck. This movement didn't slow up the stick's motion at all, but it was perceptible—getting the face of the stick blade more "open."

I mentioned this.

"Right," Jean said. "Maybe I'm taking something off the power of the shot when I do that; but you have to remember that I'm not taking slapshots from the blueline or beyond it. I'm usually shooting from thirty feet away or less. The defenseman who's blasting away from the point may be hoping for a deflection more than anything else. He just wants to be around the net, hoping that the man in front will get his stick on it. Plenty of goals are scored like that. But when I shoot, I'm usually in pretty good scoring position, and I'm shooting to score, not looking for a deflection. Not many people have noticed that little adjustment I put in there. I do it instinctively, I think, in an attempt to put a little hook on the puck—to make the shot a bit lively, not just a dead straight line."

"Do you do that on all the different shots?"

"With the wrist shot everybody does it, I believe. There isn't the same blasting action on the wrist motion, and you're much more conscious of the way the puck lies on your blade. When I take a slapshot, that stick waggle has to come unconsciously or not at all. But with the wrists moving, I can feel a much greater degree of control over the puck. The wrist shot is the most important shot, I think, and the one young players should concentrate on."

"That's funny," I said. "When I go out to the rink on winter afternoons all I see is kids banging slapshots off the boards."

"It's an impressive sound," Jean said, "and I guess it shows off your strength, but you won't score with it as much as with the wrists. That banging noise tells the story. When the puck goes in the net, you don't hear any banging."

He started flicking wrist shots from around twenty-five feet out, and he was getting plenty of power into them. When I remembered the face-offs, and the way he moved the puck on passes, I wasn't surprised to see how much zing there was in the movement on the puck. Actually I shouldn't say he was flicking his wrists, because he doesn't use a flipping, lifting motion; that would put too much loft on the puck and reduce its speed and liveliness. Like a good golfer or baseball player he seems to roll his wrists to impart power. The flicking action is too jerky and hesitant to result in either accuracy or smooth power.

"For a left-hand shot like me," he said, "the left hand, the hand further down the stick, is the power hand, and the right is the control hand. When you roll your wrists, you shouldn't jerk the stick, and lift the blade, or you may top the shot. And if you dig too far under the puck it may simply flip into the air. It's a pretty delicate adjustment, and you only learn to make it after long practice. As far as shooting goes, the best advice I can give is to practice the smooth, even wrist shot more than anything else; it's the shot that will get more results than any other."

"It isn't a looping shot," Jean said, "and it has to come fast. The backhand, that's different. Most of the time when you're shooting from the backhand you'll be off balance and in a hurry, usually because you've gone to the backhand to evade somebody who's checking you closely. And the whole physical action of the shot is reversed. Instead of that lower-down power hand's *pushing* the stick, it's *pulling* it or sweeping it. It's practically impossible to get the same power on a backhand shot as on a forehand, and nobody uses it by choice. It's a strategic move, and it has to be more of a sweep or a flick than anything else. Even at that you can get something on it if you work at it. Just like the other ways to shoot, it needs as much control as you can manage. I think the most important thing with the backhand is not to lift it too much. A really fine backhand, like Red Berenson's, can look almost like a forehand, and it's usually a short sweep of the blade, not a flick."

Jean grinned, looking as though he remembered plenty of duels in the goal-mouth. "One special kind of backhand comes when you've had to come in very close to get the goalie to move and you've gone by him. If you've got the reach, you can go to your backhand and nudge the puck to the open side. There, of course, it's more like putting than anything else; you don't want to whack at the puck, a little tap will do it. Whack at it in a hurry and you may bounce it against the goalpost. I've had that happen, and I've felt foolish afterwards. In as close as that you want complete accuracy. You just show the goalie the puck on your forehand, and when he moves you draw it back to you, go to the backhand and go to the open side."

I've seen Jean do exactly that hundreds of times in games, when it looked so relaxed and easy that I figured that I could do it myself. After this Sunday morning session my eyes were opened, and I knew that the play as he described it required infinite precision and delicacy and I thought again of the snake's tongue, flicking in and out so fast that the eye couldn't follow it.

"I think that about covers things," I said, and we skated to the boards. Jean was warmed up. I could see that. But he wasn't taking any deep breaths, the way I was. It made me think of the referee and the linesmen in the NHL. They're out there for the whole game without substitutions, and they must do plenty of skating before the night is over.

"Are those officials pretty good athletes too?" I asked Jean.

"You bet they are. Some of those guys are wonderful skaters, and you know they're apt to be a bit older than the players. The officials in the NHL are hand-picked, and they can all stay right with the play. They have to.

"Now and then you'll find that one of the officials is having an off night, getting out of position and missing a call here and there," he said. "But for the most part they're right on top of the play, and they all skate very well. Sometimes I wonder how they can do it—stay out there right through the period, when the players are taking shifts."

I had one or two last questions to ask Jean while he was getting his skates off. I noticed that he used the same make of skates as I do, something that pleased me, perhaps irrationally, and I wanted to know whether he had any special comments on his equipment. There was, as it turned out, one very interesting thing about his skates.

"I wear a half-size larger on the left foot. Whenever I'm breaking in a new pair of skates, I always feel perfectly comfortable on the left foot as I've worn them for a bit. But I almost never get the right foot to feel exactly right, no matter how long I wear the skates, even though the boot is smaller than the left one. Look here!"

He held out his skates for me to examine. Sure enough, the left was a nine, and the right an eight-and-a-half. And the left boot looked—this is hard to describe—as though it had taken the individual shape of his foot more distinctly than the right. The left boot was a bit more worn and sliced up.

"Let's see your feet," I said, and I looked at them closely. The left foot wasn't so much bigger than the right as more developed muscularly—the difference between a part of your body that you use a lot and one that you use less.

"You know what?" I said. "I'll bet that's because your left foot is doing so much more of the work in your skating. After all, you stop on the left foot, most of the time you take your shot off the left foot, and you turn around to that side much more than to the right. I'll bet you're putting the weight on the left foot eighty percent of the time."

There was no doubt of it; the difference in the muscle development was obvious.

Jean said, "I wouldn't be surprised if most people find it hard to fit both feet exactly with a standard pair of skates. After all, you can't walk into a store and ask the salesman to give you one size nine and one size eight-and-a-half. There's another thing. Two years ago the skate manufacturers changed the design of the toe cap on the skates I use; they switched from steel to a new plastic which is stronger and a bit lighter. And I can feel the difference still. The plastic leaves just that little bit of extra room in the toe. I found it quite hard to get used to, for a surprisingly long time. I don't exactly think about the fit of my skates when I'm playing, but I know when I'm not perfectly comfortable." He looked at his feet with a grin. "I guess there isn't much to be done about it."

"Do you wear the same skates all the time?"

"No. I usually use two pair at a time, switching them from game to game, sometimes even between periods if I'm not satisfied with the edge of the blades. Two pair will do me for half a season, then I'll work in two more. And no matter how carefully I break them in, one skate fits better than the other."

It seemed to me that a really enormous force must be exerted over a long time to make a significant difference in the size of the two feet; but the difference was there, visible to the eye. The twenty years of stopping, turning, putting weight into the shot, have left their mark physically after all.

The small discovery somehow seemed to me to mean something important about Jean and his career. Here's a man whose style in his life and his work is just about perfect, who does what he's meant to do with utter grace in a way that makes physical strain and the necessity of endurance seems invisible. And yet he too has paid for his style and grace; the twenty years of effort have left their mark on him, even on Béliveau.

That pleasant informal workout on the ice was one of the most unusual occasions of my life, because of the even decency and friendliness of its tone. Jean does things so well—it sounds extravagant to say this but it's true all the same—that other people do things well too. He makes you look good.

Our Hockey Is Hotter than Your Hockey

BY BRYANT URSTADT

Bikini Magazine sent me down to Corpus Christi, Texas, in 1999 to report on the explosion of minor-league hockey teams in the South and Southwest. Then *Bikini*, as was the fashion at the end of the nineties, disappeared completely, and this piece went homeless, until now. Reading it again, I still think it's pretty good.

To those readers who feel that an editor including his own writing in an anthology represents egomania run amok in the worst way, I profoundly agree, blushingly apologize, and, once I am famous, promise to be more modest.

★ ★ ★ ★ ★

When you fly into Corpus Christi, Texas, you come in by twin-engine plane, grumbling in over an endless panorama of fields. Every once in a while you spot a monster tractor with four double-tires and an enclosed cab in the middle of one of the fields. The fields are square, and the roads around them run in a huge grid, with every now and then a curve, just to break up the monotony.

Then you're over tidal flats and in among the refineries, their stacks spouting white smoke and flame as they burn off the bad oil. Right up until you land, there's no city in sight, none at all. The plane lands and stops in the middle of the runway. Across the tarmac, palm trees surround a low airport building like the ones on poor tropical

221

islands. Stepping out of the plane, a hot wet breeze hits you. And all of this combined with the smell of burning oil makes it seem like a joke that you've come here to see ice hockey.

The Corpus Christi IceRays, who didn't exist a year ago, play hockey in Corpus's only arena, which is a rodeo barn. It's called the Memorial Coliseum. It doesn't look like a coliseum. It looks more like a small shed for storing garden tools. It, too, is surrounded by palm trees and you could throw something very heavy from the front door into the Gulf of Mexico.

How small is the Coliseum? It's so small that the Zamboni has to be stored outside, in the parking lot. It's so small that the announcer doesn't have room to sit facing the ice. His chair is wedged in sideways by the glass, and unless he turns his head ninety degrees, he faces the bench. The Coliseum is so small that the IceRays don't even skate on a full-size rink—it's about fifty feet too short, and maybe fifteen too narrow. But the IceRays call this a home ice advantage. They're used to the odd size of their rink. They're also used to the fact that the boards on the north end are slanted about twenty degrees, so that cleared pucks take crazy bounces, sometimes popping straight out into center ice. The door to the lockers doesn't close properly either, and a good check there can be murderous, sending the checkee out onto the concrete outside of the rink. And the IceRays have also gotten used to the fact that a fairly dense fog can show up any time, due to the warm air coming off the sea just outside the coliseum doors. It could be coincidence, but the fog always seems to be thickest around the other team's goalie.

People start showing up for the games early, to watch the warm-ups. Women in tight dresses get seats near the entrance to the locker room, so they can be seen by the players as they go out onto the ice. Before the game the women wander around the Coliseum, and befriend the rented cops who tell them they can't cross the little ribbon separating the stands from the lockers.

When journalists go to visit the IceRays, they sit up in the press box, which a couple of fans built. It's made of plywood painted black and is just behind the highest row. Its only convenience is a cheap telephone. Behind this box sit Jake Stephens, the broadcaster for the local radio station; Mark Button, who writes up the games for *The Corpus*

Christi Caller-Times; and maybe one or two other people representing the visiting team.

For tonight's game, IceRay forward Tyler Boucher is doing the color on Stephens's broadcast. He's a casualty of the vicious level of play in the minors, particularly in the Western Professional Hockey League. His face has been broken twice, both by sucker punches thrown in recent games. "I don't get it," he tells me. "I've been getting hit in my face all my life, and all of a sudden it's breaking." As Boucher squeezes past Button to get to his seat, Button points to the screen on his laptop, saying that he's already written his lead for the next day's story, due ten minutes after the game. It reads: "Tyler Boucher wouldn't have gotten hurt if he wasn't such a pussy."

It's a joke of course, and Boucher makes some comment about beating the crap out of Button. It is a hypothetical fight, but one that Button would never win, though he has maybe six inches on Boucher, who is 5′6″.

Boucher slips into his chair next to Stephens. Boucher has a lot to talk about. The Austin IceBats are one of Corpus's biggest rivals, and, like the IceRays, fancy themselves a tough team. As if to prove it, they fought some of their own fans outside their stadium in the fall. The teams are also in a battle for first in their division. Boucher usually plays on the same line as Roger Lewis and Brad Wingfield. They're all under six feet, and they all play to get under the skin of the other team. In addition to being short, Roger Lewis scowls a lot, earning himself the nickname "The Angry Troll," and giving his line the name "The Troll Line."

The game is about to begin. Down by the lockers two IceRays staffers, Canadian guys named Kevin Simpson and Paul Beaudoin, are inflating a giant black stingray and wheeling a fog machine into place. After the opposing team has skated out, the lights go down, and the building starts to get loud. The building is always sold out, and all 3,292 fans have usually arrived by the start of the first period. The inflatable stingray is set up around the door to the lockers, forming an arch with its wings. Kevin switches the fog machine on. A strobe starts flashing, now the only light in the building. The IceRays cheerleaders, the Ice-Girls, prance out and form a gauntlet in their shorts and silver-sequin tops, jiggling their white pom-poms. The opening riff from Van Halen's "Panama" blasts through the speakers. Then, the IceRays come out. With the strobe going they look like a silent movie. The fans roar. The noise is so great that it sounds like someone is checking your ears for infections with a nail.

Despite all the lights and music, the IceRays get off to a slow start. Twenty-five seconds into the game, the IceBats score. The rest of the period is a battle. Though the opposing goalie looks like a monster sighted in the dim reaches of a smoking bog, he's playing well—"standing on his head," as hockey players like to say. Finally, IceRays defenseman Regan Harper ties it up at the very end of the period, scoring off a beautiful feed from forward Chris Robertson. Both players are standouts on the team, professionals who rarely make a mistake. The fans get so excited they throw seafood out onto the ice—stingrays to be exact.

The second period starts out rough, and stays that way, despite the leisurely time-outs called by the referee so that maintenance men can clean the fog off the glass with squeegees. The IceBats are hooking and slashing everywhere. The game is starting to look like one of the battle scenes in *Braveheart*.

Neither side scores, frustration snowballs, and violent things start to happen. First, 18-year-old forward Quinten van Horlick, known as "Cueball," drops his gloves and takes on IceBats forward Craig Johnson, who has about six inches and 60 pounds on van Horlick. Cueball is quickly knocked to the ice, but skates off in a cocky way anyhow. Hockey is played for about a minute. Then Roger Lewis, "The Angry Troll," takes on Rob Hutson, who also has several inches and many pounds on the scowling Lewis. Lewis is quickly knocked down. Though the game is still tied, the IceRays are getting pounded. Intermission comes. The game is still tied at one.

For entertainment at intermission, a remote-controlled blimp sails around the rink. On its side is a photograph of a chiropractor who looks just like Chuck Norris. Despite this tranquil entertainment, neither the fans nor the players are calmed, and as soon as the third period opens, the game continues its downward slide into goonery. Just into the third, Brad Wingfield, in the first fair battle of the night, takes down IceBat Dan Delisle.

Then, with four minutes to go, Geoff Bumstead and Pavel Evstigneev, from Moscow, set up Craig Coxe with the go-ahead goal, bringing the score to IceRays 2, IceBats 1.

Coxe is the oldest player on the team. He's a tall guy with hair so spiky that he always looks like he's just taken his helmet off. Wherever the end of the hockey line is, he's got to be near it. It might be here in Corpus Christi. Back in the 80s, Coxe played for the Vancouver Canucks along with the IceRays' coach, Taylor Hall. Coxe was an enforcer, the player who kept the other team from roughing up his team's stars. Some of his fights are legendary, like the one he had with Detroit's Bob Probert in 1988. It's often called the greatest hockey fight of all time.

The younger players on the IceRays grew up watching Coxe's fights live and on tape. Bob Quinnell, a 26-year-old defenseman for the IceRays from British Columbia, watched Coxe fight as a kid. "He was like a hero to us," Quinnell told me. "We had his fights on tape, and we watched them over and over. We'd rewind them, watch them in slow motion, count the punches."

But Coxe has stopped fighting. He's trying to score now. He's 35, which is something like 75 in hockey years. He doubles as starting forward and assistant coach. The job of assistant coach is a largely honorary position, but Coxe does give some advice out now and then. Earlier in the season, Quinnell fought a guy on the Fort Worth Brahmins. After a few punches, Quinnell and the other guy stood holding each other's jerseys—"all tied up" as Quinnell put it. Quinnell isn't an enforcer, and he had no idea what to do next. Then he heard a voice from the bench. Coxe was saying, "Uppercut, uppercut." Quinnell administered the prescription and won his bout.

As for Geoff Bumstead, he's a fighter on his way up. Everyone calls him "Bummer," and he's also an enforcer, or, a "thumper." Bumstead, from Winnipeg, has two passions, hockey and boxing, which makes him a pretty good thumper. He's 5'10" and most of his 215 pounds are crammed into enormous forearms. Before each game he tapes his wrists and writes "Lato" on the tape. It's the same thing Mike Tyson's trainer writes on Tyson's wrists. Of the younger players who like to fight, no one likes it more than Bumstead. He also scores some goals, which is the other part of hockey, and the part which has earned the IceRays a spot at the top of their conference.

Soon after his go-ahead set-up, as if to prove he really was an all-around player, Bumstead challenges Shawn Legault, the IceBats captain, to a duel, flinging his gloves to the ice. Captain Legault declines Bumstead's invitation. Bumstead is known to knock people out. The crowd yells themselves hoarse with approval as Bumstead is ushered off the ice.

The two teams never really get back to hockey. As soon as Bumstead is gone, and the puck is dropped, defenseman Sean Peet goes after Legault. Legault has been performing some mighty stickwork on the IceRays all night, gouging what he could when he could.

Peet gets knocked down, too, and the game veers out of control, if it was ever in control, and if it was ever a game. As Legault and Peet are being led off the ice, IceRay's rookie Clint Collins goes mad. There's no other good explanation for what he does, which is to jump off the bench after Legault. A linesman jumps in and holds Collins back, but not for long enough. Legault heads for the lockers and the linesman lets Collins go. Collins races after Legault, and follows him at a run up into the lockers, moving in that funny lumber that skaters use off the ice. Following Collins now is pretty much anyone remotely connected to the game—Bumstead, Peet, the ref, the linesmen, the rest of both teams, the trainers trailing their towels, security, both goalies, all trying to get through the alley leading to the lockers.

The crowd goes into an ear-splitting frenzy. It's as if your ear is now being cleaned by a nail attached to an air hammer. Fans are yelling themselves hoarse. They're pounding on the glass behind Austin's bench, peppering the few remaining players with obscenities. When the teams return, some girls in tight tank tops start giving the IceBats the finger, and a guy with a ponytail challenges the IceBats' coach to a fight, which unfortunately never happens because some rent-a-cops show up and haul him away. And over it all, the announcer plaintively calls, "Dr. Cone, please report to the locker room area."

This is all pretty much the way Coach Taylor Hall likes it—tough. He played for a couple of years in the NHL, with the Vancouver Canucks and the Boston Bruins, and, as he puts it, "I didn't like playing against tough teams. They scared me." He knew what it was like to have to dig a puck out of the corners to either side of the enemy goal, after it was helpfully tossed down there by one of his defensemen, while a big defenseman from the other side bore down on him at full speed, along with an extra thirty or forty pounds.

Taylor Hall came down to Corpus in 1997 to start a hockey team. Bringing hockey to Texas has been both a lot easier and a lot harder than Coach Hall, or anyone else, expected. It was easy to find the fans. Something about hockey seems to speak to the Texas character. In 1992, there were no hockey teams in Texas. Seven years later, there are 12. Over three million people have already paid to see WPHL games, and the IceRays have sold out every home game this year. That's just in Texas, incidentally. Hockey has been storming the south in general at about the same rate. Neighboring leagues, like the now-huge East Coast Hockey League, have sprouted 28 southern teams in ten years.

When the league debuted in 1996, plenty of fans showed up for the first games, but they left after the second period, figuring it was over. When management convinced them to stay for the third period, they were again disappointed. They thought there was going to be a fourth period. Teams in the league have gotten calls for seats on the forty yard line.

Though finding the fans has been a cinch, building the infrastructure has been trickier.

Take the flaming Zamboni. Texans haven't had much experience with ice-cleaning machines. Waco has a team, the Waco Wizards, and last fall their Zamboni burst into flames in the middle of the ice. The operator leapt out and ran for safety while the machine burned and melted a hole for itself. They had to cancel the game. The Waco Zamboni, by the way, is sponsored by Chapman's Bail Bonds. Their logo is painted across the side. It reads, "You Ring, We'll Spring."

Intermission entertainment has had its rough spots, as well, if you consider having to kill a cow on the ice a rough spot. A team in central Texas hosted a guess-the-weight-of-the-cow contest. They brought the cow out on the ice. The cow slipped and broke its leg. They had to put the cow down right there.

*   *   *   *   *

After home games, the IceRays go down to Buckets, a cathedral-like sports bar with thousands of televisions hanging from the ceiling and a fleet of pool tables in the back room. You can imagine Buckets being jammed during spring break, but most nights it looks huge and empty. On game nights, Buckets puts up a sign saying, "Tonight: IceRays Party!" and plays that night's game on the constellation of TVs. The players get their food for free, and pay half what the drinks cost. They leave big tips. Though their average salary is a measly $350 a week, there are lots of perks like these. The players hardly ever have to pay for anything. They live in team-owned apartments, even play for free on the local golf course.

At the bar they scarf down huge bowls of pasta and drink bottles of light beer. Usually they're "wheeling" some girl. As with most teams, they speak their own language. To wheel is to hit on, though it implies some degree of finesse. Women are frequently called "donkeys." Sometimes they're called "dollies." If they're hot beyond belief they're called a "dolly lama."

At Buckets, they wheel donkeys but it's not very challenging. The women come up and introduce themselves on some vague pretext, delivering a message from someone who knows someone slightly or something like that. Sometimes they just stand there. They're almost all blond and made up as if it were their wedding. A lot of fans show up and just kind of watch the players from afar. The players sit in groups. They all wear the same thing, black track suits with white stripes on the shoulders. Sometimes the IceGirls come over and chat.

At about one in the morning the players dribble back to the stadium, where the Boneshaker is waiting. The Boneshaker is the team bus. The problem with starting a league in the vast void of the West is that it's a long way between cities. Some of the rides can last for 16 hours, each way. The IceRays don't have a special bus for these grueling odysseys. Their bus is just like the ones that whisk Japanese tourists through cities, except maybe crappier. A tacky graphic on the side of the bus reads, "Funtime Tours," but there is nothing fun about trying to sleep on this bus. There is one puny bed in the bus, all the way at the back, and Coxe gets it, because he's been a pro for the most years, not that anyone would be able to take it away from him anyway. The rest of the players have to improvise. Some of them have built plywood and foam contraptions that span the space between the seats. Others just lay their foam out on the floor and sleep under the seats. To get to the bathroom at three in the morning, you have to walk over all the sleepers, your feet on the backs of the seats, your head bent and scraping the ceiling.

Before they leave, the players say good-bye to girlfriends and wives or whomever they picked up that night and file into the bus, holding their enormous bundles of foam. The faces of Lewis and van Horlick and Wingfield are swollen from punches. Coxe stands outside until the last possible moment smoking one of his Marlboros. Some of the more rabid fans show up just to watch them board the bus, bringing a box of candy and soda and a fresh bag of real Texas beef jerky. Three of these fans drive a giant black Suburban and will follow the bus to Lake Charles, Louisiana, tailing it like they were the secret service. Jim, the owner of the black Suburban, gives the bus driver a walkie-talkie, and throughout the night he and the bus driver will radio back and forth, saying stuff like, "Looks clear up ahead. I'm increasing my speed to 70." The jerky is much appreciated. Coach unwraps it and throws the sticks to the players, who scramble for it like stray dogs.

Everyone is tired and a little shocked at what happened. Three-and six-game suspensions were handed out like game souvenirs, and Bumstead, Collins and Peet are all staying home. Collins is off the team.

Still, it's not too grim a scene. Quinnell comes on to the bus smiling, because he's just wheeled what seems to be the dolly lama of dolly lamas. He sits up front near the coach. As the other players get on they tell Quinnell how hot she was. The bus finally pulls out and starts for Lake Charles, ten hours away. Corpus Christi is so small that the bus leaves the city behind immediately, but the oil refineries seem to stretch on forever, silver installations like space stations, with flames spitting from the tips of smoke stacks. Somewhere beyond this wasteland is the next game.

The Healing Power of Hockey

BY JOHN STACKHOUSE

In 2001, *Globe and Mail* journalist John Stackhouse spent months work-ing on a fifteen-part investigation into race relations in Canada, specifi-cally between European and aboriginal Canadians. Stackhouse found every kind of triumph and disaster, but one of the most moving install-ments in the series described his discoveries about hockey in the Opaskwayak Cree Nation. The OCN, despite the odds, had put together a dominant junior team, relying on many native players, challenging stereotypes held by both native and European alike.

One of the players on the team Stackhouse wrote about was Terence Tootoo, and the events surrounding his life after the story was published confirmed the extremes of joy and sadness about which Stackhouse wrote. Terence Tootoo died by his own hand in 2002. And yet his brother, Jordan, went on to play for the Nashville Predators. He is the first Inuit ever to make the NHL.

★   ★   ★   ★   ★

The final words of "O Canada" as it's sung in Cree are still reverberating in the rafters when the arena's overflow crowd begins hurling the high-pitched invective that every junior hockey team traveling to northern Manitoba has come to dread.

"Hey, loser!" a big man from the Opaskwayak Cree Nation (OCN) shouts at visiting goalie Reg Legace, from Winkler in Mennon-ite country far to the south.

"Faggot!" adds a man from The Pas, a dreary mill town across the Saskatchewan River from the reserve.

"Pull yourself before it's too late!" yells "Mouse," another native man who is perched behind the Winkler net and hammering the glass with a puck to throw Legace off his game. Mouse is the goal judge.

The verbal deluge seems to work. Less than a minute into game two of the provincial finals, the home team's star forward, Justin Tetrault, a Métis, takes a pass from captain Terence Tootoo, who is Inuit, and blasts it home.

Before Mouse can flash the red goal light, the Gordon Lathlin Memorial Centre is shaking with the sound of air sirens, noisemakers and the woodsy voices of 1,248 people from two communities that once were the most racially divided in Canada. To the sounds of Bachman Turner Overdrive—*You Ain't Seen Nothing Yet*—the Crees, Métis, whites and a few Inuit embrace in the stands, and on the ice.

For the next two hours, the native-owned arena facing The Pas across the river will rock with delirium as the Opaskwayak Cree Nation Blizzard trounces the Winkler Flyers and build a commanding lead in their run for a third straight provincial championship—a feat not seen in Manitoba in nearly thirty years.

But in the racially mixed stands, most people know that the Blizzard's sudden dominance is about much more than hockey. In this isolated town and reserve, which straddle the Saskatchewan River 600 kilometers northwest of Winnipeg, the team has built a bridge that people once thought impossible.

It was near the arena site thirty years ago that a Cree woman named Helen Betty Osborne was murdered after being sexually assaulted by men from The Pas.

The horrible crime was followed by one of the darkest periods for race relations in modern Canadian history, as the entire population of The Pas joined in a notorious conspiracy of silence. For a decade, townspeople who knew the killers refused to identify them. Finally, one of the attackers, unable to bear his guilt any longer, went to the police.

Just a generation later, the native-owned Blizzard has used a mixed-race team and integrated home crowd to start a new chapter for both the town and reserve.

"I really believe it was the hockey club that bridged the divide," says Gary Hopper, mayor of The Pas, which is one of the Blizzard's top corporate sponsors. "When the team was announced, people bought season's tickets [he has two] and all of a sudden there was white sitting beside native, a total mix, and new friendships developing."

Amazingly, he says, "You would be hard pressed to find two communities that get along better."

Although only five years old, the Blizzard has left its mark on the record book, trouncing established clubs from the south game after game. Before the 2001 playoffs, it won 50 or 60 regular-season games with players from so many communities that the coach called it "the United Nations of hockey."

It is also one of the struggling Manitoba Junior Hockey League's (MJHL) few financial successes. Not only does the team sell out most home games, its bruising style of hockey packs so many arenas on the road that it has been credited with saving a league that, ironically, once ostracized Cree players.

In wins, pennants and box-office receipts, the OCN blizzard may be the most successful new sporting franchise on the Prairies. Which may be the reason people still wonder, when the hugs and high-fives are finished, why Perry Young killed himself.

The story of the Blizzard's lightning success, the harmony it has restored and the tragic loss of the best hockey player the reserve has produced in years has its source in a river of racial tension that persists despite the Cinderella story on ice.

Born almost a decade after the Osborne murder, Perry Young grew up on a reserve that knew little of the antagonism or poverty that had shaped its past. Like most of the 1,500 residents, he lived in a sub-division of compact prefab homes, played on the reserve's nine-hole golf course and attended its $9.5-million school.

People on both sides of the river still marvel at the transition. Only a generation ago, they had a situation that was as close as Canada could get to the Deep South. The 7,000 residents of The Pas never crossed the river to the reserve, and the natives went to town only to shop, drink or go the movies, where they sat in a separate section.

The division was about more than segregation; it spoke to the belief in both communities that the Crees were inferior people. Band councillor Henry Wilson remembers going to watch westerns with his boyhood friends and, even though they had to sit in the Indians-only section, "when we came home, every one of us wanted to be cowboys. No one wanted to be an Indian."

Discomfort turned to antagonism in 1971 after the Helen Betty Osborne killing, which became international news and the subject of a film. Whites still joke about "HBO, The Movie," in which an entire town was presented to the world as conspirators to murder.

But while the killing further divided the communities, more fundamental changes also were under way. Once bold enough to call itself "Chicago of the North," The Pas was in steady decline as its timber-based economy wilted.

Across the river, a more positive change was afoot: OCN was emerging from the Osborne case as one of Manitoba's more forward-looking bands. Money from a land-claim settlement with the federal government was invested in a modern hotel, high school, the hockey arena and the region's biggest shopping mall, a dream of the late chief Gordon Lathlin, who had tired of having his people ignored by shop-keepers in The Pas.

The new school and rink meant that white and Indian kids rarely saw each other, not even for peewee hockey. Rather than share the ice, Cree teams drove to Thompson about 400 kilometers away for tournaments, while The Pas kids went to Winnipeg.

The reserve's new mall proved to be almost as divisive. Local shopkeepers—the ones who had refused to serve natives—claimed that, with an IGA grocery store, Saan department store, Tim Hortons and Shell station, it would siphon off their business. Vandals smashed the mall's windows.

But no one lost business. Instead, retailers on both sides of the river began to see a steady rise in traffic as the mall helped the twin communities become a shopping magnet for northern Manitoba.

Then the Crees began lobbying for a junior hockey team.

Ever since The Pas had lost its beloved Huskies when the old northern Manitoba league folded in the 1980s, no one from the town had been willing, or able, to provide financing for a new team. The Crees, for once, were in a better position, with a $50-million-a-year business operation to backstop a franchise and a game plan to sell junior hockey to the north.

The struggling MJHL was not so sure. Its teams were so leery of making the long bus trips north—to "Indian country," as they called it—that they demanded that OCN pay travel costs for visiting teams. The band agreed, and the league responded by waiving its usual waiting period. Instead of two years, OCN was asked to have a team on the ice in four months.

The arrival of a Junior A franchise on the reserve was about the biggest day of Perry Young's life. He and his brother, Mike, were the stars of their midget team, and eagerly awaited the tryouts. The band council had told everyone that the new team was very much about giving opportunities to local boys like Perry, who was quickly nicknamed "the Pride of OCN."

But the band also believed in success; after all, it had built a small-business empire. It decided to hire the best coach and managers, regardless of race, and soon there was pressure from many reserve residents to recruit players the same way.

"How OCN operates is epitomized by this team," says Jim Smith, one of the Blizzard's founders. "We get the best management we can."

The band put up $100,000 to bring a coach and a general manager from Saskatchewan. It renovated the dressing rooms and training room to semi-pro standards. And it allowed the new management team to scour Western Canada for the best players.

Perry Young was among the first cuts. Still, with 16 natives on the first year's roster, the Blizzard became known as a native team. As a result, all the players discovered how some Prairie people really feel. On road trips, they were jeered as "welfare bums" and "drunks." In one arena, security guards were stationed in the sections where Blizzard fans sat. A now-defunct Web site claiming to represent the MJHL went so far as to state that OCN home games were always sold out because "they're all on welfare."

Even when the Blizzard shocked the league by making the playoffs in its debut season, the racism did not let up. Phillip Albert, a player from remote Norway House, says an opposing coach once yelled "fucking Indian" at him. His childhood friend, Clifford Scatch, says another coach called him "a brown, buck-toothed Indian," but it didn't bother him. "Racism, I'm used to it. I've had it my whole life. If I ever hear a remark, I let it blow by."

In time, the Blizzard came to be seen as some kind of ghetto for native players. Jerry Mosiondz, an assistant coach, noticed that other teams were offering to trade their own native players. "They usually say, 'We think he would fit in there,'" Mosiondz says. "I ask, 'If the boy's a good hockey player, why doesn't he fit in with you?'"

Still, the more the Blizzard won, the less the Crees seemed to care about affirmative action on the ice. When the team, in its third season, set a league record for wins and captured the provincial championship, the fans clamored for more star players to help reach the national finals. The Cree management agreed, and dropped its goal to have a roster two-thirds native.

By last year, the team that once dressed 16 native players was down to six, and only one who was local—a Métis boy from The Pas. Coach Kerry Clark (brother of former Toronto Maple Leafs captain Wendel Clark) used his connections across Canada, and a handsome budget from the Crees, to acquire the best players under 21 he could find.

By season four, Perry Young, the Pride of OCN, was one of those players. He came to training camp with added strength and speed—and pressure. When he did not get as much ice time as other players, local fans, including his uncle Danny, who was on the team's board of directors, demanded to know why. Clark told the board that Perry routinely arrived late for practice, sometimes still drunk from the night before.

Then, a couple of months into the season, Perry simply stopped showing up.

Clark struck his name from the roster, and was called a "racist" to his face at a community meeting. But most people supported him. They liked the championship banners draped over centre ice—it gives their kids something to dream about, they said. They also liked being the center of Manitoba hockey's attention, and they enjoyed driving to distant places such as Winkler and watching their team whip the opposition.

Perhaps most of all, they liked the idea that townspeople were driving to the reserve for entertainment, and paying for it. Last year, the arena's concession stand alone contributed almost $50,000 to OCN minor hockey teams, which traveled to Long Island, N.Y., and British Columbia and this winter plans to go to Sweden.

In time, Perry Young faded from view and the team did not hear much about him until the summer of 2000, when his girlfriend had a baby boy. She then kicked him out of their house, telling him to sober up before he could move back.

That September, while on a binge, Perry pushed his way into the house, took a carving knife from the kitchen and, in front of his girlfriend and baby, stabbed himself five times in the heart. His mother, Marlene, reached the scene within minutes, but he was already gone.

To this day, she believes that the hockey team bears some responsibility for her son's suicide. She feels that its emphasis on winning has overshadowed the many social problems that native kids often carry. If Perry drank, it was because he had to carry the expectations of a community, she says.

"They did say local boys break the rules, come late. I've heard people say it about our kids: 'They're drunks. They're lazy. They're no good,'" Marlene says. "Who are they to judge that these [nonnative] Blizzard don't break the rules? They turn around and treat them better than our kids."

So now she refuses to let her eldest son, Mike, try out for the Blizzard (he plays for the Southeast Blades, the province's only other junior native team), and talks about leaving the community so that her youngest, 10-year-old Garrett, can play elsewhere.

The day after OCN's big win, racism seems to be the last thing on anyone's mind as the Blizzard board a chartered bus bound for Winkler, seven hours south across a dreary table of farmland, frozen lakes and forests still sprinkled with snow. Because its fans have booked every room in the area, the team will spend the night in Winnipeg.

Even so, the coach is in a good mood, joking about what southern Manitoba's Mennonites may do to his team. "Be careful," he warns the players, who seem more interested in a copy of *Playboy*. "I hear the Winkler fans will throw Bibles at you."

For the rest of the journey, there is little to do but watch videos and play *Survivor* trivia. Other than race, there is not much to distinguish them, as they sit shirtless so they can display their pecs and abs. They are all 16 to 20, and most have dyed their hair blond—but not Steve Mac-Intyre, a Saskatchewan farm boy, and Ryan Braun, from a remote northern Cree reserve. They have shaved their heads.

The players like to say they stay as one, on the ice or off. Even the natives prefer to have billets across the river in The Pas, where houses typically are less crowded than on the reserve. But there are subtle differences, which the native players quietly say why their numbers are so few.

The team's top Cree scorer, Jamie Muswagon from Cross Lake, about 300 kilometers northeast of The Pas, says he and the other native players like to go hunting and ice fishing together. They don't need a license, for one thing and out in the wild, they can talk freely about the isolation that shaped their upbringing in hockey.

Muswagon first left home to play in Brandon, west of Winnipeg, but at 16 he felt so alienated that he went back to Cross Lake every other weekend. Many native hockey careers end at the midget level because leaving a close-knit community proves too painful.

The native players also talk about Perry, but only a little. They agree that he broke the team rules. He missed practices. He drank heavily. Some of them understand why, but that does not mean they want to pay a price on the ice because of it. "Some of our players don't buy into the 'program'—the drinking, the after-hours stuff," says Jim Smith, the team's early backer. "Sometimes the youth, they may have the talent, but not all that it takes to be a hockey player."

But slowly, he believes, the Blizzard's discipline is rubbing off on a younger generation. "They're starting to understand hockey is not just a sport, it's a lifestyle, the development of a human being."

Others are not so sure, not when so many aboriginal players must struggle while growing up on remote and often socially dysfunctional reserves. Even athletes face the same stigmas, says former team manager Derek Fontaine, who played professional hockey. "The thing that pisses me off," he says, "is that, once a native kid has a couple of beers, he is given that stereotype: He's a boozer."

Fontaine now manages the Southeast Blades, which last season carried 14 native players as well as Perry Young's brother, Mike, but had the worst record in the league, just seven wins in 64 games.

As the Blizzard bus passes through the first scattered settlements between Manitoba's big lakes, and another action-thriller video begins, a few players at the back eat potato chips and talk about their own struggles with hockey off the ice.

Braun, a brick-like forward from the hamlet of Wabowden, northeast of The Pas, had to drive with his father 100 kilometers every day to his midget team's practice and games in Thompson. Most of his friends couldn't count on a parent to make the same trip. Finally, his own parents tired of the driving, and paid $400 a month to billet him with a Thompson family, on top of the $1,300 a year for equipment and arena fees.

Tootoo, the Inuit team captain from the Northwest Territories, faced a greater challenge while learning to play in Rankin Inlet. The town had an arena, but not enough players to form two teams, so everyone played pickup hockey. Tootoo didn't learn a set position until he moved to Thompson at 16, and the coach benched him for chasing the puck all over the ice.

He made the transition well enough to lead the league in scoring, but he knows how many people feel. "I kept hearing things like, 'You guys aren't going to make it.' There's a lot of 'downs' in native communities—drugs, alcohol."

But he does not despair for aboriginal kids—they just have to be tougher, he says in body and spirit. He has not forgotten what his father told both him and his brother, Jordan, who plays for the Brandon Wheat Kings: that hockey could be their ticket out of Rankin Inlet.

"I have no respect for those kids who just give up," he says. "I see those guys when I go home for the summer and they're doing nothing. If you give up, you'll be a nobody."

The bus reaches Winnipeg by late afternoon, leaving the team enough time for an all-you-can eat buffet and an amusing drive through the red-light district before reaching their hotel by dark. They head to Winkler, near the U.S. border, the next day.

Until then, coach Clark does not want any more distractions. He fears that his players will buckle under the pressure of Winkler, whose rich soil produces more than an abundance of grain. The farming town is home to a big Mennonite church, pleasant subdivisions and a sprawling recreation park with its own water slide. Winkler and The Pas could be in different provinces.

Clark jokes again about the prosperous Mennonites as the bus turns into the hotel, but then turns serious. The game "has nothing to do with race," he says. "It has everything to do with who you are. I look at it as I'm trying to coach hockey, not coach color. There's only one way to pass a puck. There isn't a white way of passing."

He is an outsider, but this view seems to be gaining acceptance in the two communities his hockey team has brought together. Once angry and segregated, they are carefully seeking out new ways to work together. For example, in summer OCN dancers perform at the rodeo put on by Kelsey, the rural municipality that surrounds the reserve and The Pas. Kelsey's residents are mostly nonnative farmers, but they have hired the reserve to provide firefighting services, while the reserve is paying for half of a new Anglican-run homeless program in The Pas.

Together, the town, reserve and Kelsey also put together a successful bid for the 2002 Manitoba winter gams, and are now lobbying for a bigger regional health centre. Almost without fail, the major, the chief and the reeve show up at each other's events. The chief refers to Hopper as "our mayor," and Hopper gives visitors lapel pins both for his town and OCN.

The co-operation goes beyond public relations. When rural teens mugged some natives in The Pas and declared themselves to be a gang called "White Power," the heads of the three communities met the kids (who had been tracked down by the RCMP) and their parents to discuss what had happened. No charges were laid. White Power has not been heard from since.

This once-improbable racial unity appears in Winkler when the Blizzard arrives for the game. Half of the spacious new arena, with its orderly stands and well-stocked snack bar, is filled with well-dressed local people. But on the other side, behind the visiting team's bench, there must be 700 raucous OCN fans, with their obnoxious air horns and vulgar chants.

Against the crisply painted white stands, their dark and light faces resemble a northern patchwork; their denim jackets and cowboy hats an alien costume in the pristine south; their melding of Cree and English insults a bizarre dialect. By contrast, the most radical offering from the Winkler side comes before the game, with an electric guitar version of "O Canada."

The action begins and Winkler takes the lead, but the Blizzard fans do not let up. "Legace: You're a LOSER!" they shout at the goalie, whose standing-room-only hometown crowd can muster only a few prep-school cheers in return.

"Go white go!" the Winkler crowd shouts, referring to the color of their players' jerseys, not their skin, as one by one the fleet-footed Flyers are hammered into the boards.

By the third period, the Blizzard's awesome hitting power has filed down the Flyers like a jagged piece of metal. OCN ties the game, and then, a few minutes into overtime, Jamie Muswagon, the star scorer from Cross Lake, puts it away.

The home crowd turns silent and leaves, trying to ignore the many hues on the other side blowing horns and waving banners.

The next evening, Winkler's chance to cheer ends with the opening anthem. The Blizzard score three times in the first 11 minutes. In effect, the series is over, and in the third period, goalie Reg Legace comes out of the game—to a huge ovation from the OCN fans.

After just five years in business, the Blizzard had won their its Manitoba title. They go on to lose to Saskatchewan's champions, the Weyburn Red Wings, in the qualifying round for the national championship tournament. But not without a fight. About 400 OCN fans, including a group that chartered three small airplanes, traveled to southern Saskatchewan for the series, which ends four games to two.

But by winning the three consecutive provincial titles, the OCN did what no Manitoba team has done since the 1970s—since before Perry Young was born, since the days when two nations were segregated in The Pas cinema, since the time of Helen Betty Osborne.

Once an easy target for racists, the Cree Nation is now home to a feared champion. They are on top of their province, and want to show it in a new way.

After the season, Kerry Clark quit to take a job in the Western Hockey League. The Blizzard promptly recruited a new coach, Glen Watson, from the WHL and told him to win the championship yet again. He will have to do so without Terence Tootoo, who has graduated from the junior ranks, turned pro and gone even farther south to the Roanoke Express of the East Coast Hockey League.

But remarkably the Blizzard's Cree stars all turned down offers to move to stronger leagues. They prefer to stay with a native-owned team, playing on native land, most likely dreaming of yet another title. It is hardly an impossible dream, considering that this season the team is off to the best start in its history—20 wins and just one loss going into Friday night's game against the Dauphin Kings.

The fans had nothing less in mind when they packed the gravel parking lot outside the Lathlin arena for a tailgate party before the season opener. As barbecues crackled, and beer flowed freely, people from The Pas and OCN mingled as if there had never been a divide between them—as if there were no Saskatchewan River separating one community from the other.

The mayor was there, along with the chief, and on the bridge over the river a long line of cars traveling from the town to the reserve, to an arena both call their own.

Slap Shot

BY NANCY DOWD

The movie *Slap Shot* (1977) has become a part of hockey's culture, having influenced the sport's conception of itself as much as it simply reported on life in the minor leagues in the 1970s.

A loud suit worn by a player is still called a "Reg Dunlop," in honor of Paul Newman's pricelessly gaudy wardrobe. "Old Time Hockey" is a byword on the rink, in the broadcasting booth, and in the locker rooms, used loosely to describe just about anything interesting that happens in hockey, although in the film it is meant to convey an ideal of skill and character in opposition to the goonery that is always threatening to swallow the game.

The movie is often noted for pegging parts of the sport with lasting accuracy. It was written by Nancy Dowd, whose brother, Ned, played for the Johnstown Jets in the early '70s (and appears in the film as Ogie Ogilthorpe). Dowd traveled with her brother and the team for a month, and had him record conversations on the bus and in the locker room. Dowd later went on to win an Oscar for the script for *Coming Home*.

Reading just the last fourteen pages of a script can be confusing. For those few who haven't memorized every character's name, here's a list, in order of appearance:

Jim CARR: The broadcaster covering the Charlestown Chiefs.
Dave "Killer" CARLSON: The squirt who steps up to become a goon.
REGGIE Dunlop: Coach and captain, played by Paul Newman.
Ned BRADEN: The gifted center who will not fight.
UPTON, AHERN, DROUIN, DENIS, WANCHUK, Billy Charlebois:
Miscellaneous supporting players.
JACK, JEFF, and STEVE: The immortal Hansen brothers.
Joe MCGRATH: The double-dealing manager of the Chiefs.
FRANCINE Dunlop: Reg Dunlop's soon-to-be-ex-wife.
LILY Braden: Estranged wife of Ned Braden.

★   ★   ★   ★   ★

INT. [INTERIOR] REGGIE'S CAR - AFTERNOON

Stunned by events mumbling to himself and in general
freaking-out, Reggie flips on the radio to hear Jim
Carr, the jock-sniffing radio announcer, chatting
up the Chiefs and the upcoming championship game.
Reggie turns his car into the steep hill which de-
scends into the horrible city of Charlestown.

> CARR (v.o.) [voice-over]
> Killer, are you worried that Syra-
> cuse stickman Tom "Doctor Hook" Mc-
> Cracken will be seeking revenge
> tonight?

> CARLSON (v.o.)
>   (modestly)
> No Jim, because when the going gets
> tough, the tough get going.

INT. RADIO BOOTH

> CARR
> I was watching some kids play hockey
> the other day, five and six-year-
> olds, just little mites, and this
> one little kid says to the other,
> "I'm Killer Carlson" and then he

picked up his little stick and just
creamed the other kid. How does that
make you feel, Dave?

                CARLSON
Well, you know, Jim, to me that little kid probably woulda done that
anyways because of bad upbringing in
the home or whatever.

                CARR
That's very interesting, Dave.

                CARLSON
If I can be serious for a minute,
Jim. I just want say that no matter
how this game turns out tonight, I
owe all that I am to Reggie Dunlop,
our coach, who's had the greatest
influence on me aside from the Swami
Baha, whose positive thinking
records have been a great help
to me.

                CARR
Positive thinking records?

                CARLSON
Yes, Jim, they're available at any
religious record store and, you
know, I know that thousands of people in Charlestown have lost their
jobs with the mill closing, and I
see them walking around the streets
depressed all the time. I just wanta
say that you unemployed folks can
get a whole new lease on life from
these records. You can erase everything from your mind and nothing
will bother you anymore and you can
just go out there and cream that
other guy in your business life.

Carlson has taken one of the records and puts it on the turntable—an unctuous east Indian accent is heard.

INT. REGGIE'S CAR

> SWAMI (v.o.)
> Be one with the universe. Allow your
> mind to become the detached observer.
> Nothing is important. Do not worry.
> Be happy.

> REGGIE
> (depressed)
> Oh, Jesus. What a fuckin' nightmare.

He turns off the radio, pulls the car over to the side and rests his head on the wheel a moment. He reaches a decision, backs up and turns on a side road.

EXT. BRADEN CABIN - AFTERNOON

Reggie pulls up before a cabin set back a hundred yards from the road. Reggie walks up to the cabin, knocks on the door, no answer, peers in the windows, postgraduate funk and nobody home. There are dishes lying on the kitchen table.

> REGGIE
> (calling out)
> Ned! Ned!

No answer. There appears to be no one around but Reggie has caught a glimpse of—a tall figure stomping through the woods next to the house. Reggie runs into the woods, shouting after the figure.

> REGGIE
> (screaming)
> Ned, you can come back, you can do
> anything you like. It's all over. I
> don't give a shit. We're going for

the stinkin' championship, man. It's
the last fucking night. You don't
have to fight if you don't want to,
Ned. It's up to you, man.

Nothing.

>   REGGIE
>   (shouting)
> I've had it with this show biz crap.
> I don't know what hit me but as I'm
> driving over here, I says to myself,
> "Who cares about Florida? Screw the
> sale. It's not worth the price." You
> were right, Ned. And we're gonna win
> the fuckin' championship tonight
> fair 'n' square. And it's gonna be
> that old time hockey. None of this
> wrestling shit. I want you to be
> there. We could play the game of our
> lives tonight, Ned. We could be fly-
> ing. Remember that feeling?

There is nothing but the silence of the woods. Dis-
couraged, Reggie heads back toward the car. Suddenly, he remembers something else.

>   REGGIE
>   (shouting)
> Ned, Lily's been at my place. She's
> terrific. We've been having a hel-
> luva time.

Reggie gets into his Mustang.

EXT. [EXTERIOR] WAR MEMORIAL PARKING LOT - NIGHT

Reggie pulls his Mustang into the parking lot. The
Charlestown fans already waiting in the parking lot
are dressed for blood. The big championship. Obscene
signs show their hatred of the enemy, their adulation of the Chiefs. Outlandish costumes, crazy hats,

beer bottles gripped like weapons. A uniformed po-
liceman, his cap on backwards, is twirling his re-
volver on one finger, while chug-a-lugging a Stroh's
beer. Fans are pouring whiskey into their beer cans.
Reggie walks toward the home team entrance, the am-
bulance careens around the corner, the driver waving
at Reggie.

> REGGIE
> (loathing)
> Oh Christ.

INT. CHIEFS' LOCKER ROOM — NIGHT

Reggie enters the locker room—out of breath and
late. In anticipation of victory, someone has
decorated the room in toilet paper. The foxy
Sparkle Twins (and Billy Charlebois) are
sprawled—on the massage table, gripping their
ever-present Instamatics. Killer Carlson is wearing eye makeup and an earring. The Hansens are
beating up the soda machine. Reggie watches the
scene, somber.

> REGGIE
> (to the twins)
> Beat it.

They look at him, startled.

> REGGIE
> Go on. Get out of here.

They leave, giggling. The team looks at Reggie, puzzled by his mood.

> UPTON
> Where's Braden?

> REGGIE
> Death in the family. Somebody passed
> away.

                    AHERN
Who?

                    REGGIE
His mother.

                    AHERN
Yeah?

                    REGGIE
She's been sick for years.

                    CARLSON
             (getting depressed)
Yeah?

                    JACK
We're gonna win for Braden's mom
tonight, guys.

                    JEFF
Yessirree!

                    STEVE
Ned's dead mom.

                    JACK
She's in heaven!

                    CARLSON
             (to Upton)
I thought he benched Braden.

                    UPTON
Yeah, but that was before he heard
about his mom.

                    CARLSON
Right, I forgot.

                    REGGIE
We _are_ criminals. We _are_ goons.

                              JEFF
                           (cheery)
          That's us.

                              REGGIE
          We deserve to be in jail.

Reggie is getting confused looks from various
Chiefs—but the Hansens are still raring to go.

                              STEVE
          Get 'em.

                              REGGIE
          I've been a fool.

                              JEFF
                           (concerned)
          Not Reg.

                              REGGIE
          We're followers, led by the nose.

Outside, the stomping in the area is growing louder.
Reggie gestures toward the noise.

                              REGGIE
          They're followers. And you know what
          that makes all of us?

                              JEFF
                           (trying)
          Chiefs?

                              REGGIE
                         (enunciating)
          No. Sheep.

                              STEVE
          Get 'em.

                    REGGIE
              (speaking slowly,
         looking right at the Hansens)
    Reg was wrong.

                     JEFF
                  (pitiful)
    Nail 'em?

Ned has entered but Reggie doesn't see him yet.

                    REGGIE
    Nope. No more nail 'em. Nail 'em is
    finished. We're gonna win this one
    fair 'n' square. Old time hockey.
    The long tradition of Dit Clapper,
    Toe Blake, Eddie Shore, The Soviet
    Union. Old time hockey.

The Hansens are soundlessly, dementedly mouthing
the words "Old time hockey."

                     JACK
    Ned's back, Reg.

                    STEVE
                (stage whisper)
    Poor Ned.

                     JEFF
    His mom—
    (he can't bear to say the fatal word)

Reggie quickly puts his fingers to his lips suggest-
ing they be discreet.

                     JACK
                  (to Ned)
    We're doing it for her, Ned. Old
    time hockey.

Braden gives the Hansens his scum bag stare. Without a word to anyone he begins to dress for the game.

>   REGGIE
>   (addressing the club)
>   Ned was right. Violence is for suck-
>   ers. Violence is killing the sport.
>   If things keep going this way, hockey
>   players will be nothing but actors,
>   punks. We can't let that happen.

INT. WAR MEMORIAL ARENA — NIGHT

The crowd is waiting for the two teams to make their entrances. One section of the stands is filled with people holding snow shovels. The crowd is screaming "Let's go!"

>   ANNOUNCER (v.o.)
>   (laughing)
>   Ladies and gentlemen, our national
>   anthem.

The organist with the Charlestown High Band as a backup is blaring out the Chiefs' theme song, an original composition, "You Stink," which goes some-thing like this: You stink, I said you stink, you stink so baaaad.

McGrath, looking confident and ebullient and smok-ing a cheap cigar, is sitting with eight middle-aged men in top coats, felt hats, and note pads. Bedlam as the Chiefs skate piously to their bench.

>   REGGIE
>   (gazing up at the stands)
>   They love us.

Now the Syracuse team is making their entrance. Syracuse has recruited for the occasion the worst retired goons in the history of the Federal League.

ANNOUNCER
Playing for Syracuse, Ross "Maddog"
Madison, defense . . . .

Madison, tired, old and awful skates out.

UPTON
(paling)
Jesus, I thought he'd been suspended
for life.

ANNOUNCER
—Clarence "Big Chief" Swamptown,
center . . .

Swamptown, a full blooded American Indian with scars
that would do credit to a German derelict, skates on
. . . The Chiefs are appalled.

ANNOUNCER
—Andre Sussier, defense . . .

Sussier, with a neck like a leg, skates on the ice.

AHERN
Where did they get them?

ANNOUNCER (v.o.)
And from Moose Jaw, Saskatchewan
where he now runs a donut shop, Number Four, the former penalty minute
holder of the Federal League,
Gilmore Tuttle.

Tuttle skates to the Syracuse bench; he carries his
stick over his shoulder like a shovel. The Chiefs
are in shock.

The Syracuse Captain, Tim "Dr. Hook" McCracken (the
player upon whose head Reggie had placed a bounty
earlier) is wearing a black cape; he is making little

Z signs in the air with his hockey stick. McCracken, sneering and laughing, skates over to the Chiefs' bench, leaps four feet into the air, clicking his blades in Reggie's face.

                    REGGIE
                (staring at Syracuse)
        Wrestlers.

The last Syracuse man on the ice has a blond afro; he is about twenty-one and there is no expression in his eyes and not a tooth in his head.

                    UPTON
        Oh Jesus. They let him out.

                    DROUIN
        I don believe dis.

                    CARLSON
        Ogilthorpe.

                    AHERN
        Oggie.

The crowd is going berserk.

                    REGGIE
                (oblivious)
        Let's go, guys.

INT. CHIEFS' ARENA

The Hansens are trying to play what they have conceived to be old time hockey, no violence, pure sport. Jack Hansen is faced off with McCracken who has taken eighteen Bennies.

                    MCCRACKEN
                (to Jack)
        They don't call me Dr. Hook for

nothing. I'm gonna carve you like a
turkey. I'm gonna operate.

INT. CHIEFS' ARENA

The Chiefs are getting slaughtered on the ice.
Syracuse is not so much interested in scoring as in
creaming the Chiefs. The imported goons are wreaking havoc while the Chiefs are trying to play
straight. In the stands McGrath is screaming at
them. The men with him look disgusted. The fans are
outraged.

> JACK
> (screaming; his eyes shut tight)
> Eddie Shore. The Soviet Union.
> Rocket Richard. Old time hockey.

McCracken sucker punches him. Jack makes an exaggerated gesture of turning the other cheek.

INT. CHIEFS' ARENA

The score is 0—0, Reggie is out of it. He is barely
noticing that Syracuse is slaughtering his men.
Oggie Ogilthorpe is jumping up and down like a go-
rilla on the Syracuse bench.

> OGILTHORPE
> (screaming)
> Kill, maim, kill, kill, ha ha.

The horn blows ending the period. In the stands Mc-
Grath hurries down the aisle.

INT. CHIEF'S LOCKER ROOM BETWEEN PERIODS

The Chiefs are a mess. Jack Hansen is examining the
front teeth he holds in his hand. Braden is staring
transfixed at the floor, so that his nose won't
bleed on his uniform.

                              REGGIE
                           (absurd)
          Let's go guys. Let's get that
          speed. Eyes open. Better passing
          Better passing. This is a big
          period for us.

                              JACK
                   (trying to be positive)
          Old time hockey!

Denis LeMieux who has resisted 108 shots on goal in
twenty minutes is climbing into his locker; he has
not removed his mask.

                              DENIS
               Non, non, non, non . . . .

Billy Charlebois is staring horrified at the black
eye on his gorgeous face.

                              UPTON
          I'm too fuckin' old to be playing
          this way.

                              REGGIE
          Come all the way back with that
          winger. Let's go. Tonight's the
          night.

                              BRADEN
                         (mumbling)
          Awful. Awful. Awful.

Killer Carlson is in shock; he is also bleeding.

                              CARLSON
                         (quietly)
          I gotta call the Swami.

Joe McGrath in the worst White Rabbit suit of his
long miserable life has run into the locker room.

                    REGGIE
    More co-ordination. I want to see
    more co-ordination.

                    MCGRATH
                    (shrieking)
    We're losing!

                    BRADEN
    Ah, the subtlety of this man.

                    MCGRATH
    They're burying us alive!

                    REGGIE
                    (ignoring McGrath)
    I want a big rally. Big rally.

McGrath is jumping up and down next to Reggie—trying to get his attention.

                    JEFF
    Eddie Shore. . . .

McGrath is hyperventilating, wringing his fat wrist.

CORRIDOR — ARENA

Two women are hurrying into the arena. On close inspection we see it is Francine and a miraculously
transformed Lily—teased hair, lots of makeup, tight
dress, fur coat, charm bracelet. The works.

INT. CHIEFS' LOCKER ROOM

                    MCGRATH
    Piss on Eddie Shore—You're blowing
    it! Every scout in the NHL is out
    there looking for talent, for win-
    ners. All my publicity. Years of
    fashion shows, telethons, Rent-a-
    Chief—for nothing!

The dazed expression has left Reggie's eyes. He looks at Braden.

> MCGRATH
> They came to scout the Chiefs—the toughest team in the Federal League. Not this bunch of pussys!

> JACK
> Dit Clapper?

Jeff is trying to be nice to the soda machine by massaging it. Braden is watching Reggie. Nobody else is conscious enough to have taken much notice of McGrath who is stomping out of the locker room.

> REGGIE
> (without missing a beat)
> Let's face facts: there's something to be said for the American way. The pioneers. The Bi-Centennial. I know violence has been getting a bad name lately. Why is that? There's nothing fake about retaliation and revenge. They're as old as time itself.

> BRADEN
> Here we fuckin' go again.

> REGGIE
> Where would civilization be today without winners?

INT. CHIEFS' ARENA — NIGHT

A huge brawl is in progress. The Chiefs are killing Syracuse. Oggie Ogilthorpe, happy as a clam, is destroying the penalty box where he has been shackled.

OGGIE
                  Maim, maim, maim, maim. Ha ha.

Ned Braden is sitting all alone on the Chiefs' bench,
his hands folded across his chest. The brawl is
brought under control and Reggie flops next to Braden.

BRADEN
                  No fuckin' way, you old has-been.
                  No fuckin' way.

But someone in the stands has caught Ned Braden's eye.
It is Lily Braden. Braden can't believe his eyes. He
stares at her transfixed. She waves at him with a daz-
zling smile. The Upton line comes staggering off the
ice and Braden goes over the boards, still staring at
Lily, a crazy, spaced smile starting to form.

BRADEN
              Oh no.

He skates slowly onto the ice, as the line starts a
face-off, staring up his wife, slowly peels off one
glove and tosses it suggestively into the audience.
McCracken breaks the face-off giving Braden an evil
stare. Now Braden is throwing his other glove into
the stands, peeling off his shirt. McCracken skates
over to the referee.

MCCRACKEN
                    (pointing to Braden)
                  Make him stop that.

REF
                  Don't talk to me in that tone of
                  voice.

MCCRACKEN
                    (to Ref)
                  Listen, you. I'm protesting this
                  disgusting display.

                    REF
          Protest? Protest, my ass. What d'you
          think you are—in college? You don't
          protest. You play.

                    MCCRACKEN
                 (grabs the Ref)
          Make him stop it or we're leaving.

                    REF
          Get your paws off me, Scarface.

The crowd is digging Braden as he starts a Dick
Bretens routine, stripping off his shirt, whirling it
over his head and letting it fly into the audience.

                    LILY
                 (applauding)
          Take it off! Take it off!

The organ thunders into a strip grind routine.

                    MCCRACKEN
                 (beside himself)
          Stop him! This is a serious game.
          This isn't a freak show.

                    REF
          What do you mean a serious game?
          Huh? What are you talking about?
          This is hockey.

Braden is stepping out of his shorts, now whirling
his garter belt over his head. Lily and Francine are
both cheering. Reggie is just enjoying the hell out
of it. McCracken has now grabbed the Referee by the
shirt.

                    MCCRACKEN
          You're afraid of these perverts,
          aren't you?

                    REF
        Watch out, punk, you're hitting the
        tape.

McCracken and the Ref are nose to nose.

                    MCCRACKEN
        Clean up this fuckin' game. Make him
        stop that.

                    REF
        Who the hell do you think you are?

Braden's suspenders are sailing into the stands—
his shoulder pads, knee and shin pads are going,
too.

                    REF
        I'll give you ten seconds to get in
        that fuckin' face-off circle, or you
        forfeit.

                    MCCRACKEN
                     (to Ref)
        Forfeit, my ass!
                 (slugs the Ref)

                    REF
        That's it. Get out!

The Ref is screaming "Get out, get out" over
and over as he skates to what's left of the
scorer's box and emerges with the huge Lakeland
Trophy.

                    BRADEN
                   (screaming)
        My fan club meets in a phone booth.

Clad only in his jock strap, Braden is skating tri-
umphantly around the ice.

                              REF
                         (to Reggie)
                    Here ya go, ya bum!

The Ref is shoving the Lakeland Trophy at Reggie as
the War Memorial Arena erupts into mayhem, dead
chickens and rabbits thrown on the ice, air horns,
pitched snow shovels. One of the Hansens is slamming
at the trophy with his stick. The Chiefs have won
the championship.

                            BRADEN
                         (screaming)
                My fan club meets in a phone booth.

EXT. CHARLESTOWN STREET — NEXT MORNING

The victory parade. Charlestown has gone berserk—
the pandemonium of a one-horse town reconfiguring
itself as the birthplace of champions. Reggie,
Braden (still in his jock strap) and Lily (still the
Francine look alike) are seated on the back of an
open used Volkswagen Rabbit—waving, smiling at the
crowds.

Wanchuk, Ahern and Carlson are sitting on a float—
necking with Miss Charlestown and her court. The
streets are lined with cheering people. The three
Hansens have a float of their own. The motif is a
huge pair of eyeglasses.

Reggie has spied an old beat-up Mercury fighting the
parade in the opposite direction—a U-Haul (chock
full of furniture) hitched to its stern. Reggie
jumps off his used convertible to talk to the
driver.

                            REGGIE
                         (out of breath)
                    You leaving?

FRANCINE
(exasperated)
What do you think I'm doing with the
U-Haul?

REGGIE
(elated)
Francine, I've got some great
news.

FRANCINE
(gesturing toward the U-Haul)
Listen, I'm getting charged by the
hour for this thing.

REGGIE
The Minnesota Night Hawks—I'm gonna
coach 'em. The Big Apple.

FRANCINE
Someone's playing a practical joke
on you, honey.

He reaches into his jivey leather suit and waves a
letter at her.

FRANCINE
(sighing)
Reggie, I'm holding up traffic.

REGGIE
The Chiefs are history but
the minute I get to Minnesota
I'm gonna send for all these
guys. We're a solid act. This
is the start of something very
big.

In the b.g., a Girl Scout group is presenting Lily
Braden with a bouquet of roses.

LILY
Hi, Francine.

FRANCINE
Hey, honey.

Francine turns back to Reggie and starts the engine of her used Mercury.

REGGIE
You don't have my number.

Francine smiles: she's always had his number.

REGGIE
(quickly)
You can always call me care of the
team. You may need money. Maybe
things won't work out. We gotta
lotta years between us, Francine.
Some hard miles.

FRANCINE
I know.

On that one phrase, Reggie has caught a glimmer of hope but just behind them an irate fan has begun to honk his horn.

REGGIE
Shut up, you fuckin' fathead.

FRANCINE
I've gotta go.

REGGIE
You do? Well, you could always come
up to Minneapolis if things don't
work out. Remember—the Night Hawks.

                    FRANCINE
     Bye, Reggie.

                    REGGIE
             (whispering to her)
     I could make a fortune.

Francine is smiling her mysterious detached smile.
She reaches out and strokes his cheek. The April sun
has caught her lacquered nails. Francine is waving
good-bye.

Reggie clambers back on the float carrying Braden
and Lily.

                    LILY
     Is she coming?

                    REGGIE
             (grins, confident)
     For sure.

EXT. CHARLESTOWN — DAY

In the distance, Francine and her U-Haul have hit
the horizon (the upward trail out of Charlestown).
Reggie (waving) and Lily and Braden (embracing)
cruise through Charlestown in their open car. The
other Chiefs float nearby.

                    THE END

Permissions Acknowledgments